Consuming Urban Culture in Contemporary Vietnam

Vietnam is currently undergoing a metamorphosis from a relatively closed society with a centrally-planned economy to a rapidly urbanising one with a global outlook. These political and economic transformations have been the catalyst for an exciting ferment of activity in popular culture, with those involved benefiting from the diversification in patterns of consumption, the slowly increasing levels of wealth and the gradual freeing up of state control over the activities of the populace.

Consuming Urban Culture in Contemporary Vietnam sheds new light upon the social and cultural changes presently occurring in Vietnam by exploring the realm of Vietnamese popular culture and urban life in a world that has been increasingly affected by global flows of ideas, capital and products. The book provides insights into the dynamic relationship between the recent economic and political changes in Vietnam and the rapidly transforming aspects of urban experience including street life, music, media, magazines, novels, television, dance, film and leisure activities.

Contributions to this interdisciplinary collection come from scholars engaged in the most up-to-date social research in Vietnam, as well as some of Vietnam's most popular cultural producers who are forging new ways of imagining the present, while at the same time actively engaging in re-interpreting the past.

Lisa B.W. Drummond is Assistant Professor in Urban Studies at York University, Toronto.

Mandy Thomas is Deputy Director and Senior Research Fellow at the Centre for Cross-Cultural Research at the Australian National University.

Consuming Urban Culture in Contemporary Vietnam

Edited by
Lisa B.W. Drummond
and Mandy Thomas

RoutledgeCurzon
Taylor & Francis Group
LONDON AND NEW YORK

First published 2003
by RoutledgeCurzon
11 New Fetter Lane, London EC4P 4EE

Simultaneously published in the USA and Canada
by RoutledgeCurzon
29 West 35th Street, New York, NY 10001

RoutledgeCurzon is an imprint of the Taylor & Francis Group

Typeset in Baskerville by Taylor & Francis Books Ltd
Printed and bound in Great Britain by TJ International Ltd, Padstow, Cornwall

British Library Cataloguing in Publication Data
A catalogue record for this book is available from the British Library

Library of Congress Cataloging in Publication Data
A catalog record for this book has been requested

ISBN 0–415–29689–7

Contents

Illustrations

Contributors

Dang Nhat Minh has established a reputation in Vietnam and abroad as the most outstanding Vietnamese filmmaker today. He is an international award-winning director with a skill for portraying social change through the everyday experiences of Vietnamese subjects. His film *Returning* has won numerous international awards including prize for best director at the Pacific and Asian Film Festival in Sydney in 1995. In 2001 his film *Season of Guavas* received international recognition and acclaim.

Lisa B.W. Drummond is an Assistant Professor in Urban Studies at York University in Toronto. Lisa's doctoral research at the Australian National University was on everyday life and social change in urban Vietnam. She has worked in Vietnam since 1991 and lived there for six years, undertaking research as well as being employed on development projects with bilateral and multilateral donors and NGOs. Her earlier research was on women in the informal sector in Hanoi, and her most recent work is on the transformations in Vietnam's urban society.

Adam Fforde, an economist with long experience in Vietnam, is now working in the South East Asian Studies Program at the National University of Singapore. His interests are mainly to do with institutional change and interactions between social and economic affairs. He works as an academic researcher and as a development consultant through Aduki Pty. Ltd. Fluent in Vietnamese, he studied the language at Hanoi University in 1978–79. He has spent more than eight years living and working in Vietnam. He studied music theory and voice with Pham Quy Duong in Hanoi during 1990–92 and has been called 'a serious amateur electric bass player'.

Martin Gainsborough is a British Academy Post-doctoral Research Fellow in the Department of Politics and International Studies at the University of Warwick. He wrote his PhD thesis on politics and economic reform in Ho Chi Minh City, where he lived from 1996–99. He is the author of 'Political Change in Vietnam' in *Democratisation* (Polity Press for the Open University 1997) and has published widely in journals and periodicals. In addition to his academic work, he has an active consultancy portfolio doing research for the Economist Intelligence Unit, Business Monitor International as well as a number of private sector clients. From 1992–94 he was the Asia-Pacific Editor for the international business consultancy firm Oxford Analytica.

Peter Higgs graduated from the School of Social Work UNSW in 1988, then worked for a number of years as a community development worker on an inner-city public housing estate in Melbourne. Between 1993 and 1995 he lived and studied in Hanoi, Vietnam where he completed research for a Master of Arts at the Victoria University of Technology in Melbourne on footpath trading in Hanoi. Since 1996 he has worked with the Centre for Harm Reduction at the Macfarlane Burnet Institute for Medical Research and Public Health on action research and community development projects with ethnic Vietnamese injecting drug users in Melbourne, Sydney and Vietnam.

Stephen McNally is a doctoral candidate in the Department of Anthropology at the Australian National University. His research orientations include development discourses, the anthropology of development practice, gender and development, and the political economy of HIV/AIDS in the third world. His experience in Vietnam includes fourteen months of fieldwork in Hanoi (1996–97) where he also worked as a development consultant for Deutsche Gesellschaft für Technische Zusammenarbeit (GTZ).

Pham Thu Thuy is a research scholar in Asian History in the Faculty of Asian Studies, Australian National University. She has been reading about and doing research on Vietnamese popular culture and popular religion for the last eight years. She is also a Research Assistant in the Department of Political and Social Change, Australian National University. She has translated a paper called 'The Changing Face of Vietnamese Cinema', published in David G Marr (ed.) *The Mass Media in Vietnam* (1988).

Phan Thi Vang Anh is a popular novelist who won the 1994 Vietnamese Writers Association Award. Her stories about young people's lives in contemporary Vietnamese urban settings, of love and family friction, have wide popular readership throughout Vietnam, and are of particular appeal to young women. Her stories strike a chord with Vietnamese youth whose dilemmas exemplify the social impact of the society-wide transformations. Her most famous story 'When People Are Young' deals with the issue of youth suicide within a contemporary world devoid of ideals and purpose.

Alexander Soucy completed his doctorate at the Department of Anthropology, Research School of Pacific and Asian Studies, the Australian National University, in 2000. His dissertation focused on gender and religious practice in Hanoi and was based on research conducted in the period from January 1997 to September 1998. He is presently documenting nineteenth-century photographs of Asia for the Canadian Centre for Architecture in Montreal.

Cheryl Stock is an Associate Professor and Head of Dance at Queensland University of Technology, prior to which she had a long career as an

Australian dancer, teacher, choreographer and director, creating over forty major works and working in twenty-seven countries. Cheryl was the founding Artistic Director of Dance North, one of Australia's leading contemporary dance companies from 1985 to 1995. In 1995, she was awarded two medals from the Vietnamese government; for services to dance in Vietnam and for services to the women's movement. Currently Vice-President (Pacific region) of the World Dance Alliance – Asia Pacific Centre, Cheryl has undertaken eighteen cultural exchange programs in Asia, of which twelve have been in Vietnam. Her doctoral thesis, *Making Intercultural Dance in Vietnam* was awarded in 2000 and was the result of collaborating with Vietnamese artists in Hanoi over a ten-year period.

Philip Taylor, an anthropologist, is a research fellow at the Research School of Pacific and Asian Studies, Australian National University. His research on the impact of national reunification, socialist reforms and economic liberalisation policies in Ho Chi Minh City and the Mekong delta appears in *Fragments of the Present: Searching for Modernity in Vietnam's South* (Allen & Unwin 2001). He is completing a book on pilgrimages and popular religion in Vietnam and a study on ethnic and religious minority cultures in Vietnam's Mekong delta.

Carlyle A. Thayer is Professor of Politics, University College, University of New South Wales at the Australian Defence Force Academy and concurrently, Deakin University's On Site Coordinator at the College of Defence and Strategic Studies, Australian Defence College. He is a political science specialist who has been studying Vietnamese politics for over thirty years. He is the author and editor of fourteen books and major monographs including *The Vietnam People's Army under Doi Moi* (ISEAS 1994), *Soviet Relations with India and Vietnam, 1945–1992* (Oxford University Press 1992, with Ramesh Thakur) and *War by Other Means: National Liberation and Revolution in Vietnam* (Allen & Unwin 1989).

Mandy Thomas, an anthropologist, is Deputy Director, Centre for Cross-cultural Research, Australian National University. She has published widely on the overseas Vietnamese communities in Australia, including the book *Dreams in the Shadows: Vietnamese-Australian Lives in Transition* (St Leonards, Allen & Unwin 1999). She is also the co-editor of *Alter/Asians: Asian-Australian Identities in Art, Media and Popular Culture* (2000). Her research interests are in migration and embodiment, the flows of Asian popular culture, and social and political change in Vietnam. She has also been involved in numerous development consultancy projects in Vietnam and elsewhere in Southeast Asia.

Acknowledgements

This book originated from a series of energetic discussions within the Vietnam Studies Group at the Australian National University. These exchanges about the compelling transformations in contemporary Vietnamese society and the relatively small amount of scholarly material available on the subject paved the way for the *Vietnam Update* in 1998. Unlike previous yearly updates which dealt with the contemporary political and economic changes in Vietnam, this conference focused almost entirely on everyday life and popular culture in urban centres. For the first time, not only academics but also Vietnamese cultural practitioners involved in the production of contemporary film, music, television and literature were brought together to debate the transformations in city life.

Our deepest thanks go to the Ford Foundation and its Vietnam office for its generosity, specifically for its financial support for the 1999 *Update* conference. This funding allowed us to bring a diverse group of social scientists and cultural producers from as far afield as Vietnam to Australia for a highly memorable and challenging meeting.

We thank Thuy Pham for her hard work in assisting with the organisation of the conference, in her excellent translations during the proceedings and in her continued involvement in liaison with the Vietnamese participants during the publication process. We also acknowledge the assistance of David Koh and Yen Musgrove who readily contributed their ideas, enthusiasm and translation skills when they were needed. We are grateful to Ben Kerkvliet and David Marr who provided excellent advice and assistance throughout the conference and in the development of the publication. We thank all those in the Vietnam Studies Group at the Australian National University for their generous support and for making the conference such a stimulating and lively occasion.

We are indebted to Beverley Fraser and Oanh Collins from the Research School of Pacific and Asian Studies at the Australian National University for their efficiency and good humour in assisting so adeptly with the Update organisation and the publication process. Jan Mullette and Joan Silk helped us greatly with the preparation of the manuscript and colleagues at the Institute for Cultural Research provided a stimulating working environment in which to bring ideas to practical fruition. We thank Jane Gibian and Amanda Wise for their excellent editing skills, flexibility and patience in dealing with each of the chapters in the final stages of completing the book. Appreciation also goes to the Division of Social Science, York University, for providing a collegial and supportive space in which to pull together this volume in the final stages.

Our thanks to Rachel Saunders, Emma Howarth and Carol Baker at RoutledgeCurzon for the refreshing ease with which they assisted us with the publication. The anonymous reviewers provided some excellent comments which helped all the authors revise their chapters and ultimately led to a much richer volume. A different version of Thomas's chapter was published in *Urban Studies* in 2002 and the feedback she received from the journal's assessors is gratefully acknowledged as is the journal's permission to publish the paper in a different form.

Finally, we thank the authors themselves for making our collaboration such an enriching one and for enduring a long process which included several sets of revisions and a multitude of emails. Ultimately, this book aims to reveal the ways in which the Vietnamese cultural landscape is being refashioned and reshaped under major social and economic change. Only the vivid first-hand accounts of these processes from scholars and cultural workers engaged in research as well as cultural production and consumption on the ground in Vietnam has made this endeavour possible.

Lisa Drummond, Toronto
Mandy Thomas, Canberra
March 2003

Chapter 1

Introduction

Mandy Thomas and Lisa B.W. Drummond

Present-day Vietnam: contradictions and dilemmas

Everyday cultural life dramatically reflects and embodies changes in society at large. In this volume, a range of authors discuss the impact on everyday lived experience of the key political and economic transformations that have occurred in Vietnam over the last few years. Since the late 1980s, Vietnam has undergone a metamorphosis from a relatively closed society with a centrally planned economy to a rapidly urbanising one with a globalising cultural outlook. As the experience of other modernising Southeast Asian nations has shown, however, it is nigh impossible to open oneself up to global flows of capital without also opening oneself up to global flows of culture and information. It is because of this that Vietnam is on the brink of becoming a fully fledged media culture in which the popular narratives and cultural icons are reshaping political views, constructing tastes and values, crystallising the market economy and 'providing the materials out of which people forge their very identities' (Hartley 1996: 1). These changes have been the catalyst for an exciting ferment of activity in the domain of pop culture. Artists, musicians, writers, television producers and film directors have all benefited from the diversification in patterns of consumption, the slowly increasing levels of wealth and the gradual freeing up of state control over the activities of the populace.

Street culture in the cities of Vietnam is one in which street vendors carrying baskets of fresh produce from their farms jostle with young men in crisp, white, business shirts rushing to their offices, where *cyclos* carry groups of students loudly communicating on their mobile phones, where the pavement noodle shops double as internet cafés and the latest glimmering paintjob on a motorbike is being admired by a group of savvy young consumers. The streets in urban Vietnam are predominantly youth-focused, reflecting the demographic situation in which well over half of the population is under 16 years old. However, it is not so much the age of people that marks the cities as being forward-focused and energetically engaged in the future, but the technologies, music, fashion and leisure activities which symbolise a population urgently acquiring the emblems of modernity. At the same time traditional practices are being modified and transformed, religious practices reinvested with meaning and traditional arts and crafts revived.

The papers collected in this volume represent the work of not only many scholars who are carrying out some of the most exciting social research in Vietnam today, but also some of Vietnam's most popular cultural producers who are forging new ways of imagining the present while at the same time engaging actively in reinterpreting the past. In Vietnam, the embrace of pop culture has arisen simultaneously with a nostalgia for modes of life swallowed up by modernity's relentless progress. The quest to preserve, to salvage, comes precisely at that moment when the sense of inevitable global homogenisation and subsequent extinguishing of cultural diversity is at its most compelling.

But this volume does not just provide a celebration of contemporary cultural life and artistic creativity in Vietnam, it also reveals a dark side of Vietnamese urban existence. There has recently been an explosion in the incidence of marriage breakdown, HIV/AIDS, drug and alcohol abuse, petty crime and teenage suicide, particularly in vulnerable and minority groups. At the same time, wider evidence of 'social unrest' – as manifest in demonstrations and other forms of civil disorder in both urban and rural areas – reveals, among other things, a country struggling to confront the brave new world of economic restructuring with which the region has now been forced to engage. The Asian economic and political crises of the last few years have wreaked some havoc in Vietnam, cutting down many promising economic, political and social signifiers of movement forward. The papers in this volume reveal the diverse ways that Vietnam is culturally and socially negotiating the future.

Money and consumerism: new forms of longing

The dramatic changes in the Vietnamese economy, begun by *doi moi* (the economic 'renovation' policy of 1986) and fuelled by increasing levels of international investment and aid in the early nineties, have had a profound impact upon the social life and consumer practices of the Vietnamese populace, particularly in the cities. Shopping centres are springing up in every major city. In early 2002 the luxurious Trang Tien Plaza in Hanoi was opened on the site of the former spartan Hanoi State General Department Store on Hoan Kiem Lake as a very visible demonstration of the evolution in consumer tastes of the last decade. Not only has there been an increasing availability of consumer items, particularly imported ones, but these consumer items are being taken up as markers of success. Whereas in the early eighties most families used bicycles for transport, today motorbikes are prevalent. Not only are they widespread, but certain brands and engine capacities are keenly sought after. Fashion has developed to such an extent that girls now go on shopping expeditions after school to look at the range of new fabrics and styles available. The market for popular culture in the form of music and film has expanded to include not only regional musicians and films but also some US and other international products. When the film *Titanic* was released in 1998, thousands of pirated video copies of it were readily available in Vietnam (where first-run movies are not released) and teenagers were seen wearing Leonardo DiCaprio T-shirts. There is a housing boom throughout the country with cement factories recording a dramatic increase in sales and the opening up of homeware stores for the wealthy. Private clubs with bars and sports facilities are also being opened with membership prices many times more than the average yearly income.

The emerging more affluent youth market is hungry for products, but always with a Vietnamese flavour. Global trends such as cafés have taken off but with their own unique Vietnamese twist. For example, what is being called the Vietnamese Starbucks, the chain of more than 400 Trung Nguyen cafés, was started by a young entrepreneur as the first nation-wide franchise.[1] In Hanoi one of these cafés seats over 400 people and at weekends attracts hundreds of young people on motorbikes.

Changing consumption patterns have been interwoven with popular holidays and festivals. At the same time as the interest in state-organised events such as May Day celebrations has seriously declined, pilgrimages and religious festivals are flourishing. With the rise of popular festivals comes an array of consumer practices associated with leisure activities – tourism, drinking, eating, souvenir purchasing and the enjoyment of popular entertainment such as karaoke, music and dancing. While the Tet and Autumn festivals remain the holiday highlights of the Vietnamese calendar, celebration of Christmas and the Western New Year has in recent years become popular. In 2002, Valentine's Day had its first obvious commercial presence, with greeting cards stores and chocolate sales registering the moment (Jim Kennedy, *New Haven Register*, 14 February 2002).

It is clear that consumption has become one of the prime leisure activities of the urban population. However these new patterns of spending have revealed new social divisions and hierarchies. While sales of gold have skyrocketed, there has been a rise in petty crimes such as bag-snatching and pick-pocketing, increasing use of illegal drugs such as heroin and a flood of contraband goods from across the border in southern China pouring into the markets. There has also been a surprising lack of development of manufacturing industries. So while the pleasures of purchasing have been enjoyed by a few and there has been a proliferation in advertising, the continuing economic woes of the country have not been positively affected by such a change in spending patterns.

The changing media and new technologies

In a recent volume on the media in Vietnam, Marr (1998) argues that the mass media has undergone a radical face-lift over the last decade and has fuelled consumer interest in new products. If the media is, as Hartley suggests, 'a visualisation of society' (1996: 210), then the recent foray into media culture is a dramatic turnaround from that which existed previously.[2] Until the policy of renovation (*doi moi*) was instituted in 1986, the Vietnamese media had the role of spreading propaganda and consequently focused less on reporting news than on educating the populace.

As evidenced in the memoirs of northern journalist turned political refugee, Bui Tin, many journalists from 1954 onwards were integrated into the party and felt honoured to be spreading the party's messages (Bui Tin 1995). Public criticism of the regime in the north has been apparent mainly in literature rather than in journalism, and writers such as Duong Thu Huong and Nguyen Huy Thiep, who examine forms of social deterioration and dislocation, have often found themselves censured by the party.[3] In general, however, the nationalist cause and the socialist ideals were promoted through the arts, which were 'to be purged of the perfidious influence of Western bourgeois culture and provided with a new focus, nationalist in form and socialist in content' (Duiker 1995: 181–2). In the south after 1975, journalists and writers were singled out for particular punishment by the party, with many sent to forced labour camps or imprisoned (Jamieson 1993: 364). Awareness of the power of the printed word has led the party to harness journalists and writers to its cause at the same time as it harbours a tenacious suspicion and distrust of their products.

At the time of writing, reports in the major Vietnamese newspapers remain dominated by party-related events highlighting activities which represent the socialist society of Vietnam as a success. Other stories that predominate in the newspapers are those that convey moral lessons or provide information on public issues of health and safety. Although there are increasing media reports of corruption, crime and social upheaval, these are often framed so that the information appears to be for the protection of the masses and thus such reports continue to represent the party as a body interested in rooting out social and political 'problems'. While criticism may be directed at officials, the leaders of the party and the overriding system of rule never come under direct attack, nor are they placed under the critical spotlight.

Since *doi moi*, there has been a dramatic increase in the number of newspapers and magazines available. Journalists have also been permitted to investigate cases of wrongdoing by police and local party officials as well as instances of high-level corruption. However, there is still a demand for greater freedom of the press. Journalists are in the difficult situation of serving two masters, of wanting to attract a readership at the same time as not being permitted to exacerbate political instability.[4] While there are no private presses and all publishing has to be licensed by the Culture and Information Ministry, there has been a widening range of material available as well as a dramatic rise in the overall number of publications, including foreign literature. The shift from a 'public relations state' (Schudson 1989: 160) to one in which the public takes an active role in the choice of media information they receive has been bumpy and the media has on occasions reverted to dictatorial state control (see Hiang-Khng Heng 1997; Unger 1991).

The growth in television ownership has coincided with more sophisticated and varied programming, with some popular programmes capturing a large audience (see Drummond, this volume, Chapter 10). In recent years the number of illegal satellite dishes has grown rapidly, with the public's demand for a more diverse range of information such as that which they can now see on channels such as Star World, Star Sport, MTV, Discovery, Cartoon Network, CNN: 'Chinese satellite dishes have flooded the domestic market, selling for just $100 each and enabling users to receive transmissions from Hong Kong, China, Indonesia and Australia. Others include dishes from Taiwan, Korea and the US' (Bich Ngoc, *VIR*, 16 August 2002).

Throughout Vietnam, there is a revival of the radio, particularly programmes that feature listener participation, for example *Green Wave*, an hour-long weekly youth programme in Ho Chi Minh City which is 'credited with setting the pace for Vietnamese musical tastes' (Margaret Cohen, *Far Eastern Economic Review*, 3 January 2002). But perhaps the greatest media intrusion into the social and political life of the country will be the internet. The popularity of the internet is growing rapidly. Although Vietnam has only 250,000 internet subscribers, due largely to high sign-up costs and user fees (Reuters, 8 August 2002), internet cafés are exploding in number to accommodate the number of young people wanting to chat on-line and surf the net. While it is still too early to see what impact the net may have on consumption patterns and upon political change, the state has tried to censor its use and limit circulation of some types of information through nation-wide firewalls (electronic filters) (Knight Ridder News Service, 2 September 2001). However, in reality electronic political censorship is difficult, with politically sensitive material easily being sent via email, fax and radio. How successful such manoeuvres will be in the long term, given the ability of the internet and its users to 'work around' such obstacles, is uncertain, although it is fair to note that the Singapore government has seemingly implemented this method with on-going success.

While the use of new technologies such as mobile phones and text messaging is common throughout the region, communication via technology has also grown and in particularly Vietnamese ways. In Ho Chi Minh City, for example, 'chat phone cafés' are becoming very popular, as reported in the following news article:

> These days, the tables at Chat Phone Cafe in Ho Chi Minh City are filled with twenty-somethings who talk not among themselves, but into telephones. Customers visit the cafe specifically to talk to complete strangers over the phone. These cafes, which could be considered the Vietnamese version of a telephone club, have become increasingly popular among young Vietnamese. Chat Phone Cafe, Vietnam's first telephone cafe, is run by former journalist Dang Hong Tuyen and her husband. The cafe has eight two-person tables equipped with one telephone. The idea to open the cafe came to Tuyen, who mainly covered domestic issues during her 15-year career as a reporter, when a 17-year-old girl approached her for advice after she broke up with her boyfriend. Tuyen recalled that the girl had told her that she wanted someone to listen to her problems. For an annual membership fee of 50,000 dong, clients can register their telephone numbers with the cafe, along with their age, gender and interests. Currently, Chat Phone Cafe has about 1,000 members. Telephone numbers are managed by the cafe. Visitors inform the cafe of the type of person they would like to talk to.

> The cafe then pairs them up with a suitable candidate from their members, whom visitors are introduced to over the telephone.
>
> (Kenichi Okumura, *Yomiuri Shimbun* (Daily Yomiuri), 16 April 2002)

While romance fuels the motivation to engage in these forms of communication, an epiphenomenon of these changing practices is the opening up of spaces for critical discussion and sharing of ideas. Internet cafés, coffee shops and leisure sites will undoubtedly also be key sites for the fuller development of civil society in Vietnam, with students playing an increasingly important role in initiating social and political change and taking on new forms of media and technology.

Popular culture: youth and radical transition

Although the media is changing, the state still does not see information as a marketable commodity or as entertainment. The development of celebrities in Vietnam thus requires something in addition to media support. Consumers must engage with tangible cultural products of the icon. The advent of market economics and globalisation brought the notion and practice of pop culture with icons and cultural products to Vietnam. Throughout the country, celebrities are being memorialised in obtainable objects, the media only providing the initial catalyst for interest in an individual. Celebrities are brought into the home embodied in artefacts.[5] These posters, cassettes, soap operas, CDs, videos, or even T-shirts with the pop image or name of the celebrity emblazoned on them are freely available in Ho Chi Minh City and Hanoi.[6] Unlike neighbouring socialist China which witnessed Mao revolutionary paraphernalia turned into a massive pop industry of T-shirts with slick slogans, posters with New Age images and cover designs for rock music CDs (Barmé 1996), Vietnam has not 'Warholised' Ho Chi Minh's heritage. The commodities associated with popular icons are usurping older mass cultural icons such as the ubiquitous bust of Ho Chi Minh or lapel pins/badges of the emblems of the socialist state.[7] It is evident, therefore, that with the rapid increase in the availability of consumer items, the attraction to celebrities is growing. At the same time, as the relationship between popular icons and commodification is intensifying, there has been a corresponding decrease in the circulation of the iconography of the socialist regime.

Presently, a startling change in public culture and media accessibility is underway in Vietnam. The growth of a heterogeneity of popular figures who appeal to youth is significant because of the noticeable contrast between this range of interests and significations compared with the figures that are popular with the older age group. Here, so-called 'globalisation' has not been a homogenising influence but rather the reverse. For older people there was an intense narrowness of interest in public personas but for young people there was a vast array of contrasting, fluid identifications (for example, in a recent survey one young man listed 'Bill Gates, Fidel Castro' as his favourite non-Vietnamese celebrities – a seemingly opposed set of individuals – see Thomas 1997; Thomas and Hiang-Khng Heng 2000). In the same survey, local celebrities listed by young people were much more homogenous. By contrast, the foreign celebrities listed were spread over a range of fields and interests and seemed to vary with an unpredictability that indicates the sudden flooding of the discursive field of fame with a ready population of personas. This suggests that a populace newly exposed to celebrities and without having had the time or opportunity to build on-going relationships with these icons, readily identify with a diverse range of images. This is not to say that Vietnamese youth are 'undiscriminating' when exposed to foreign media images, but rather that the situation is indicative of their intense and growing fascination with overseas celebrities and the gradual diffusion of the power of few public figures to a larger and more diverse field of personas.

Here, the enjoyment of certain cultural forms and the 'capacities for pleasure and conceptions of pleasure' are mobilised by a configuration of cultural and historical meanings (Mercer 1986: 66). That is, what is considered to be 'entertaining' at any given moment is contingent upon cultural systems of meanings at particular sites. Until very recently the powerful intervention of state upon the desires and needs of the populace was successful in implementing a regime of pleasure associated with nationalist ideals. Following Mercer (1986: 55), the imposition of desires upon the populace is part of a wider political arena in which there is some persuasion, some resistance and some negotiation. So the present popularity of football players in Vietnam, like the earlier attraction to national figures, is inseparable from the dominant ideology of the moment and the everyday cultural and social worlds of the individual consumer. These celebrities, all popular icons, are meaningful because they are hieroglyphs, instantiations of worlds in the making, of tastes, ideologies and relations of power in the wider social environment of Vietnam. The very different responses of younger people to questions about their media interests indicate the sea-change in attitudes about the role of artists as public personas.

Nostalgia: the 'rural' in the Vietnamese imaginary

Increased mobility is one of the most important changes for rural residents in the last decade. This has come about from a freeing up of internal travel restrictions, improvements in the transport sector, an opening up of markets and a need for labour in the newly developing urban manufacturing and service industries, as well as from the dismantling of the rationing system which kept people in their registered place of residence. While some wealthy or educated urban Vietnamese have been able to travel overseas, this form of travel remains the domain of very few. The biggest impact on mobility has been within the country itself, creating a free-flowing movement of people seeking to sell their goods, looking for work in the cities, moving to be with family, as well as for internal tourism and pilgrimage to religious sites (see Higgs, Chapter 5 and Soucy, Chapter 8). This movement has, however, come at a time when the image of rural life in Vietnam resonates increasingly strongly as a site of the nostalgic imagination.

Although 'urban culture' is beginning to be circulated widely throughout the country and therefore permeates its predominantly rural population (see Drummond, Chapter 10), urban culture also expresses a profound and heavily romanticised vision of rural life and 'the village' around which it is centred. This romanticisation is a consequence, as it has been in other countries of the region (see Logan 1994; Barmé 1996: 321) and at various times around the world, of a growing discontent with the alienation and anomie of urban and industrial life. Such discontent is not necessarily new in Vietnam; the cultural focus on the countryside has long been a feature of Vietnamese society (see Drummond 1999). In the present circumstances, what is striking is not only the ability of this expression of imagined nostalgia to reflect discontent with urban/modern life, but the circulation of these images beyond an urban audience to a large rural audience with newly acquired access to the media of popular culture.

It is a common perception in Vietnam that the opening up of Vietnamese society to global flows of culture and information has had a profound impact upon traditional values. There have indeed been changes in moral outlook, behaviour and personal relationships, and the ideals and principles of previous generations seem no longer appropriate or relevant in the new social and economic environment. The rise of what seems to many to be money-worship and the erosion of traditional values generate fear and uncertainty, especially for those who have not benefited from the changes and may perceive that they have been left by the wayside. Increased mobility, urbanisation and globalisation and their concomitant poverty, economic hardship and uncertainty about the future have given rise to a nostalgic longing for a more spiritual, more meaningful and balanced co-existence among a large section of the population. The gap between urban and rural lifestyles and incomes seems irrelevant to these idealised images. Romanticised views of the village and rural society have represented the city as the site of materialism, superficiality, spiritual alienation and corruption. The rural images, by contrast, project a sense that the countryside is the repository of traditional values, national identity, that life in the village is more peaceful and that relationships there are based upon emotion rather than money. This dichotomy is represented well in Dang Nhat Minh's film *Returning* (see Dang and Pham, Chapter 12). Here the south is a metaphor for the city and the north a metaphor for the countryside. Hanoi represents culture, peace, calm and warmth; Saigon represents commerce, the rat-race, the corporate ladder, corruption and a lack of feelings. These contrasts between north and south are common in both the media and in popular literature, and to some degree reflect the urban/rural contrasts.

It hardly needs stating that, for most, this nostalgic longing refers to an era or rural way of life that they do not know personally because they are too young and because it no longer exists (if it ever did). Yet the state has made culture, and by implication a nostalgic culture, a major policy initiative (the 1997 Communist Party Plenum focused on culture). This preoccupation with culture is significant in state efforts to address these issues of social dislocation indirectly through the instigation of nostalgia and the manipulation of cultural images to create a sense of shared national culture and cultural pride.

Views from afar: the diaspora and the fetishisation of democracy

Right up until the present, the north has struggled economically rather more than the south. Historically, northerners criticised the south for consumerism and moral corruption both during and after the American involvement in Vietnam. This characterisation of the south as harbouring decadence, a loss of spiritual values and as being a society corrupted by materialism still persists. The situation at present in Vietnam is that it is the fifth poorest country in the world, with a GDP per capita of only US$400 per year *(http://www.dfat.gov.au/geo/veitnam/vietnam_brief.html)*. Not only did many northerners head south in 1954 to escape communism but, after that time, there were many economic and political migrants who left Vietnam altogether (from the north and the south) and went to some of the world's richest countries. This differential between the economic position of those in Vietnam and those who left has to be remembered when considering the relationship between overseas Vietnamese and their relatives back home.

While there are obvious regional, class and gender distinctions among migrants from Vietnam, it appears that the distinction that is made between those remaining in the homeland and those living overseas is often the 'difference that makes a difference' (Levi-Strauss, 1969) to Vietnam-born people. This difference often outweighs other differences although inevitably there are individual cases in which class, in particular, overrides other markers of identification. As occurs with most migrant groups, class and educational status in the homeland are given entirely different positions in the land of settlement. In the case of Vietnamese, discrimination in employment opportunities and structural change in Western economies have combined to place most Vietnamese in marginal socio-economic positions in their host societies (see Viviani 1996). Nevertheless, this marginality is invisible when examining the relations between homeland and diaspora and there is frequently a bilateral valuation of those who have left as having a higher economic and political status relative to those who remain in Vietnam. Certainly, the impact of overseas remittances from relatives to family members in Vietnam has had an impact on these issues of power and status as well as important nation-wide economic effects: during 2001 overseas remittances were estimated to reach US$2 billion (*Vietnam News*, 16 November 2001).

At the present moment, we are continually being called upon to reflect upon the status of 'the nation' in the rapidly transforming social and political theatre of globalisation. Appadurai, in his 1996 book *Modernity at Large*, argues that there are two constitutive features of modern subjectivities – the media and migration. He suggests that both the media and migration offer new resources for the construction of imagined selves and imagined worlds; that as these two processes move people imaginatively out of their local, regional and national spaces, they set up a transnational flow of experience. On flights to Vietnam there are always overseas Vietnamese returning to visit families and birthplace, peering anxiously out of the windows for that first sight of the landscape: Is it what they remember? Has it changed? There are also tourists expectantly reading their Lonely Planet guidebooks. There are a few businessmen in suits, looking slightly bored and tired, checking out their appointments in their slick black filofaxes. And then there are a group of people composed of those who work for non-governmental organisations (NGOs), media organisations, academics and other cosmopolitans. The interactions between the cosmopolitan elites and the returning migrants are almost non-existent. Western tourists, for example, do not turn to the overseas Vietnamese to ask what places they should see in Vietnam but closely question other tourists who have travelled to or worked in Vietnam. Among the business people, academics and NGO workers there are very few overseas Vietnamese. This curious division between two types of transnationals – the diasporic and the cosmopolitan – expresses a complex contemporary social set of interrelationships. In the increasingly heterogeneous transnational social field, there are distinct hierarchies and divisions and it is cosmopolitan elites who appear to have the advantage.

It is important here to point out the power of the construction of the West as consumer-oriented and 'the Rest' as not. While the north/south division in Vietnam is linked to the Vietnam/the West opposition in this regard, these links and boundaries are ambiguous and unstable. Further, while overseas Vietnamese are decried as embodying a decline of Vietnamese moral values and contamination by the consumerist global culture, in actuality, local Vietnamese complain about this transformation within their own country. For example, in discussing the contemporary northern writer, Nguyen Huy Thiep, the Vietnamese scholar Nguyen Hung Quoc writes:

> The majority of his short stories concentrated on one main theme: criticising the alienation of man under the socialist regime.... Nguyen Huy Thiep pitilessly unveiled all the misery, degradation and ridicule of mankind and the complete collapse of morals and feelings between men. Money reigned supreme.... There was no brotherhood, no fraternal feelings. There was no love, no feelings between husband and wife. Only trifling and mean calculations about money.
>
> (Nguyen Hung Quoc 1991: 22)

The perception of many overseas Vietnamese is that there has been a degradation of spiritual values, a result of the socialist regime which effectively cut the country off from Western influence for more than a decade. Western values and lifestyles have often been the focus of attack by those that decry the changing nature of the Vietnamese family in the West and the rhetoric of externalising of the causes of decay has worked at reinforcing a boundary that has always been unstable. Vietnam belongs irrevocably to what Edward Said (1979: 55) once called an 'imaginative geography and history', which helps overseas Vietnamese 'dramatise the difference' between themselves and those left in Vietnam. This difference is most felt to arise in the political and economic domains, in which the communism of Vietnam is demonised to a degree that overseas Vietnamese often view their homeland as inexperienced in the ways of the consumer West, however clearly the history of Vietnam points to long-term engagement with the world beyond: the overseas Vietnamese were no strangers to capitalism when they left Vietnam.

There is frequently a desire on the part of overseas Vietnamese to help their families under a regime they may despise. Giving gifts to family back home then is an inherently political act and for many is the only legitimate form of resistance. This is because fighting the regime in Vietnam is seen as fighting the forces of communism with capitalism, with the 'power of modern consumption processes' (Miller 1995: 3). In Vietnam there is still a good deal of political control over consumption as well as an association between consumer items and decadence or 'social evils'. Many autobiographical accounts of those who fled suggest that, under socialism in Vietnam, one could express opposition to the regime through the accumulation of objects which on many occasions which might be used to pay for a departure. Not only were people defining themselves through these items, they were also strategically creating contrasting categories – the free West of abundant consumer pleasure versus the repressive, colourless communist bloc more interested in production from vast, inefficient, state-owned enterprises than in consumer freedoms and choice. Here, as Slater (1997) argues, Western consumption has come to represent not only material wealth and the satisfying of fantasies of accumulation but is equated with the notion of personal freedom. As gifts allow individuals to insinuate certain symbolic properties into the lives of the gift recipient, so overseas Vietnamese often wish to place the desire for consumer products within families in the homeland and suggest that there exists an independent and prior desire for goods which they are attempting to satisfy. As one overseas Vietnamese individual mentioned: 'If my family see what they could have if Vietnam were a democracy they may want to do something about it, these gifts may make them more politically aware' (Thomas 1999: 74). Here, the gifts are viewed as a type of Trojan horse, which could lead to the disruption of the political system in Vietnam. Like the colonial quest to civilise, there is a faith that commodities can invoke profound social transformation (see Comaroff 1996: 19). The impact of both the money and the ideas of overseas Vietnamese upon their homeland thus should not be underestimated, but must always be seen as part of the process whereby democracy and capitalism are often fetishised (and believed, mistakenly, to be in opposition to what presently occurs in Vietnam). However, both the Vietnamese economy and the present-day political arrangements are becoming much more blurred and contradictory.

Contributions in this volume

The papers in this volume are arranged thematically, though such an arrangement is necessarily arbitrary as many of the topics are connected in various ways to several of the themes. Part I groups a number of papers which provide much-needed overviews of the socio-economic issues backgrounding the social transformation and cultural issues of contemporary urban Vietnam. In Chapter 1, Carl Thayer examines the political situation of the late 1990s, charting the role of Party Secretary General Le Kha Phieu in the events of 1997–2001. Thayer argues that Le Kha Phieu's term was a period of what he calls 'reform immobilism', a preoccupation with political stability which overshadowed economic concerns, limiting decisive action on issues such as the impact of the Asian financial crisis and effective anti-corruption measures. Adam Fforde considers the local–global implications in analysing Vietnam's current economic situation, as well as addressing the cultural aspects of Vietnam's economic problems. Fforde highlights the important differences and similarities between Hanoi and Ho Chi Minh City as he discusses the two cities' emerging middle classes and their economic histories. His chapter offers not just an overview of the economic changes in the country but argues that Vietnam's particular style of development is reproducing a set of cultural styles in which certain aspects of Vietnamese traditional life – such as music, fragrance and food – are given primacy. The discussion of Hanoi and Ho Chi Minh City reflects the central role these two cities play in Vietnam's urban system and their popular characterisations: Hanoi, the seat of national government, and Ho Chi Minh City, the country's economic engine; Hanoi, the bastion of socialist conservatism and Ho Chi Minh City, the heart of reformist thinking. But Martin Gainsborough re-examines this popular characterisation of Ho Chi Minh City as 'reformist'. As a result, he offers an insightful analysis of local politics in the southern urban centre which challenges the usual reading of that city.

Part II consists of papers which more directly address issues of everyday life in the cities, opening with Peter Higgs' look at sidewalk trading, which has blossomed since the introduction of *doi moi*. Higgs observes how urban residents of Hanoi have responded to changing economic circumstances as evidenced by the small-scale trading activities of one neighbourhood over a period of six years. Pham Thu Thuy examines newspaper cartoons which tread the fine line between social commentary and political criticism. She provides an analysis and 'de-coding' of cartoons appearing in two of the country's most popular newspapers, offering insights into the ways in which cartoons convey deeper socio-political messages and critiques. One of the most common billboard themes in Vietnam today is that of the risks of contracting HIV/AIDS from certain dangerous activities. In Chapter 7 Stephen McNally looks behind the billboards at the social location of the sex industry in Vietnam and how HIV/AIDS is changing, or not, the way in which people engage in sexual activity via the sex industry.

In Part III four papers examine facets of popular culture, often overlooked in favour of so-called 'mass culture' (*van hoa dai chung*) which is interpreted by the state as largely rural in nature. Urban culture and contemporary cultural identity is examined in each of the chapters (as, in various ways, in all the chapters here). As strictures against religious practice have eased, religious rituals are resurfacing in everyday life. Alexander Soucy examines the engagement of young urbanites in religious pilgrimages, generally more popular than the usual religious activities, and considers the construction of these as 'entertainment', as well as their underlying religiousity. Both Soucy and Philip Taylor consider the shaping of 'tradition' in popular cultural practice. Taylor discusses the cultural medium of *cai luong* opera and uses its contemporary performance to question Ho Chi Minh City's construction as lacking in cultural traditions or eager to shed them in pursuit of profit. Moving from specific practices to general trends, Lisa Drummond and Mandy Thomas contribute papers which consider, on the one hand, the growing media culture disseminating images and icons for widespread consumption and on the other, increasing contestation over urban development as an indication of an emerging 'public sphere'. Drummond looks at the circulation of images of urban life throughout the country via television. The very popular weekly soap opera-style serials which Drummond examines often portray life in contemporary urban Vietnam and encourage particular understandings of how social relations 'ought' to be enacted. Thomas focuses on the mixing of popular culture with activities in public spaces as well as a series of protests over property development and urban planning, arguing that these protests – this contestation – are evocative of a new, civil society. Public spaces are designed for specific activities and meanings by the state, but even though policed, use of those spaces for undesired activities and counter-meanings cannot be completely eradicated; as 'transgressions' are increasingly tolerated, a sense of a 'public sphere' is developing.

The papers in Part IV move from the analysis of popular culture to the production of it. Dang Nhat Minh, one of Vietnam's best-known film directors, both within and outside the country, offers a filmmaker's view of the social transformation Vietnam is experiencing. Through a discussion of his 1995 film *Returning*, which won several international awards, Dang Nhat Minh explores the social and cultural dilemmas facing Vietnam in its attempt to transform its economy and join, however reluctantly or restrainedly, the international community. Award-winning writer Phan Thi Vang Anh reflects on her own experiences of writing and being a writer in the second paper in this section. Phan Thi Vang Anh also uses interviews with other writers to examine the social role of novelists in Vietnam and the ways in which various writers tackle the social issues of transition. Finally, in a paper on professional dance, Cheryl Stock analyses the tensions and dilemmas facing the arts in Vietnam. Although the arts have supposedly been liberated from direct state control under *doi moi*, to some extent they have traded one set of problems for another, most of them revolving around the trade-offs between commercialisation and artistic goals.

As has been noted in several instances, Vietnam is a country with dual first cities: Hanoi, the capital and the administrative and cultural centre, and Ho Chi Minh City, the economic centre. Given the comparative paucity of work on contemporary social conditions in urban Vietnam in general, it is not surprising that the papers presented here reflect this narrow urban emphasis on Hanoi and

Ho Chi Minh City, as so much still remains to be written about these dominant and fascinating places. Nonetheless, despite a situation in which it is still relatively difficult to secure permission to conduct research in urban centres outside Hanoi and Ho Chi Minh City, there are other Vietnamese cities where the trends, flows and impacts discussed in this collection of papers are also experienced. The second-tier cities, of which Haiphong, Danang and Hue are perhaps the best known, are no longer the stagnant backwaters they have long been considered. These cities and others – including Bien Hoa, Can Tho, Quy Nhon and Nam Dinh – are becoming lively centres in cultural as well as economic terms. As Vietnam becomes increasingly urbanised, these sites will increase in importance. We hope that future research on contemporary urban life in Vietnam will address the general and particular experiences of everyday life and culture throughout Vietnam's swelling urban hierarchy.

Conclusions

One of the key themes that arises in this volume is that of the cultural hybridisation that is occurring in Vietnam. By hybridisation we are not suggesting that two pure forms – indigenous traditional culture and Western influences – are intermeshed but that tradition itself is hybridised and also that external cultural influences must always be indigenised in culturally meaningful ways – they are not just taken on board uncritically but selected and transformed.

A second theme is the widespread ambivalence throughout Vietnam about the changes taking place, an embracing of change at the same time as there is a critiquing of it. Cultural producers are themselves experimenting with describing and documenting the social changes that are taking place, with providing a mirror for society. The people's actual practices of consumption indicate both the inability of national culture to meet their consumer aspirations and a desire for the diverse products of late capitalism at the same time as reflecting an ambivalence towards the development of a consumer culture.

A third thread is the operation of informal, non-state cultural activities. While the operation of social networks in opposition to formal institutional activities is not new, the development of a civil society in Vietnam is relatively recent in the post-war period. The alternative communities that are arising began in the realm of business, with private companies flourishing in the early 1990s. Now the lack of state control of these business ventures has expanded into other areas – groups of women, for example, will arrange to hire a mini-bus together and travel with a group to visit pilgrimage sites over a period of several days; a rural community, tired of waiting for the local party to invest in improving the local hospital, will arrange the funds themselves and organise the improvements; or families will organise the setting up of a private day-care centre and hire their own staff. Now that these activities have expanded in ways too diverse to be controlled by the party, more and more individuals are pushing the boundaries of activities and behaviours and the state is powerless to prevent further, more significant, political and economic change.

At the beginning of the new millennium Vietnamese cultural life has become increasingly affected by global flows of ideas, capital and products. It is too early to gauge the impact of such an expansion of international capitalism into Vietnam but it is clear that many of the institutional structures are being put under threat and the ideas about what constitute contemporary Vietnamese identity are being continually contested and re-negotiated.

Notes

1 The cafes are quirkily decorated. – '…glittering Christmas lights, Crayola-coloured chairs, a pop music soundtrack – are undeniably trendy. For the stream of customers crowding into Trung Nguyen cafes across Vietnam, it's a potent combination of coffee chic and "ca-phe sua", Vietnamese for "coffee with milk" or, in this case, strong espresso served over a syrup of condensed milk. The entrepreneur behind this business, Dang Le Nguyen Vu, says, "I visited some Starbucks outlets in the United States. I think Starbucks and Trung Nguyen share some similarities. But we are planning to make Trung Nguyen coffee shops with typical Vietnamese features, which reflect our culture, design and service style,".

(Tini Tran, AAP, 22 April 2002)

2 This and the next section contain material published in a different form in Thomas (2001).

3 The phenomenon of politically critical literature has historical roots in the colonial period when, in the 1930s in the north, a group named *Tu Luc Van Doan* (Self-Reliance Literary Group) wrote novels which critically assessed the inequities arising from colonisation (Duiker 1995: 179).

4 While there is no censorship office, journalists are expected to exercise self-censorship, a situation which offers significant pitfalls for those who misread the tolerance levels of the party. A recent and widely publicised example is that of the editor of a finance and economics newspaper who published 'state secrets' in the form of an article about the activities of the State Bank.

5 It is worth commenting here that it is only the Vietnamese and regional products which are affordable and accessible. As yet, the availability of products associated with European and American celebrities is minimal. An integral component of the new appeal of celebrities in Vietnam is that they signify a consumer world beyond Vietnam and are a material representation of capitalist democracies. In this way, the cultural products associated with fame have become a visualisation of modernity, or as Hartley suggests, 'of the promise of comfort, progress and freedom' (1996: 200). Because of the lack of non-Asian consumer items, it has been East Asian popular culture in Vietnam that has most clearly symbolised the possibilities and desires for affluence, accumulation and personal freedom, and in doing so has conjured up new forms of society for the Vietnamese populace.

6 Examples are the Hong Kong 'Cantopop' stars Jacky Cheung, Leon Lai, Andy Lau and Aaron Kwok, all of whom who have a very large following in Vietnam and attract large numbers to their concerts.

7 The mass culture icons of the socialist era were not really products in a marketplace but units in a socialist distribution system which also indicates a differentiation between what was the 'mass' culture of the past and the 'pop' culture of today.

Bibliography

Appadurai, A. (1996) *Modernity at Large: Cultural Dimensions of Globalisation*, Minneapolis: University of Minnesota Press.

Barmé, G. (1996) 'The Irresistible Fall and Rise of Mao Zedong', in G.R. Barmé (ed.), *Shades of Mao – The Posthumous Cult of the Great Leader*, New York: M.E. Sharpe.

—— (1999) *In The Red: On Contemporary Chinese Culture*, New York: Columbia University Press.

Bui Tin (1995) *From Cadre to Exile: Memoirs of a Vietnamese Journalist*, Chiang Mai: Silkworm Books. (First published as *Following the Trail of Ho Chi Minh: The Memoirs of a North Vietnamese Colonel*, London: Hurst.)

Comaroff, J. (1996) 'The Empire's Old Clothes: Fashioning the Colonial Subject', in D. Howes (ed.), *Cross-Cultural Consumption: Global Markets, Local Realities*, London and New York: Routledge.

Drummond, L.B.W. (1999) *Mapping Modernity: Perspectives on Everyday Life in Vietnam's Urbanising Society*, Australian National University, Canberra (unpublished PhD thesis).

Duiker, W.J. (1995) *Vietnam: Revolution in Transition*, Boulder, San Francisco and Oxford: Westview Press.

X Hartley, J. (1996) *Popular Reality: Journalism, Modernity and Popular Culture*, London, New York, Sydney and Auckland: Arnold.

Hiang-Khng Heng, R. (1997) *Media in Vietnam and the Structure of its Management*, unpublished paper.

Jamieson, N.J. (1993) *Understanding Vietnam*, Berkeley, Los Angeles and Oxford: University of California Press.

Levi-Strauss, C. (1969) *The Elementary Structures of Kinship*, London: Eyre and Spottiswoode.

Logan, W. (1994) 'Hanoi Townscape: Symbolic Imagery in Vietnam's Capital', in M. Askew and W.S. Logan (eds), *Cultural Identity and Urban Change in Southeast Asia: Interpretative Essays*, Melbourne: Deakin University Press.

Marr, D.G. (1998) *The Mass Media in Vietnam*, Political and Social Change Monograph, Canberra: Australian National University.

Mercer, C. (1986) 'Complicit Pleasures', in T. Bennett, C. Mercer and J. Woollacott (eds), *Popular Culture and Social Relations*, Philadelphia: Open University.

Miller, D. (1995) 'Consumption as the Vanguard of History: A Polemic by Way of an Introduction', in D. Miller (ed.), *Acknowledging Consumption: A Review of New Studies*, London and New York: Routledge.

Nguyen Hung Quoc (1991) 'Fifteen Years of Vietnamese Communist Literature (1975–1990)', *Journal of Vietnamese Studies*, 1(4): 11–25 (trans. Hoai An).

X Said, E. (1979) *Orientalism*, New York: Random House.

Schudson, M. (1989) 'Towards a Comparative History of Political Communication', *Comparative Social Research*, 11: 85–112.

Slater, D. (1997) *Consumer Culture and Modernity*, Cambridge and Oxford: Polity Press.

Thomas, M. (1997) 'Diana at the Cultural Interface: The Appropriation of Diana's Story in Vietnam and in the Vietnamese diaspora', in Re: Public (eds), *Planet Diana: Cultural Studies and Global Mourning*, Sydney: University of Western Sydney.

—— (1999) 'Dislocations of Desire: The Transnational Movement of Gifts within the Vietnamese Diaspora', *Anthropological Forum*, 9(2): 145–61.

X —— (2001) 'Public Spaces/Public Disgraces: Crowds and the State in Contemporary Vietnam', *Sojourn: Journal of Social Issues in Southeast Asia*, 16(2): 306–330.

Thomas, M. and Hiang-Khng Heng, R. (2000) 'Stars in the Shadows: Celebrities, Media and the State in Contemporary Vietnam', in Yao Souchou (ed.), *House of Glass: Culture, Modernity and the State in South East Asia*, Singapore: Institute for South East Asian Studies.

Unger, E.S. (1991) 'Media and Society: Sociocultural Change in Vietnam since 1986', in D. Forbes, T. Hull, D.G. Marr and B. Brogan (eds), *Doi Moi: Vietnam's Renovation Policy and Performance*, Political and Social Change Monograph, Canberra: Australian National University.

Viviani, N. (1996) *The Indochinese in Australia 1975–1995: From Burnt Boats to Barbecues*, Melbourne: Oxford University Press.

Part I

The background to recent changes

Chapter 2

Political developments in Vietnam

The rise and demise of Le Kha Phieu, 1997–2001

Carlyle A. Thayer

This chapter reviews major political developments at the elite level in Vietnam during the stewardship of Vietnam Communist Party (VCP) Secretary General Le Kha Phieu (December 1997–April 2001). Political developments are considered under six major headings: the rise of Le Kha Phieu, rural unrest, economic crisis, political dissent, corruption and internal party politics. The chapter ends with a brief discussion of the ninth national party congress and the selection of Nong Duc Manh as the new Secretary General of the VCP.

The rise of Le Kha Phieu

In 1995–96 the VCP was beset with intense factional in-fighting between conservative ideologues and reformers in the run up to the eighth national party congress scheduled for mid-1996. The ideologues targeted reformist Prime Minister Vo Van Kiet, particularly after Vietnam and the United States normalised relations. Conservatives were angered by a confidential memo Kiet had prepared for the Politburo in which he asserted that confrontation between socialism and imperialism had given way to multi-polarity and future conflicts were more likely to be based on material interests than class struggle (Vo Van Kiet 1996). Politburo member Nguyen Ha Phan led the counter-attack by circulating widely a criticism of Kiet's views. Conservative ideological views were also written into the draft Political Report being prepared for submission to the eighth congress.

Phan had the backing of Politburo member Dao Duy Tung. Tung was widely expected to replace Do Muoi as party Secretary General at the eighth congress. However, on the eve of the congress, it was unexpectedly announced that Phan had been summarily expelled from the Politburo. He was charged with concealing information about his past in his party file, with holding 'erroneous economic views' and leaking Kiet's memo (Greg Torode, *South China Morning Post*, 27 April 1996). Tung was rebuked for attempting to influence unduly the selection of new Central Committee members and was retired. Given these extraordinary circumstances, delegates to the eighth congress agreed to keep the party's ruling troika (Do Muoi, President Le Duc Anh and Vo Van Kiet) in office until mid-term (late 1998).

During the final quarter of 1996 it became clear that growth in Vietnam's economy was in decline for the first time since *doi moi* was adopted in 1986. In mid-year a currency crisis in Thailand triggered a regional financial crisis. At the same time Vietnam experienced mounting peasant unrest in Thai Binh province, a stronghold of the revolution. In December 1997, at the fourth plenary session of the VCP Central Committee, Vietnam's leadership transition was brought forward. The plenum accepted the resignations of Do Muoi, Le Duc Anh and Vo Van Kiet from the Politburo and approved by an overwhelming majority the nomination of Le Kha Phieu as Secretary General. The plenum elected four new members to the Politburo – two conservatives and two reformers.[1] Le Kha Phieu immediately reconstituted the five-member Politburo Standing Board or inner cabinet. Phieu, as party Secretary General, became ex officio its head and was the only incumbent to remain. The new members included state President Tran Duc Luong, Prime Minister Phan Van Khai, Chairman of the National Assembly Nong Duc Manh and party trouble-shooter Pham The Duyet.

Who exactly is Le Kha Phieu? Phieu was born in Thanh Hoa province in central Vietnam in December 1931. He joined the party in 1949 and the army a year later. Phieu graduated from the military university and attended a course at the National Political Academy for high-level party cadres. His career path has been essentially that of a political commissar with responsibility for ideological indoctrination. Phieu had no direct experience with economic matters nor had he travelled abroad widely. Phieu's career had much to do with his commanding officers in Cambodia, Le Duc Anh and Doan Khue, who both went on to serve as ministers of national defence and as members of the Politburo. It was under their patronage that he was brought to the centre of national power.

Phieu was first elected to the VCP's Central Committee in June 1991 at a time when socialism had collapsed in Eastern Europe and was in disarray in the Soviet Union. Three months later he was appointed head of the army's General Political Department where he directed the ideological campaign against the threat of peaceful evolution. In 1992 Phieu was appointed to the Secretariat. This marked an important shift in his career path from the military to the party. Shortly after he was appointed to head the party's Internal Political Protection Commission where he dealt with internal security and disciplinary matters. It was his staunch defence of ideological rectitude that won him support in the party and military. Phieu has been a consistent proponent of strong administrative, internal inspection and control measures to combat corruption.

In 1994 Le Kha Phieu was elected to the Politburo and was re-elected in 1996. It then appeared that Phieu was being groomed for the top party job. He began to appear in public more often. He also addressed a variety of groups including the media and intellectuals. It was noticeable that he moderated his ideological rhetoric and grew increasingly confident when speaking in public about a variety of socio-economic issues.

In 1986, with the death of party leader Le Duan, the era of the party 'strong man' ended. Duan had served in office for an unprecedented twenty-six years. His successor, reformist Nguyen Van Linh, served only one five-year term. Linh's successor, Do Muoi, served six and a half years before he stepped down. Phieu was the first Secretary General who was not elected by a national congress.[2] Phieu came to the office of party Secretary General without a strong patronage network to support him. If Phieu were to serve out his term in office and gain re-election for a full five-year term, he would have to broker consensus among the contending factions within the party and successfully meet the policy challenges facing Vietnam. Phieu failed and was retired in April 2001.

Rural unrest

In 1997–98 Vietnam was rocked by a series of peasant disturbances. The first reported rural incident occurred near the Hanoi airport in February 1997 when hundreds of local peasants resumed their protests about the confiscation of land for use as a luxury golf course. Earlier clashes had occurred in May and December 1996 (Reuters, 31 December 1996).

In 1996, in Thai Binh province, local authorities were inundated with hundreds of verbal complaints, written petitions and letters of denunciation regarding widespread corruption, the exaction of illegal taxes and fees, requests for 'voluntary labour' and abuse of power by local officials (*Nhan Dan*, 8 September 1997). Local officials were accused of diverting funds raised for social welfare and developmental purposes into their own pockets. These complaints and petitions went unanswered in the main.

During the months between April and July 1997 Thai Binh was rocked by an escalating series of protests by farmers from 128 villages in six of the province's seven districts. Initially the protests were peaceful. For example, in late April 1997 several thousand villagers marched to their district seat to lodge complaints about alleged financial irregularities by members of their village people's committee (*Tien Phong*, 4 October 1997). The protests escalated during May and turned violent in June and July. Hanoi was forced to dispatch 1,200 special police to restore order (Deutsche Presse-Agentur, 25 July 1997; hereafter DPA). In several incidents peasant demonstrators grabbed riot shields from the police and smashed their megaphones. The demonstrators laid siege to a district compound and other government offices. Cadres were seized for questioning and several were beaten; some local officials fled the province for their own safety. In one extreme case the homes of local officials were set on fire.

The largest demonstration reportedly took place in late May/early June when an estimated 3,000 persons from thirty-three communes gathered in the Thai Binh province capital to protest against corruption by local party cadres (Jeremy Grant, *Financial Times*, 7 June 1997). These protests broke out when local officials attempted to raise the amount of contributions required for public works projects (Associated Press, 19 February 1998; hereafter AP). In another incident, local farmers protested against local officials who had allegedly pocketed compensation money paid by a foreign oil company drilling near the coast. Provincial authorities called in military units to restore order but local unit commanders balked at suppressing the protests. Instead, they deployed the army to provide an armed escort so drilling equipment could be removed safely from the area.[3]

According to official accounts, by the end of June fifty-three village officials in Thai Binh province had been either suspended from office or otherwise disciplined, and thirty other local officials were under investigation. Party leaders in Hanoi sent Politburo members Le Minh Huong and Pham The Duyet to make on-the-spot evaluations of the situation (Reuters, 21 October 1997; AP, 10 November 1997; and Agence France-Presse, 9 November 1997; hereafter AFP). In October, the Politburo ordered party and state officials in Thai Binh to undergo criticism and self-criticism (Reuters, 21 October 1997). As a result, the head of the Thai Binh province People's Committee and the provincial party chief were relieved of their duties.

It was only in late January 1998 that the unrest in Thai Binh was declared over. A dozen local farmers were detained for prosecution while more than twenty cadres (out of thirty-seven village officials) were disciplined (AP, 19 February 1998). All in all, 300 officials were 'dealt with' and more than forty prosecuted. The disturbances in Thai Binh had far-reaching implications because they occurred at a time when there were signs of a national economic downturn and because they took place on the eve of the fourth plenum where leadership changes were on the agenda.

Disturbances were also reported in Ha Tay province in the north, Dong Nai province in the south, and Military Region 4 in the centre. In 1997, seventy-five incidents were reported in Ha Tay mainly involving land rights and land management issues (*Nhan Dan*, 30 March 1998). In November 1997–January 1998, Thong Nhat district, Dong Nai province, was the scene of several land rights protests by Catholic villagers (AP, 10 November 1997; Reuters, 5 February 1998). And finally, in December 1997, it was reported that Quang Tri and Thua Thien-Hue provinces in Military Region 4 had experienced 'disturbances and violent incidents' provoked by unnamed 'religious elements' (*Quan Doi Nhan Dan*, 9 December 1997). Rural unrest was also reported in Tra Vinh and Hoa Binh provinces in 1998 but details are lacking.

Economic crisis[4]

In December 1997, at the same plenum at which Le Kha Phieu was elected party Secretary General, the Central Committee reviewed the Asian financial crisis and its likely impact on Vietnam. This meeting was symptomatic of Vietnam's policy response over the next two and a half years. Party leaders asserted that Vietnam would determine the pace of its economic reforms in order to ensure that political stability and Vietnam's unique national character were preserved. In their view, Vietnam would be spared the worst effects of the financial crisis because of the inconvertibility of the dong and the fact that Vietnam's economic integration with the region was at a comparatively low level.

The fourth plenum identified Vietnam's problem areas as declining foreign investment, low domestic saving rates and the lack of export competitiveness.

The causes of Vietnam's economic woes, as the plenum acknowledged, were of its own doing – corruption and wastage, bureaucratic red tape, high overheads, arbitrary and inefficient decision-making, and a Byzantine licensing process. By way of policy response, the fourth plenum reaffirmed Vietnam's commitment to accelerating 'comprehensive and uniform renovation' as the best way to overcome the country's economic problems. Priority was assigned to improving Vietnam's economic efficiency and international competitiveness, attracting foreign investment, mobilising domestic capital, austerity in government spending, and reform of the state banking and financial systems. The plenum resolved to negotiate a trade agreement with the United States, but was cautious, however, about opening up Vietnam's capital market. It set unrealistically high targets of 9 per cent for GDP growth and 26 per cent for exports.

Le Kha Phieu presided over ten plenary sessions of the Central Committee during his tenure in office. It is clear that concern over political stability and party unity continually trumped economic worries. This led to 'reform immobilism' (Thayer 2000). When economic matters were raised, Vietnam's political leaders stressed the mobilisation of internal resources and piecemeal reforms in preference to advice from external donors such as World Bank, International Monetary Fund and United Nations Development Program to step up the pace and scope of reforms. Vietnam also rejected out of hand conditional financial inducements by international financial institutions to underwrite the costs of reform efforts.

In July 1998 the Central Committee's fifth plenum declared that Vietnam had achieved a 'big success' in maintaining political stability. GDP growth was lowered to 6 per cent while exports targets were lowered by more than half to 10 per cent. The plenum stressed the importance of mobilising domestic capital resources to make up for the shortfall in foreign investment. Perhaps more surprisingly, the plenum focused mainly on ideological and cultural issues.[5]

At the start of the fourth quarter 1998, foreign investment continued to plunge, exports fell short of target, foreign reserves came under pressure and inflation rose. In a speech to the sixth plenum/first session (October 1998), Secretary General Phieu argued that 'economic development for next year is unpredictable and the regional economic crisis might become a political crisis with a world-wide impact'. The plenum set priority on agriculture, rural development and the revitalisation of agricultural cooperatives. It called for the mobilisation of domestic savings and funds from overseas Vietnamese as sources of investment. This was the first Central Committee plenum to fashion a policy response to the impact of the Asian financial crisis on Vietnam's economy (Thayer 1999).

In 1999 Vietnam was hit by the secondary impact of the Asian financial crisis. Foreign investment continued to fall, export growth stagnated and Vietnam began to lose its competitive edge. Over the past two years Vietnam had given lip service to its promises to curb corruption, to carry out a thoroughgoing reform of its banking and financial sectors and to improve the climate for foreign investors. More than one-third of its 6,000 state-owned enterprises (SOEs) continued to lose money and another third managed to break even only because of subsidised credit from banks and preferential access to land and trade quotas. Moreover, only 39 SOEs had been privatised, well below the target of 150.

One major indication that Vietnam was gripped by reform immobilism was its handling of negotiations with the United States for a bilateral trade agreement (BTA). Quite simply, the debate about the pace and scope of economic reforms, and the degree to which Vietnam should open up its economy and expose itself to the forces of globalisation, became inextricably tied up with consideration of the draft BTA. A draft agreement was negotiated in July 1998, but at the eleventh hour Vietnam pulled out of the signing ceremony scheduled for September 1999. When the Central Committee reviewed the draft of the BTA at its eighth plenum in November 1999, vested interests in the SOE sector and the military maintained their strong opposition. Prime Minister Phan Van Khai was forced to admit that he could not obtain consensus and threw this hot potato back to the Politburo.

As the debate wore on, party conservatives eventually became convinced that, in order to achieve their objectives of industrialising and modernising Vietnam by 2020, they needed to reverse the marked decline in foreign investment and step up the rate of economic growth. The first indications of change appeared in 2000 when Vietnam issued new implementing regulations for the Law on Foreign Investment (amended in June) and gave approval to long-delayed plans to open a stock exchange. Of greater significance, however, was the decision by the tenth plenum (26 June–4 July) to continue with regional and global integration.[6] Immediately following the plenum, the new Trade Minister journeyed to Washington where a final accord was reached. The BTA was finally ratified by Vietnam's National Assembly and the United States Congress in late 2001.

Political dissent

In late 1997/early 1998 Vietnam's one-party regime came under challenge by intellectual critics and political dissidents. Foremost among the dissidents were Tran Do, Nguyen Thanh Giang and a group of intellectuals known as the Dalat Circle. Tran Do was a native of Thai Binh province with impeccable revolutionary credentials. He was a retired general and former head of the Central Committee's Ideology and Culture Department. He became increasingly vocal after peasant unrest broke out in Thai Binh. In late 1997, prior to the fourth plenum, Tran Do penned an open letter to Vietnam's top leaders which he offered as his contribution to the upcoming ninth party congress. Do's open letter contained a trenchant critique of Vietnam's political system and pervasive corruption. The VCP responded by vilifying Do in the press. He then wrote a letter to *Nhan Dan* to demand the right of reply.

Early in 1998, Hoang Minh Chinh wrote an open letter calling for a dialogue between the party and intellectuals. Chinh was a prominent revolutionary figure who had been imprisoned twice for his outspoken views (AFP, 5 and 14 February 1998). He also called for the establishment of multi-party democracy in Vietnam. 'In order to establish a democracy, there is a need to … deeply reform the Communist Party of Vietnam and courageously and cautiously restore the multi-party and plural system in Vietnam', he concluded. Shortly after, geophysicist Nguyen Thanh Giang circulated an open letter in which he denounced 'red capitalists' within the VCP who were 'promoted, subsidised and protected by the proletarian dictatorship' (AFP, 14 March 1998).

The significance of this new wave of political dissent is that it came at a time when rural unrest had provoked debate within the party about the extent to which economic reforms should be expanded into the political sphere. While the protest letters written by Hoang Minh Chinh and Nguyen Thanh Giang could be dismissed out of hand, someone of General Tran Do's impeccable revolutionary background and prestige could not be dismissed so easily. Significantly, Le Kha Phieu, as the newly elected party Secretary General, paid a private visit to Tran Do's home to discuss his suggestions. Afterwards Hanoi's propaganda organs noted that Tran Do's letter was 'consistent with internal party debate' and represented a minority view' (Jeremy Grant, *Financial Times*, 13 February 1998).

This propaganda spin belied reality. Tran Do was in fact put under surveillance, members of his family were harassed, and foreign journalists were actively discouraged from contacting him. The question of Tran Do's treatment was even raised at Secretary General Phieu's first press conference broadcast live in May 1998. Phieu disingenuously denied that Do was under house arrest. After the fifth party plenum in July 1998 party officials openly resumed their criticism of Tran Do's writings.

In January 1999 Tran Do was expelled from the VCP. This provoked a round of protests and the resignation from the party of Colonel Pham Que Duong, former editor of *Tap Chi Lich Su Quan Su* and a party member since 1948 (Radio Free Asia, 19 January 1999). Ha Si Phu, one of the Dalat Circle of political dissidents, wrote to Tran Do congratulating him on his expulsion. In April 1999 police confiscated Phu's computer and printer. That same month, in another challenge to the authorities, Tran Do unsuccessfully submitted an application to publish a private newspaper. In June 2001 security police arrested Tran Do in Ho Chi Minh City and confiscated a draft section of his memoirs. Do responded by writing a letter of protest to the Vietnam Association of Writers. In January 2002, the Vice-Minister of Culture and Information issued a decree instructing police to confiscate and destroy publications that did not have official approval; this included Tran Do's three-volume memoirs.

In 1999 Vietnamese security authorities had to contend with the increased use of the internet by political dissents. In March, Nguyen Thanh Giang was detained for two months for 'propaganda against the socialist regime' because his critiques were widely distributed on the internet. After his release he was placed under house arrest. In August 2001 the government passed a decree that set stricter regulations on internet cafés and imposed fines for illegal internet usage. In April 2000 police once again raided the home of Ha Si Phu and seized his computer and several diskettes. Phu had been in touch via email with anti-communist pro-democracy activists in France and was in the process of drafting a pro-democracy declaration. Phu was accused of making contact with overseas groups and 'betraying the fatherland'. Phu's arrest provoked a protest by five dissidents – including Hoang Minh Chinh and Nguyen Thanh Giang – who released an open letter to the National Assembly calling for his release and for democratic reform. The biggest crackdown against political dissenters took place in September 2001 when police in Hanoi and Ho Chi Minh City arrested fifteen leading activists including Hoang Minh Chinh and Nguyen Thanh Giang. In the months preceding the ninth congress, several dissidents adopted a new tack. They began to criticise the government, and Le Kha Phieu in particular, for having given away Vietnamese territory in boundary negotiations with China.

Le Kha Phieu was unable to end political dissent or to win the trust of dissidents. Indeed, sections of the VCP were sympathetic to the views of the dissidents and supported their right to air their views. This served to undermine Phieu's authority, but no criticism was more potentially damaging than allegations of conceding too much land to China in border negotiations.

Corruption

The VCP identified corruption as one of the main issues that could undermine its legitimacy. There was consensus in the party that corruption must be ended and the guilty punished. There was a tendency, however, to protect high-ranking officials. In practice, the attempt to weed out corruption became something of a political football within the party.

In addition, the National Assembly became somewhat more assertive in seeking accountability from ministers. In September 1997, for example, its deputies rejected newly elected Prime Minister Phan Van Khai's nomination of Cao Si Kiem as Governor of the Vietnam State Bank due to his association with several scandals and debt management problems in the banking sector the previous year. In May 1999, National Assembly deputies demanded that Phan Van Dinh, the head of customs, be sacked because of scandals involving officials from his department. Dinh was dismissed in October.

In 1998 the system of lodging written complaints and letters of denunciation was reformed. This resulted in a marked rise in citizens' complaints about corruption. In a celebrated case in May 1998, for example, eleven party veterans signed a letter alleging that Politburo member Pham The Duyet and his family benefited from corruption and shady property deals during his tenure as Hanoi party boss.

In March, the VCP announced a pilot scheme to allow farmers to monitor decisions by local officials and giving them more say in village and commune budget matters. Nevertheless, corruption by local officials continued to provoke public demonstrations outside government offices or the homes of high-ranking officials. It was especially noticeable that rural farmers were prominent in these protests. In April 2000, for example, thirty farmers from Dong Thap province staged a two-day protest against corruption and abuse by local officials outside the VCP headquarters in Hanoi while the Central Committee was in session (Reuters, 18 April 2000).

In May, ten demonstrators from Ho Chi Minh City, Thua Thien-Hue and Vinh Phuc provinces staged a protest outside the National Assembly. They carried placards accusing local officials of selling off communal land and thus forcing them off their land (AFP, 23 May 2000). These same issues featured in September 2000 when more than 100 people from the Mekong Delta and Central Highlands conducted a protest outside a government office in Ho Chi Minh City where an inter-ministerial working group was meeting to settle citizens' complaints (Reuters, 28 September 2000).

About 100 farmers from three northern provinces including Thai Binh staged a four-month (August–November) public protest against corruption and grievances against local officials outside the office of the Prime Minister (Reuters, 19 October 2000; Rajiv Chandrasekaran, *Washington Post*, 3 November 2000). In March the following year, 500 ethnic minority people from Son La province gathered outside Ho Chi Minh's mausoleum to publicise their views on a local land dispute. And in February 2002, a group of women peasants all wearing hats bearing slogans denouncing corruption by local state and party officials demonstrated outside the Hanoi home of Prime Minister Phan Van Khai. Remarkably, they were permitted to continue their protest during the official visit of China's President Jiang Zemin (AFP, 27 February 2002).

Under the leadership of Le Kha Phieu the VCP decided to tackle the issue of corruption by launching a two-year campaign of criticism and self-criticism of its 2.3 million members. The issue was first broached at the sixth plenum/second session (February 1999) which decided that a national campaign was the best way to counter the degradation in the party's ranks caused by corruption, excessive bureaucracy, individualism, and internal disunity (Reuters, 1 February 1999; AP, 2 February 1999). The object of the campaign was to rid the party of its degenerate members and restore unity (Reuters, 2 February 1999). The criticism campaign was officially launched on 19 May 1999, the anniversary of Ho Chi Minh's birthday. Initial progress was reviewed by the eighth plenum in November 1999.[7] A statement issued by the plenum stated that Central Committee members Ngo Xuan Loc and Cao Si Kiem had each been issued a reprimand. This is the lowest form of party discipline.[8] In addition, the plenum recommended that Loc be dismissed from his post as Deputy Prime Minister. Loc was implicated in a scandal surrounding the Thanh Long amusement park in Hanoi and for his role in encouraging speculation in the cement market in 1995. Loc was a key advisor to reformist Prime Minister Phan Van Khai. In December, the National Assembly dismissed Loc from his state post. Cao Si Kiem had earlier been dismissed as Governor of the Vietnam State Bank for mismanagement of loans that resulted in an explosion of bad debts.

In recognition of public concern about corruption, Vietnam held a number of high-profile court cases to publicise the fact that it was taking action. In the so-called Tan Truong Sanh case, seventy-four persons were indicted for smuggling. Two persons, including a customs official, received the death penalty in April 1999. The second celebrated case was the Minh Phung EPCO affair in which seventy-seven defendants were charged, six of whom received the death penalty for defrauding the state of millions of dollars in a banking scam. In 2000, Phan Van Khai set up five commissions to investigate corruption and land disputes in fifteen provinces. A report released in October 2000 called for action against sixty-two officials. In September 2001, six government officials were convicted for corrupt land dealing involving the Thanh Long water park. (*Nhan Dan*, 8 September 1997). And in November of the same year, the Lai Chau provincial court tried twelve persons on charges of bribery and embezzlement of funds from government development projects. In April 2002, fifty-nine persons went on trial in Ho Chi Minh City for bank fraud.

Internal party politics and the demise of Le Kha Phieu

Le Kha Phieu (Thayer 2001b) came to power in unique circumstances. He was not elected party Secretary General at a national congress. The fourth plenum (December 1997) which elected Phieu party chief also appointed the former ruling troika as advisors to the Central Committee. In this role they cast a long shadow over Phieu by regularly attending high-level policy meetings. Do Muoi, for example, retained his office in the headquarters of the VCP. During Phieu's first year as Secretary General, Muoi not only attended meetings of the Politburo but continued to sit at the head of the table. In September 1999 party conservatives successfully lobbied Do Muoi to intervene to postpone the signing of the bilateral trade agreement with the United States.

Phieu reportedly became frustrated at the constraints on his power and began to seek ways of shoring up his position. At the eighth national congress (1996), party statutes were amended to abolish the Secretariat (a powerful administrative body) and replace it with a Politburo Standing Board. In an unscripted development, delegates at the congress rejected giving the Standing Board executive authority. Its powers were limited to providing advice to the Politburo. The ninth plenum (April 2000) revisited this issue with an eye to drafting recommendations for the next congress. Three options were tabled: direct election of the Politburo Standing Board by the Central Committee; re-establishment of the Secretariat; and retention of the Politburo Standing Board alongside a revived Secretariat. See below for further discussion (AFP, 19 April 2000).

In May 2000, Le Kha Phieu made an 'official visit' to France and Italy. He was reportedly irritated that he was not treated on the same protocol level as a head of state. On his return to Vietnam his advisers began canvassing the idea that Phieu should occupy the posts of party Secretary General and state President concurrently along the lines of China's Jiang Zemin. Phieu also suggested amending the party statutes to abolish the position of advisor to the Central Committee.

Le Kha Phieu, as noted above, was not a 'strongman'. In order to be successful he had to play the role of consensus-maker among the party's factions. However, Vietnam's system of collective leadership continued to constrain the decision-making process and resulted in reform immobilism. In 1999, the VCP became embroiled in particularly bitter in-fighting over leadership questions. The Central Committee's sixth plenum/second session (January–February 1999), for example, was held amidst intense speculation that major changes in party and state leadership would take place (AFP, 24 January 1999; Reuters, 25 January 1999). The meeting could not reach a consensus and the leadership question was deferred (AFP, 1 February 1999; Reuters, 3 February 1999). The next Central Committee meeting, the seventh plenum (August 1999), had to be postponed five times due to factional in-fighting.

Because of Phieu's weak and indecisive leadership, Prime Minister Phan Van Khai became the victim of continual sniping by party conservatives who repeatedly criticised him for not rooting out corruption among his ministers. Party conservatives zeroed in on Ngo Xuan Loc, one of Khai's close confidants. When Loc ran afoul of Le Duc Anh, Anh instigated a press campaign attacking Loc for corruption. As noted above, Loc was reprimanded by the Central Committee's eighth plenum in late 1999[9] and later dismissed as Deputy Prime Minister. In the midst of this bickering, Khai revealed he was unable to obtain a consensus on the draft trade agreement with the United States and was referring the matter back to the Politburo. Shortly after, Nguyen Thai Nguyen, one of Khai's aides, was placed under investigation for unspecified violations of the law. In March 2000, Hanoi-based diplomats reported that Prime Minister Khai, 'frustrated by the steady erosion of his power through the removal, sacking and jailing of close associates ... tendered his resignation ... but the party refused to accept it for fear of sending the wrong signal to the world' (Chanda 2000b).

The question of high-level corruption was discussed at the Central Committee's ninth plenum (April 2000). As a result of the direct intervention by Do Muoi, Ngo Xuan Loc was rehabilitated. Shortly after the plenum, it was announced that Loc was appointed special advisor to the Prime Minister for industry, construction and transport – the same responsibilities he had as Deputy Prime Minister. Nguyen Thai Nguyen's case did not turn out so well. In October 2000, he and three other persons were sentenced to jail for having conducted a 'witch hunt' against Vo Thi Thang, director of Vietnam Tourism and a member of the Central Committee.

As early as the seventh plenum of August 1999, Vietnam began preparations for the ninth party congress scheduled for the first quarter of 2001. Le Kha Phieu's stewardship as Secretary General increasingly came under critical scrutiny. In September 2000, Phieu endeared himself to party conservatives when he pronounced that Vietnam would follow its own course of reform and that 'socialism will triumph'. In November 2001, Phieu berated Bill Clinton during his official visit to Hanoi about US imperialism and ordered party officials to accord the visiting American president a low-key welcome. These statements were not what reformers who hoped to open up Vietnam's economy wanted to hear.

By this time Le Kha Phieu had come under fire on a number of issues. He was criticised for ineffective leadership, failure to revive Vietnam's stagnant economy, an inability to root out widespread corruption in the party, and 'anti-democratic' behaviour (because he reportedly sought to become both party leader and state president). Phieu aroused the wrath of the former leadership troika because of his efforts to abolish their positions as advisors to the Central Committee. In October 2000, they signed a joint letter to the Central Committee criticising Phieu, *inter alia*, for weak leadership (Chanda 2000a). Phieu was also accused of nepotism due to his appointment of cronies from his native Thanh Hoa province. And finally, Phieu was accused of pursuing a 'pro-China' policy, by approving concessions to China in border negotiations. An indication that Phieu's hold on the party's top post was under challenge came at the eleventh plenum/first session of the Central Committee held in January 2001. Phieu's detractors moved to promote younger officials to the Central Committee in order to achieve a better balance between the 'three generations' (under 50s, 50–60 and over 60s). They sought to prevent anyone aged 65 or older from standing for re-election. This move was widely perceived as being aimed at Phieu. The plenum decided, however, to grant exceptions to 'key cadres' (AFP, 3 February 2001).

Phieu staved off another challenge in February 2001, following ethnic minority demonstrations in the Central Highlands. In April, on the eve of the ninth party congress, the Politburo voted twelve to six to recommend Le Kha Phieu's reappointment (AP, 8 April 2001). The Central Committee's twelfth plenum (7–10 April 2001) overturned this recommendation when presented with evidence that Phieu had misused the military intelligence service to conduct wiretaps on his colleagues (AFP, 23 April 2001). The plenum voted to reprimand the minister of national defence and the chief of the general staff for their roles in this affair. On 17 April delegates to the ninth congress voted to withdraw their support from Phieu (Reuters, 18 April 2001).

Ninth congress and Nong Duc Manh's reform agenda

The VCP's ninth national congress met from 19–23 April and elected Nong Duc Manh as the next party Secretary General (Thayer 2002). Manh, a member of the Tay ethnic minority, was born in 1940 in the northern province of Bac Thai. He holds a forestry degree from the former Soviet Union and has had a long career in the party apparatus in his home province. He was first elected a member of the Central Committee in 1986. He served on the Nationalities Council before becoming chairman of the National Assembly's Standing Committee. In this latter post Manh travelled widely, to China, the ASEAN countries and to the United States. In 1996 he was nominated for the post of party Secretary General but declined to stand. He was elected to the Politburo, ranking fourth out of nineteen. Manh is viewed as a consensus-maker and as representing the ideological centre of the VCP.

The ninth congress abolished the Politburo Standing Board and replaced it with a Secretariat to be elected by the Central Committee. This was a concession to supporters of internal party democracy. The congress also deleted the position of advisor to the Central Committee from the party statutes. This decision effectively ended the behind-the-scenes influence of senior retired leaders.

The ninth congress reaffirmed Vietnam's goal of accelerating industrialisation and modernisation in order to become a modern industrialised state by 2020. The congress adopted a five-year socio-economic plan (2001–5) and a ten-year socio-economic plan (2001–10). These documents called for self-reliance, mobilisation of domestic capital, the development of Vietnam's comparative advantage, and attracting external resources in the form of foreign investment capital, new technology and managerial expertise. A key plank in Vietnam's development strategy is to alleviate poverty and overcome the wealth gap in society over the next two decades. To accomplish this objective Vietnam will have to achieve growth rates averaging 7 per cent throughout this period. In 2000 Vietnam's GDP growth rate reached 6.9 per cent, but fell to 4.8 per cent in 2001.

Since the ninth congress, Manh has presided over five plenary sessions of the Central Committee – the second (9–10 June), third (13–22 August), fourth (5–13 November) and fifth (18 February–2 March 2002). Secretary General Manh has signalled that policy implementation will be strengthened by a more proactive Politburo and by the use of party committees within the state apparatus, including the National Assembly. Immediately after taking office, Manh engineered a number of leadership changes in the areas of ideology, personnel and security by appointing Politburo and Central Committee members to key leadership roles. New appointments were made to the Central Committee's Department of Ideology and Culture, Organisation Department and Internal Security Department. Other new appointments included the Chairman of the National Assembly, Minister of Culture and Information, Deputy Minister of Public Security and Director General of the General Tax Department. A major reshuffle was carried out in the military where a new Chief of the General Staff and new head of the General Political Department were appointed.

Manh has given priority to five main areas: strengthening leadership, infrastructure development, party-building, state-owned enterprise reform, redress of ethnic minority grievances in the Central Highlands, and constitutional reform.

Notes

1 Pham Thanh Ngan, director of the VPA General Political Department; Nguyen Phu Trong, former editor of *Tap Chi Cong San*; Nguyen Minh Triet, former deputy secretary of the Ho Chi Minh City party committee; and Phan Dien, director of the VCP Central Committee Office.
2 Truong Chinh served for six months following the death of Le Duan in July 1986 and the election of Nguyen Van Linh at the sixth congress in December.
3 See *The Economist* (1997).
4 This section borrows from Thayer (2001a).
5 See Voice of Vietnam (1998).
6 *Quan Doi Nhan Dan* (2000).
7 *Quan Doi Nhan Dan* (1999).
8 According to party statutes there are three forms of internal party discipline: *khien trach* (reprimand), *canh cao* (warning/censure) and *cach chuc* (dismissal). See 'Dieu Le Dang Cong San Viet Nam' (1996: chapter eight, article 35). The previous statutes

made provision for a fourth category, *khai tru* (purge) (see *Dieu Le Dang Cong San Viet Nam* (1992: 45)).

9 *Quan Doi Nhan Dan* (1999).

Bibliography

Chanda, Nayan (2000a) 'Blowing Hot and Cold', *Far Eastern Economic Review*, 30 November: 22.

—— (2000b) 'The War Within', *Far Eastern Economic Review*, 4 May: 20.

Dieu Le Dang Cong San Viet Nam (1992) 'Hanoi: Nha Xuat Ban Su That' ,45.

'Dieu Le Dang Cong San Viet Nam' (1996) *Statutes of the Vietnam Communist Party*, chapter eight, article 35.

Economist, The (1997) 'Vietnam: Rural Descent', 13 September, 41.

Quan Doi Nhan Dan (1999) 'Thong Bao Hoi Nghi Lan Thu Tam Ban Chap Hanh Trung Uong Dang Cong San Vietnam' (Communiqué of the Eighth Plenum of the Central Executive Committee of the Vietnam Communist Party), 20 April, 1 and 4.

Quan Doi Nhan Dan (2001) 'Thong Bao Hoi Nghi Lan Thu Muoi Ban Chap Hanh Trung Uong Dang Cong San Viet Nam Khoa VIII' (Communiqué of the Tenth Plenum of the Central Executive Committee of the Vietnam Communist Party Ninth Congress), 5 July, 1 and 4.

Thayer, Carlyle (1999) 'Models to the North', *Vietnam Business Journal*, 7(1): 28–9.

—— (2000) 'Vietnam: The Politics of Immobilism Revisited', in Daljit Singh (ed.), *Southeast Asian Affairs 2000*,Singapore: Institute of Southeast Asian Studies, 311–26.

—— (2001a) 'Vietnam's Integration into the Region and the Asian Financial Crisis', in Martin Großheim and J.H. Vincent Houben (eds.), *Vietnam, Regional Integration and the Asian Financial Crisis: Vietnamese and European Perspectives*, Passau Contributions to Southeast Asian Studies 9, Passau: Department of Southeast Asian Studies, University of Passau, 17–53.

—— (2001b) 'Vietnam in 2000: Toward the Ninth Party Congress', *Asian Survey*, January/February, 41(1): 181–8.

—— (2002) 'Vietnam in 2001: The Ninth Party Congress and After', *Asian Survey*, January/February, 42(1): 81–9.

Vo Van Kiet (1996) 'Thu Vo Van Kiet Goi Bo Chinh Tri' (Letter from Vo Van Kiet to the Politburo), *Viet Luan*, Paris, 5 January 1053: 30–1, 58–60.

Voice of Vietnam (1998) 'Building and Developing an Advanced Vietnamese Culture Imbued with National Identity', *Voice of Vietnam*, 11–12 August, in BBC Monitoring, 27 August.

Chapter 3

Vietnam – culture and economy

Dyed-in-the-wool tigers?

Adam Fforde

> One of the most delicate tasks that faced the Tudors, therefore, was the creation and education of a new ruling class and the retention of its loyalty. The new men had to be prevented from moving up too fast or too far. The drive and efficiency in economic matters which brought them their wealth and power also made them harsh to their tenants and contemptuous of the common people.
>
> (Morris 1955: 25–6)

Introduction

In this chapter I examine the state of Vietnam's economy in the late 1990s and early 2000, and place this in a wider context. Despite the reputation of economics as a profoundly boring discipline, I will also try to show how important cultural elements of Vietnamese society both reflect – and also more interestingly for issues relating to economic development – have deeply influenced Vietnam's changing development style.

In the late 1990s, two main sets of problems confronted economic policymakers in Vietnam. First, the effects of the regional economic crisis and global economic slowdown, and their severe effects on inward investment flows and exports. Second, the political problems posed by high levels of rural unrest and weak employment growth, and the links between these and the pattern of savings and investment that was consolidated in the mid-1990s. Vietnam's development style, as it was emerging through the 1990s, stressed urban and capital-intensive growth rather than one that could have been more agrarian and employment-oriented. Viewed as 'style', this suggested a relative disintegration of the national political economy in favour of processes of integration into global economic and cultural systems.

Thaveeporn (1996) argued that this disintegration was to a certain extent offset by political responses, for example Public Administrative Reform (PAR), which sought a new order in the self-definition of the state and its relationships with its subjects. From this, arguably, would emerge a new developmentalism, a new 'development style', which, as elsewhere, would reflect a political response to the concrete issues generated by 'development', rather than a proactive realisation of any immanent, and thus 'objective', process, a view which is common but more than somewhat nonsensical.[1]

This chapter commences by examining the more important aspects of the Vietnamese economy in the 1990s. It starts by looking at the political 'hot points' and the associated policy responses. This is followed by a discussion of the macro-economic situation – the state of economic variables such as GDP, inflation and the balance of payments. Macro-economic stability is contrasted with the more systemic and longer-term issues related to political tensions. The section finishes with a discussion of the more general historical issues associated with market-oriented growth. This section of the discussion contrasts the political problems of the Tudors with those of the Vietnamese Communist Party (VCP), who were the 'new men' – the emerging commercially powerful – and asks what was their relationship to the rulers of the country? This brings out the fact that nation-state development has its conscious as well as its unconscious aspects, not least for a ruling group informed by the classical political economy analysis of Marxism-Leninism. What is interesting is the way in which the relative economic and social stability of the period 1998–2001 probably drew upon the perceived threats to continued stability of the position outlined in this section: state power was used to *prevent* the expected from coming to pass. This naturally stresses the subjective, and thus often unpredictable, nature of history. And to some extent, perhaps, they were successful – traps were foreseen, perhaps avoided (at least, maybe).

The second section of the paper then presents observations on some cultural aspects of Vietnam's development style as it has emerged. It takes as its point of departure the fate, not of Cassandra, but one of her (so far as I know unnamed) little sisters, whose fate was to be ignored by the god who cursed her elder sister, which had for her of course positive as well as negative aspects. A not entirely dissimilar fate confronted Vietnamese farmers and workers in the 1990s, as foreign direct investment (FDI) largely passed them by.[2] But there is always hope. Vietnam's social structure was consistent with unusually low rates of domestic savings by East Asian standards. By the early 2000s, fate seemed to have started to change in favour of the majority, as the private sector began to rapidly emerge.

To develop this line of thought, I look at three areas. First, I contrast middle-class lifestyles in Hanoi, the capital, and Ho Chi Minh City, the commercial centre. Contrary to many orthodox perceptions, it is Hanoi that emerged as the more savings-averse of the two, with, for example, a high stress upon perceived high-quality consumer durables (the Honda 'Dream' culture, for example). A predilection for consumption over the production of tradeables has important long-term implications for resource flows, as well as cultural style. Second, the cultural consequences of the development 'style' upon the emerging 'new men' in the rural areas. Here contrast is made with the English 'development style', with its heavily structured integration of emerging urban power groups into rural upper-class lifestyles. This is related to the lack of a rural property base for urban accumulation processes. Third, and most adventurously, I examine three areas where a profound localisation of global cultural processes seems to be happening. These are food, fragrance and rhythm – all areas where standards are largely unwritten, and also highly 'popular'. All have major economic meaning.

Economic update: the Vietnamese economy in the late 1990s

Politics and all that: economics 'hot points' and policy responses

The Vietnamese political economy of the 1990s was dominated by a pro-state-owned enterprises (SOEs) policy stance that permeated the society.[3] This arguably had its origins in the effects of the recovery of state resources in 1991–92. By the mid-1990s, the Vietnamese government controlled rather substantial levels of resources. And official attitudes to the 'private' sector remained at best ambiguous. To give one example, this state of affairs encouraged a widespread 'spreading of risk' by families who tried to keep one foot in state employment even when they were pushing for new opportunities in private business.

Although this policy stance had emerged in the early 1990s, in dogmatic and ideological terms, it was perfectly consistent with earlier neo-Stalinist thinking.[4] In this view, the main instruments for securing growth were, in caricature, a farming, family-based, rural economy linked to world markets through SOEs combined with substantial, inward FDI-creating joint ventures between foreign companies and SOEs. The recovery of state finances and power after the 1989–91 crisis provided one of the preconditions for attempting this policy in the mid-1990s. Other preconditions were the willingness of foreign investors to enter into joint ventures with SOEs, and the willingness of foreign aid donors to go along with the rhetoric by arguing for the reformist credentials of the government.[5]

By 1997–98, however, things were coming unstuck. There were continuing signs of local administrative breakdown in parts of the countryside. Random conversations with a wide range of sources suggested that the problems of rural unrest that had surfaced in Thai Binh province in 1997 were widespread, and, even where there was no fire, there was often a worrying volume of smoke. It is therefore quite impossible to estimate with any accuracy the extent of the problem. It is enough, though, that state power at local level, in what remains a predominantly rural economy, had been challenged. There were apparently two main political responses at national level: First, there was a re-orientation of official development priorities towards the rural areas, most marked at the second and fourth central committee plena.[6] Second, there was a re-examination of various premises of the mid-1990s development policy stance: the focus upon SOEs and their 'leading role' in the economy; the pattern of investment, especially FDI with its avoidance of the rural areas, import-substituting and high capital-intensive nature; the poor performance in job creation; and the general sense of the government's weak authority.

These two issues came together in the contradiction between the need to use state power to change the direction of various economic processes, and the concern that such power might be insufficient. It is not difficult to interpret this as a sign that, at high level, it was felt necessary that the three top economic portfolios be held by politicians of second rank yet of a certain proven capability: Pham Van Khai, Prime Minister, with overall economic responsibilities, a trained economist with long experience; Nguyen Tan Dung, Deputy Prime Minister in charge of domestic economic affairs and acting Governor of the State Bank of Vietnam, young but dynamic; and Nguyen Manh Cam, Foreign Minister and Deputy Prime Minister in charge of external economic matters.

In the late 1990s these leaders were expected to defer to senior advisors and to more senior politicians such as Le Kha Phieu, party General Secretary.[7] However, for state power to be utilised to offset the adverse political consequences of the largely *laissez faire* attitude towards state business interests and the direction of foreign investment flows, they would have had to be given their heads (although not on a platter). The relative independence of these active politicians, and their successors, was a crucial indicator of success.

Closely related to the recovery of state resources in the very early 1990s, by the end of the 1990s the main power base of the regime could well be said to be the state apparatus.[8] This combined with a widespread popular acceptance of Communist Party rule, albeit grudgingly in places. According to its own well-worked out ideology, a Communist Party in government has no natural basis for ruling a market economy. Yet rule it did.

To avoid threats it was necessary that actual and potential discontent be dealt with. Traditionally, this was by the reallocation of state resources and an acceptance of spontaneous liberalisation. By the late 1990s, the latter was no longer a viable option, not least because of the risks involved, for example, the danger, as exemplified by the Russian experiment, of a free-for-all SOE privatisation that would give ownership to managers and the old planning cadre.

A market economy, as was increasingly obvious in Vietnam as well as elsewhere, presents political opportunities that encourage the exercise of state power. Yet, in Vietnam as elsewhere, and as global processes grow in power and pace, the governing elite must confront a general complaint – that of the relative weakness of nation-states seeking to localise these processes in response to local political and social priorities.[9]

The significance of the political problems of the closing years of the decade is that, as Thaveeporn (1996) has argued, *without* an ability to exploit state power, risks appeared to be mounting. But without greater state authority there was no guarantee that *any* adopted policies could be implemented, especially if, perceiving threats to the regime, there was a shift in overall policy stance to 'buck the trend' and confront important and by now well-entrenched interests (see Kokko and Zejan 1996). The sword was blunt, and, even once sharpened, the foe remained strong.

Macro-economics and all that

Growth

Like the Philippines, but unlike most other Southeast Asian countries, Vietnam was able to maintain positive economic growth despite the 1997 economic crisis. Estimates for the most likely 1998 outcome were around the 3–5 per cent mark.[10] There was some uncertainty over these numbers, largely due to the changes through 1998, with rather rapid deterioration in the second half-year. When compared with rates reported around the 9 per cent level through most of the 1990s, the numbers indicate major contractionary forces at work. This is despite Vietnam's avoidance of the financial upsets experienced in many other countries. The reasons for this are discussed below.

The main contractionary forces operating on the Vietnamese economy through 1997–98 are as follows: first, the steep decline in FDI disbursements and signing-ups; second, the slowing of export growth; and third, the increasing need for businesses to reduce their liquid capital needs by reducing the build-up of stocks they were carrying as a result of the slowdown in output growth. According to many analysts, these trends were set to deteriorate further and so little growth could be expected in the early years of the new millennium. There was a tangible risk of negative growth.

Unsurprisingly, the situation of low or negative growth affected the government's ability to manoeuvre. Partly as a result of higher prices paid to farmers, partly owing to expansion of bank credit to SOEs in the rice export business, *inflation* accelerated in 1998. *Tax revenues* started to show a real decline, which the government dealt with both through inflationary finance and, more importantly, through *reductions in spending*. This was a fine juggling act, as claims upon state resources naturally increased (due to competition and the threat of bankruptcy) at the same time as the resources available to meet them declined.

If this were the specific conjuncture of the immediate post-crisis period, it was nevertheless clear, given a longer-term perspective, that the ready availability of state-controlled or state-influenced resources that had underpinned the emergence of the pro-SOE development model had now ended.

What to do? As is so typical, the main killing ground for increasingly outmoded political ideas was the balance of payments, in times of crisis, the area of most intense interaction with the World Bank and the International Monetary Fund (IMF). Through 1998 the decline in exports became a major issue. While growth was maintained until September, exports then began to fall. Vietnam was hit badly by the collapse in the world oil price, and by competition from many commodity exporters desperate to create dollar revenues. Yet 'objective' factors eased the political climate. Vietnam's rather diversified primary commodity export base (coffee, peanuts and seafood are three good examples) helped offset these trends. Rice exports also continued to increase.

Indeed, the government's task of restructuring to cope with the effects of the Asian financial crisis and the consequences of the earlier growth pattern started to seem rather less onerous than some had expected. Light manufacturing exports in fact showed positive growth in 1998. Textile and garments exports grew around 5 per cent. And electronics showed fast growth, mainly due to a number of assembly factories coming on line.

With the brakes already full on, imports growth was cut to well below 1995–96 levels, when free access to consumer goods which would underpin emerging 'middle-class lifestyles' (see below) pushed the country towards a severe balance of payments crisis. It was essentially administrative controls (the use of state authority to avoid the effects of corruption, for example, bribes designed to argue for special cases) that saw a reduction in imports. The trade deficit remained, however, leaving the economy dependent upon capital inflows, and these could not be expected to improve. Of central importance was the fact that the deficit improved through 1998. Exports showed an increase for the year of around 2 per cent, and imports a fall of about the same magnitude. The task facing the government, or, rather, the intensity of the crisis, thus eased in the period 1998–99.

The pattern of industrial output growth, however, showed vividly the rigidities in the system and the consequences of the pro-SOE development model. Total industrial output in 1998 showed a growth rate of around 12 per cent; however, the foreign-invested sector, which would soon produce around one-third to one-half of Vietnam's total industrial output, was still growing fastest, at around 22 per cent. This reflected, and is reflected in, rapid growth in highly capital-intensive sectors such as crude oil (24 per cent growth), cement (22 per cent), electricity (13 per cent) and rolled steel (9 per cent). Employment growth was thus limited. At this time the non-state sector was still growing the slowest of all, a pattern that was to remain unchanged until the early 2000s.[11]

Agricultural output growth remained rather high, at near 4 per cent. The production potential of the family farming system continued to show its ability to grow fast using its own retained profits. This provided a striking contrast to the poor performance of the small-scale non-agricultural sectors. Non-state industry, for example, was the slowest growing part of Vietnam's industry, and ended up showing a growth rate of around 5 per cent for the year.

The monetary economy also was remarkably stable. The crucial indicator of tensions – free market interest rates – remained at normal levels. Businesses could still get access to bank credits, although larger firms, especially SOEs, were preferred. Political pressure to support SOEs and 'favoured sons' was very important. Yet the overall macro-economic balance remained remarkably good. The exchange rate had fallen, initially in response to failed interventions and then simply to conserve reserves. The fall, from near 11,000 to near 14,000 – almost 30 per cent in fact – compared rather favourably with Vietnam's regional competitors, such as Thailand.[12]

It is likely that there had been extensive overseas commercial borrowing by SOEs and also Vietnamese joint-venture companies. Taiwan remained the largest investor, and had not experienced any major financial crisis.[13]

As throughout the 1990s in the aftermath of the macro-economic measures of 1989, a second reason for macro-economic stability was the very high degree of confidence in the banks held by the Vietnamese public. Despite the effects of the confusion of the mid-1990s and then the 1997 crisis, people continued to hold dong, but they also continued, as they had done for a long time, to hold US dollar bank accounts. These amounted to some one-third of total deposit liabilities. It was striking to see how, after various moves to encourage, if not force, a higher level of sales of dollars to the banking system, the authorities moved quickly to reassure the public that these deposits could be withdrawn freely.

The contrast between the continued integrity of the Vietnamese financial system and those of many ASEAN members was somewhat deceptive. It was the very lack of a normal system of financial markets that had protected Vietnamese businesses. The main focus of political attention, however, was that, as restructuring was pushed through as part of IMF and World Bank packages, Vietnam's competitors would increasingly benefit from more competitive fundamentals, including better human resources and physical infrastructure, as well as the normal effects of capitalism's 'creative destruction'. In fact, this tended not to happen: for example, Thailand saw the election of a nationalist government seeking to preserve domestic commercial interests (or at least some of them). Again, this tended to *ease* pressures upon Vietnamese politicians.

Outlook

Sitting in the hot seat in the late 1990s, any self-respecting economic advisor would, if asked, have had to argue that the outlook for the Vietnamese economy, in the short term, was for a period of slower, if not negative, output growth as various cumulative 'multiplier' effects impacted upon demand and output. *Exports* growth could not safely be expected to recover quickly, not least as Vietnam's regional competitors moved through their restructuring process and demand in the developed world fell. *Investment* had fallen and, with excess capacity a major issue throughout the region, FDI could not be expected to recover to 1995–97 levels in the short term. *Consumer spending* was also weak, hit by pessimism and layoffs. Again, this could only be expected to deteriorate further as stock was shed and the recession continued.

It seemed, therefore, that 1999 and 2000 were set for negligible rates of growth. Advice would necessarily have had to entail policy changes and economic restructuring under conditions of increased competition for resources. However, the rural unrest of 1997 aside, there was no open and overt 'Big Crisis' to push for change. The tensions were more to do with the political problems posed for the country as a result of its recent history and the short-term outlook. And, as we can see in hindsight, various factors evolved differently, leading to a less tense political atmosphere: the emergence of a rapidly growing private sector, the failure of Vietnam's regional competitors to force through major restructuring, the general and rather early success of macro measures to stimulate exports, domestic demand and a reigning-in of the excesses of the state business sector, among others. One can conclude, therefore, that while the mid-1990s and the 1997 Asian crisis certainly concentrated the mind, the force of these events was rather rapidly muted by the changing nature of affairs in the real world.

Development issues

It is nevertheless the case that the exercise of state power changed both qualitatively and in practice during the late 1990s. The implications of the situation immediately after the 1997 crisis need to be seen in a longer term context, and especially that of the pro-SOE development model that, arguably, had emerged in the early 1990s (see Fforde 1997).

One useful way of coming at this is from the concept of aggregate savings – i.e. total savings. While one can debate whether a high level of savings is a necessary or sufficient condition for rapid growth, it is the case that most fast-growing economies have savings as a percentage of GDP at least near the 25 per cent level. Under communist rule, such levels were rarely attained. In the mid-1990s, investment rates near that level were seen, but these were strongly supported by inward investments. As FDI declines, overseas development assistance is on the increase.

It is often argued that at low levels of incomes, savings by the population are low. In Vietnam, where farmers have little access to bank credits, most of the investments associated with agricultural output gains have come from farmers' own retained incomes, which, though not easily measured, are large. There have certainly been significant state investments in infrastructure, especially in irrigation and drainage, but these do not match the mass of resources committed by the farmers themselves. By the late 1990s, with FDI largely ignoring agriculture, these resources had yet been sufficient on their own to provide one condition for higher rural incomes. However, there existed many structures and mechanisms that were sucking resources out of agriculture, of which the widespread processing and export monopolies still enjoyed by SOEs were perhaps the most important.

Outside the agricultural sector, the Vietnamese economy remained largely dominated by SOEs, with the foreign-invested sector by now growing fast. What was striking in its absence was a dynamic, small-scale, private or quasi-private sector, growing rapidly, based upon retained earnings and soaking up large amounts of labour. One need only point to the effects upon South Korea of the 1997 crisis to see the links between the 'little picture' of economics and the 'big picture' of culture and cultural production. The relative lack of this sector, and the consequent dual importance for the newly rich of the state sector and foreign contacts, was by the late 1990s an increasingly deep-rooted aspect of the Vietnamese political economy. Reaction against it was visibly expressed in the rural unrest and imminent threat from growing numbers of unemployed. Less overtly, one can experience a tangible sense across a wide range of consumption that the initial stage of consumption of global 'goods' was coming to an end.

This issue is also usefully viewed historically and comparatively. 'Development issues' are not new, although so-called 'development studies' is. In the next sections I discuss issues related to 'class formation', the interaction between those individuals who find themselves in power over society, and changes within society. Under the dynamic and globalising conditions of the late 1990s, it is not clear just what elements of Vietnam's historical 'political culture' could inform modern strategies.

Policy issues and the 'confusion of expectations'

Much policy debate occurs in isolation from those issues outlined above. This is partly the result of its dominance by social scientists, with their rationalist and activist approach. This is especially true of economists, who are locked into a metaphor of knowledge frighteningly close to nineteenth-century physics. However, it also reflects the practicalities involved in negotiating relationships structured by concepts of the nation-state as an object of political influence and a subject capable of identifying and implementing transcendentally 'correct' policy. There are strict limits upon what can be said and done by foreign officials working in Vietnam. But what was widely expected has not, in fact, come to pass.

The Vietnamese 'market economy', it has been argued, emerged around 1989 from a period of economic liberalisation that can best be understood as a process, rather than the outcome, of purposeful policy (see Fforde and de Vylder 1996). This view, deliberately unenthusiastic about predictive exercises, nevertheless anticipated certain matters, such as the role to be played by SOEs, as being of importance and as yet 'unresolved'. It has had far more influence on the academic literature than it has had upon writings emerging from the neo-classical economic orthodoxy, for obvious reasons.

Yet the various different expectations that arose in the early and mid-1990s regarding what would happen to Vietnam point up various interesting issues. The two key groups of actors, so far as policy debates are concerned, are Vietnamese policy-makers and the overseas donor community. Their relative isolation from the broad masses of consumers, both of clear commodities and things less typically seen as such, is thought provoking. Was the SOE-focused policy contradictory, in terms of the adaptation of global product to local tastes?

For dominant groups within the Vietnamese policy-making establishment, the recovery of state resources from around 1991–92 offered a continuation of state activities that was not so very different from old ways of thinking. Basic to this was the idea that the main channels of savings should be controlled by the state.

Central-planning had argued that profits from SOEs, based upon the institutions of neo-Stalinism and controlled plan prices, should form the basis for the resource flows underpinning the plan. Now, with prices largely set by the market, bank credits and a reformed tax base could again fuel the state's development engine. The creation of 'rents' – resources that could be acquired by the chosen at very low or zero cost – was thus structurally transformed, giving the renamed State Planning Commission a new, albeit not radically different, meaning to its existence.

The SOE-focused development model that emerged in the mid-1990s fitted this world outlook. It is not at all hard to understand why Vietnam's state banks were increasingly subject to the imposition of non-commercial criteria in their lending. They were *intended* to act as instruments of state rent creation – to secure and then allocate resources for planners and politicians, not generate profit.

For the key opinion-makers within the donor community, such as the dominant cadre within the World Bank as it developed its view prior to the resumption of US–Vietnamese relations, the early 1990s, especially the period 1989–92, offered support for a vision within which the SOEs would slowly dissolve in the rising tide of emergent private-sector firms. This view was supported by the particular circumstances of 1990–92, when the state lacked resources and SOEs were being heavily squeezed. The 'hard budget constraint', when combined with an interpretation of the events of 1989 as reflecting purposive market-oriented and systemic 'reform', implied that SOEs should not be a source of worry.[14]

An additional element of this view, based upon orthodox views of the forces governing domestic and international capital movements, was that investments in Vietnam would reflect her so-called 'comparative advantages'.[15] These were said to be a cheap and relatively high-quality labour force and rich agricultural potential. If capital were to flow in these directions, then growth could be expected to be both sectorally and socially 'good', in that the rural areas would benefit and employment creation would be rapid. In fact, however, in Vietnam both FDI and domestic investments have tended to avoid these areas in favour of real estate, tourism and relatively capital-intensive industry. One reason for this was the temporary profits to be made as land became a commodity. However, it remains a key problem in the analysis of Vietnam's economic development during the 1990s.

Neither of these views has turned out to be correct. Why? Much has to do with the pattern of investment that occurred. There are at least three ways of looking at this issue. First, by arguing that there is in fact little evidence that capital flows have in fact ever been explainable in these ways. This view is now starting to influence important official thinking (in the IMF for example) (see Nguyen Manh Huan 1997). Second, by arguing that markets in Vietnam were full of entry barriers and other 'distortions', which, if corrected, would ensure that investments moved in the 'right' direction. It is certainly the case that Vietnam was full of such inhibitors to business, especially the ad hoc barriers to inter-provincial trade set up by underpaid policemen (see Nguyen 1997). Third, by arguing that almost any barrier in Vietnam could be dealt with, assuming the relative profitability of doing so is sufficient. This point of view tends to be confirmed by discussions with Vietnamese business people. It is supported by the observation that increasing competition was, and is, present in global markets for both light goods and agricultural products, with increasingly high entry barriers. For light goods manufacturers, especially those in Southeast Asia, competition from China was and is a major problem. Such exports were already suffering *before* the onset of the 1997 crisis, spurred by China's devaluations earlier in that decade. In agriculture, the trends towards biotechnological intensification and the presence of European Union-subsidised output make expected profits in agriculture low.

Whatever the truth of the matter, it is clear that the pattern of investment in Vietnam during the 1990s – contrary to donor expectations – tended to avoid politically key domains – the rural areas; light goods manufacture and small-scale private and semi-private non-agricultural enterprise. The relative failure of small-scale enterprise to emerge and grow strongly is perhaps the most striking and revealing aspect of Vietnam's 1990s' development style. Vietnam had nothing to compare with China's TVE (Township and Village Enterprises) phenomenon. It also helps to understand why aggregate savings were so low, and is the main explanation for the political tensions discussed above. It is these issues that forced the re-ordering of sectoral priorities presented at the second and fourth plena in 1996.

It was the rapid expansion of the non-state sector in the period 1989–91 that transformed the rural landscape as services returned to the streets. It also easily absorbed some 500,000 labourers shed by the state sector. However, in manufacturing, the 1990s saw very little employment growth in this sector.[16]

There is good evidence here on the nature of the non-state manufacturing sector. The 1998 Ronnas study shows that new entrants exhibited a classical model of rapid capitalist growth, characterised by extremely rapid accumulation, based upon retained earnings. There was very little borrowing from the banks and there were clear signs of emergent class formation. Unlike during the 1980s, most managers came from middle-class backgrounds.[17] However, most reported 'previous experience' as their main reason for entering private business.

This suggests that they came from the state sector, pointing to earlier processes of 'primary accumulation' as hoards were built up. Systemic extraction of resources ('expropriation', or perhaps 're-expropriation') has been viewed in radical quarters as the main characteristic of capitalist development in Vietnam in the 1990s (Greenfield 1993). Close links between accumulation and official status have been identified by Vietnamese researchers, but the lack of access to state bank credits reported by Ronnas muddies the simple picture that could be drawn from this.[18] Work of this type points to underlying processes of social change and class formation that would be quite normal. Accumulation of private wealth and economic power can be expected in any emerging market economy, whether it be Vietnam in the 1990s or Tudor England.

How, from this perspective, are Vietnamese SOEs to be viewed? Neither of the two sets of official beliefs outlined above really fit easily with the fact that very few Vietnamese SOEs reported any significant capacity to put their own equity (own capital) into investment projects, and therefore required high levels of state bank finance.[19] Since they were generating significant cash flow, where did the retained earnings go?

These arguments take us towards a re-examination of the interests driving state activities and the exact function of SOEs in the political economy. Their power to access resources controlled by the state is clear; also now evident, however, are the social and economic costs that resulted.

In the event, both of these two views can easily be criticised. The ideas that drove the pro-SOE development model, as we have seen, led to major political problems. By combining a high level of state socialisation of risk with a breath-taking self-exposure to corruption and the creation of weakly competitive businesses, the model has taken the regime into the minefields of popular discontent that we see it confronting today. The increasing foreign domination of the economy, partly the result of Vietnam's low domestic savings, which is directly related to the lack of a large private sector, adds to the mix.

An alternative view downplays the importance of state activities and looks more closely at incentives to 'watch where the money goes' (to use the maxim of the Bloomberg financial intelligence service). This, as we have seen, is revealing.

Systemic issues – the 'New Men': from Bosworth field to industrial zones?

Introduction – 'last man standing'?

The emergence of a market economy in 1989 was the outcome of a series of events, some of them policy-driven, which were certainly not widely predicted. The usefulness of the analogy with certain European histories is that the VCP, to a certain extent, found itself somewhat bemusedly and quite unexpectedly ruling over a market economy under changing conditions with which it was quite unfamiliar. Even if the rules of the new game could be learnt and understood, the style of play that would evolve, essentially Vietnamese, could hardly be predicted. That the VCP was in power was incontrovertible; in a market economy, however, to which its dogma and ideology were essentially hostile, upon what would its power rest? For a Tudor monarch, knowing that his crown had been placed upon his ancestor's head by his own hands at Bosworth field, owing power directly to nobody else, the task was clear: stay in power.

Willy-nilly, since all processes of growth imply differentiation, Vietnam's social structure and political makeup would have to change. 'New Men' would come up, with wealth based upon a range of sources, and what would be done about them? As the quote at the start of this chapter reflects, similar issues have confronted others in the past. A simple characterisation would be that most of the 'New Men' have come from positions *in* the state apparatus, negotiating with varying success new positions in the 1990s' market economy.[20] This process was naturally full of contradictions, not least of which were the rather different skills required to manage a business as opposed to a network of well-established relationships granting access to resources in various ways, fair and foul.

Savings, accumulation and economic development

As I have argued above, one main element of the Vietnamese 'development style' as it emerged was rather low levels of savings. This was mainly due to the lack of a rapidly growing private or semi-private sector. This in turn may be explained by a variety of factors: First, the general hostility of the regime to the private sector, and its favouring of SOEs; second, the high levels of competition from imports and the relatively low profitability of light goods manufacture; and third, the presence – for example in real estate, FDI consultancies and related service activities – of *alternative* outlets for capital and investment and entrepreneurial activities.

Does this really matter? The answer is at root only valid in terms of Vietnamese political priorities. These reflect, among other things, learning processes on the part of much of the population, not least those in the government.

If under the Tudors the 'New Men' were people whose 'drive and efficiency in economic matters ... also made them harsh to their tenants and contemptuous of the common people' (Morris 1955: 25–6), the evident lack of antagonistic class relations between their Vietnamese equivalents and their workforces points to a rather different 'development style' (see Chan and Norlund 1999). However, unlike their Vietnamese equivalents, these 'New Men' came from a local political set-up whose power base rested mainly upon land – something conspicuously lacking in Vietnam. For predominantly rural countries, whether Tudor England or modern Vietnam, rulers' perceptions of developments in the countryside were naturally very important.

Lenin and the peasantry re-visited: the other 'delicate task'

If one 'delicate task' to be managed was the relationship between rulers and the 'New Men', then another was the way in which the social structure of the rural areas had been changing.

It has been argued that the basic political rationale behind collectivisation was economic: the desire to avoid the creation of a new class of landlords and employers in the rural areas whose class interests would be antagonistic to the regime (see Bray 1983). It was argued that land concentration and rural proletarianisation would be necessary to attain increasing land yields. Experience in China and Vietnam since decollectivisation appears to argue, on the face of it, that large output gains can be obtained from a rural economy made up predominantly of family farms. Yet the political pressures to re-establish co-operatives 'of a new type' suggest that there was something going on in the rural areas that was seen to threaten political stability. Most likely, arguments were made that, without these organisations, small-scale new entrepreneurs would increasingly force themselves into local politics. The sense that this was the case is strong. The picture was made more complex by two features of the situation: First, the effective breakdown of the local administration and party structures in 'hot' areas, such as Thai Binh, for it is these that would guide and utilise such co-operatives. And second, the sheer lack of competitive power of co-operatives under Vietnamese conditions: Vietnam is no Denmark.

The second and fourth plena both called for a major shift in development priorities to support rural development. Yet these were not the issues raised in Thai Binh, where unrest was more to do with relations between the population and the local administration. There was thus a stalemate.

Conclusions

Two main issues confronted Vietnam as it went into the 2000s. First, coping with the need to use state power to offset gathering pressures from the politically important who felt that they had missed out on, relatively speaking, the benefits of economic growth in the 1990s. These were, to generalise excessively, farmers and the growing mass of unemployed. That they had missed out can be more or less directly attributed to a pattern of growth that resulted from a relatively free allocation of investment according to 'market forces' (Cassandra's little sister). Yet the state remained incoherent, ill disciplined and in need of profound constitutional reform (either explicit or implicit). Second, was the need to secure sufficient power to confront these very powerful external and domestic economic forces, so as to redirect resources in keeping with domestic political priorities. This 'localisation' issue is common to many governments. Vietnam, with far less to play with, confronts it in spades.

Culture and comedy – economics and the real world

Introduction – Cassandra's little sister was bored, again

A wide range of texts argue, based upon old insights from a range of classical writers, that changes in the mode of production, however that is defined, have a wide series of implications for what might be called 'cultural production' (see Introduction). At its simplest, these can be seen as being both constraining and expanding in their nature. They are constraining in that, in societies with market economies, there is an underlying tendency, unless things are put in place or preserved to ensure the contrary, to see production as production for profit. Means of production are owned, priced and used to cover costs and reward the risk-bearer, entrepreneur, bank, thug or lady who controls them. Many aspects of society (the legal, the educational, etc.) present knowledge in terms of this as the 'natural' order of things; others then critique this. Part of that critique is the realisation that, while alternatives are possible, they remain alternatives. To anybody who has a decent modern education in the social sciences, such opinions are well known. As well known should be the other side of the coin: the ways in which the implications of market economy are expanding in their nature. One may have to have cash, and earn it, but still there is a range of things, often changing, that can be bought.

I recall watching a female farmer squatting on her carrying pole, outside an urban market in Hanoi, goods sold, having her early lunch of a demi-baguette and pâté. Clearly it was delicious. It was also cheap, French in origin, suited well (in that baguettes used little oil) to Vietnamese baking techniques of the pre-market economy period, and, although the pâté would probably not have gone down well in Bordeaux, it was adapted to Vietnamese tastes. Or at least those of the customers of the particular stalls who were selling nearby.

Here it is the adaptation that is interesting, as it offers new opportunities for the outsider (me and us) to experience new variations on cultural themes that are both accessible and novel. To develop this theme, consider the standard VinaMilk Yoghurt, lightly sugared and as well distributed through cold chains by the mid-1990s as Coca Cola. Called, in Vietnamese, not anything close to the Western name but *sua chua* – sour milk – and supplemented in many shops by home-grown products, what determined the flavouring of this basic product? I do not know, but recall the taste as well as the (to my mind also excellent) cheap vanilla ice cream of suburban Australian Woolworths of the 1990s. Here one can note in passing that the emergent dairy sector designed to feed Hanoi, contracted to supply milk to VinaMilk in the mid-1990s, went to the wall when the company found that it could buy milk powder on the global market far more cheaply, and so cancelled the contracts.

Adaptation requires integration into foreign (i.e. global) processes so that basic products can be adapted; this encourages a domestication of production, so that there is scope to change what is produced (the feedback driven no doubt by profit-seeking), perhaps on the margin between local market competition and adaptation to local tastes.

This returns us to a more general issue, for Vietnam seems to confirm, in the world as it now is, the centrality of position with respect to global processes. In terms of the macro development issues discussed above, one interpretation of that economic analysis is that the political agenda in Vietnam was, increasingly, pushing the VCP towards interventions to influence these 'positions' for a range of political actors who objected strongly to the status quo. The basic issue, given the profound poverty of Vietnam, comprised the terms of access to external economic opportunities, whether directly or indirectly.

Like Cassandra's little sister, to miss out on the curse is also to miss out on divine intervention.[21]

Again, at the 'macro' level, it is useful to put into perspective the relative power of the economic forces and phenomena we are observing. Around 2000, the Vietnamese GDP was around US$30 billion, of which perhaps US$7 billion was invested. By comparison, in Australia, not the richest of Western countries, total exports, yearly, were around US$100 billion. The total value of deposits at Vietnamese banks was around US$3 billion, of which around US$1 billion was in US dollars. If, for the sake of argument, we assume that there were one million families (in a population of 75 million) with US dollar deposits, then this amounted to only US$1,000 each. And from these should be deducted the deposits of businesses and other organisations. In addition, Vietnamese salaries remained low, even in urban areas. This underlying economic weakness was a primary characteristic of the Vietnamese 'development style' as it affected emerging middle-class lifestyles.

Middle-class lifestyles, purchasing patterns and cultural issues – the Year of the Leg; Hanoi and Ho Chi Minh City compared

Those people who were enjoying middle-class incomes by the end of the 1990s had come from often very low levels only a decade previously. Food rationing really only stopped being relevant in 1990–91, and in the late 1980s a bicycle had been a major purchase. Yet it is important to see the differences between quantity and quality.

It was often remarked that a major visible sign of the differences between Hanoi, the capital, and Ho Chi Minh City, commercial hub, is the different forms of conspicuous motorised transport: specifically, that the Hanoi motorcycle market was far more status-conscious than that of Ho Chi Minh City 'where they ride things that work, rather than make them look good'. In the mid-1990s this was marked by the replacement of the Honda Dream by the Spacey, while1997 saw preferred body styles go through another set of changes, with greater emphasis upon the leg, as could be seen from the classic Spacey advertising campaign. Since these campaigns aimed at a wide range of female definitions, it was the stuff of novels and intrigue, as well as just dollars. Yet this focus was far more evident in Hanoi than in Saigon; indeed, the relative absence of such expensive conspicuous consumption in what has long been referred to as the 'individualistic, commercial, south', is intriguing.

A group who clearly benefited greatly throughout the 1990s was the salaried urban middle class. These families often have mixed incomes: father in the bureaucracy, children in a mixture of public and private sector jobs, wife possibly in trade but moving into other things as the economy liberalises. This mixed pattern is more common in Hanoi than Saigon, reflecting the opportunities for corruption, the perceived need for risk-avoidance and the greater number of public sector jobs in the capital. From a situation in the late 1980s when a bicycle was a major capital investment, by the late 1990s many of these families now found themselves close to regional middle-class lifestyles. Central to this, of course, was the radical change in attitudes to house-servants – usually called 'maids' in the Vietnamese English of the time, no matter what skivvying they had to do. Again, in 'liberating' the women of the house (and perhaps even the men) from child care, housework and other 'caring' activities, this was once more the stuff of novels and intrigues. It was perhaps comparable to the effects upon urban women of the opening up of the streets in 1989–91, as service industries blossomed (widening greatly access to goods such as the demi-baguette mentioned above).

A main lack was of course a car; other differences included housing stock, which in Hanoi and Saigon often reflected rapid 'own-construction' activities with a wide range of qualities and designs; a still near-complete lack of air-conditioned malls and other ways of dealing with the climate; and a relative lack of numbers leading to thinner markets.

The great land 'share out' of the early and mid-1990s often saw such middle classes end up with real estate having nominal values well over \$100,000. There were white goods – the prized imported Electrolux at over \$1,000 replacing second-hand washing machines imported from Japan at less than \$50 – second-hand Hondas sold to buy Dreams or Spaceys worth over \$2,500; hi-fi systems, colour TVs, VCRs etc. Domestic servants and cheap tailoring permitted wives and daughters to transform their lifestyles, as did the return of street food and ready-made meals. Style, chic, ostentation and the rest revealed the capacity of Vietnam's urban tigers to blow away most other cities in terms of pure 'front'. But, unlike in Milan, such conspicuous consumption was not based upon real and sustainable economic power – by which I mean the production of tradable goods, i.e. exports.

Yet steady incomes remained rather low: most earned around $100 a month. Few of such families were making money from small businesses. Instead, they relied upon access to handouts and shares of office 'funds' derived from the flows of resources entering the country as an accompaniment to foreign investment, aid, technical assistance and so forth, helped by the creation of assets by such measures as the sharing out of land. It was this, rather than actual income, that permitted such lifestyles.

The Vietnamese salaried middle class thus remained dependent upon rather low incomes. Sometimes, its living costs were low. Maids, for example, were paid levels sufficient to attract them from their impoverished villages. Yet, when it had to pay for the services of others members of the class – such as teachers, doctors and others – it found that salaries were high, since state salaries were deemed too low for these professionals to deliver good services without 'top-ups'. As a result, maintenance of lifestyle, and continuing purchases of important status goods, depended upon access to savings. With foreign interest and dollars drying up, the feast could be seen in danger of rapidly turning to famine. Houses, built with little debt, now started to be sold, or at least buyers were sought. Yet by the early 2000s, the boom was back as economic stability and the relative lack of other investment outlets due to stagnating stock markets saw investors bring dollars back to Vietnam's cities.

How did this group save? Throughout the 1980s, preferred media were goods, real estate, land (including rural land), education, gold and dollars. As the banks started to offer good returns, the middle class became accustomed to having savings in the banks. Not until the very late 1990s and early 2000s did small businesses really start to attract funds.

One part of the picture was a rapid increase in dollar deposits. With the state commercial banks offering reasonable rates of interest with no questions asked (unlike in the 1980s), a significant proportion of dollars were returned to the banks. Easy arbitrage meant that interest rates remained competitive with opportunities offered by overseas banks. This came to be seen as normal, for, unlike the 1980s, nobody suffered from banks refusing to pay out when asked.

The main differences between Hanoi and Saigon can be related to the different sources of income. If the main difference lies in the importance attached to conspicuous consumption, then the greater importance of 'rent-seeking' in Hanoi is striking. Hanoi, it should be noted, is most striking in its relative lack of an extensive commercial class basing itself upon the production of goods for sale on markets. Too much of the city's revenue derives from its role as the main 'gate-keeper' to Vietnam, as the capital city. Furthermore, the willingness to spend large sums on consumer durables points to an underlying sense of 'development style', relative security being based upon social position, with little desire to invest in medium-risk commercial ventures. By contrast, Saigon is more normal, with greater social mobility and a far greater interest in commerce and the production of commodities.

'Le petit Vietnam' and the 'New Men' emerging from the rural areas

All seems well, hopefully, for the new urban groups. What about those left 'down on the farm' (who seem inclined to wander in search of a better life)? How isolated are Vietnam's farmers? How cut off from the outside world? To what extent can they be seen as being kept 'down on the farm'?

One consequence of Vietnam's 'traditional socialist' past was that, unlike many other countries enduring processes of urbanisation and industrialisation, Vietnamese cities did not derive any direct income from land holdings. This was certainly a process underway during the French period, when land acquisition by rising urban groups had been powerful, both in the north and more significantly in the south, before the US-inspired Land Reform of the 1960s. But collectivisation and all its trappings effectively severed the property links between cities and the rural areas. However, since the late 1980s, if not before, this has been reversed, as profits and earnings have been invested in land. But economic links between city and countryside were, unlike in earlier times, still predominantly based upon trade and contract, not land ownership. This helps explain the nature of urban life.

It seems too far-fetched to argue that, by the end of the 1990s, Vietnam's farmers were 'isolated'. Apart from in the upland areas, by now near universal electrification and access to TV, coupled with rather easy migration possibilities, had resulted in an opening up of Vietnam and relative freedom for farmers. Issues of ideological control aside, and given the rather porous nature of control via the registration system, what did keep them 'down on the farm'?

Dominant expressions in the mass media, and popularly, regarding the nature of the village, of rural peace and its contrast with urban life and colonial conditions, are certainly reminiscent of other evocations of a 'little world', such as that of pre-war Ireland during the Free State. These notions also suit a country recovering from a period of violence and turning inward. Yet the Vietnamese population seems too desirous of aggressively negotiating its relations with the outside world to be viewed in this manner.

Indeed, the awareness of the wider world expressed by the Vietnamese rural population was and is often challenging. Praise from cadres and people alike was often given to those with 'get-up-and-go' and the capacity to get out and seek out new opportunities (the right ones, of course).

What is marked, however, is the relative absence from the ranks of the new urban middle classes of those who had 'made it' in the rural areas, those who now intended to spend the associated rewards seeking better social positions for themselves and their children. Among the successful, the few who did possess a rural background were almost always those who had got 'up and out' during the period of 'traditional socialism' (i.e. before the 1980s). Such careers were typically made in the state sector, with a strong emphasis upon education and access to positions in the state apparatus.

Unwritten localisations: rhythm, fragrance and food

In these closing parts of this chapter I want to extend the discussion into three areas, all related to the issue of adaptation mentioned above. While conditioned by the economic, of necessity they involve elements well beyond that. They draw upon the particular opportunities and constraints of a market economy, and are of (to many) inherent interest. There of course exists a substantial wider literature.[22]

The joy(s) of commoditisation – Chinese food, French house, Japanese wife, Bose speakers

In Vietnam there is a well-known expression of the 'three bests: *Com Tau, Nha Phap, Vo Nhat* (Chinese food, French house, Japanese wife).[23] This, naturally, could be modified. In any case, it excludes rhythm, fragrance and food. These are inherently interesting areas of 'localisation' since there are strong and well-developed indigenous tastes and activities that are in turn not overly conceptualised and regulated. Such a situation permits the interplay of supply, demand and evolving tastes to be observed. Below I explore briefly three areas: music, fragrance and food. Economically, all three are very important, as can be seen from the widespread purchases of hi-fi systems and tape-recorders, and the equally widespread availability of pre-recorded tapes and counterfeit CDs. Food is of obvious importance. Urban, wage-earning, young women can be found spending very high proportions of their incomes on fragrances and toiletries (up to 30 per cent or more has been reported).[24]

Rhythm – natural syncopation with no dance tradition

Musically, Vietnam poses a number of intriguing paradoxes.[25] First, the society is one of strong rhythms, both in speech, movement and indigenous music. Yet it has no popular dance tradition.[26] Second, while initially tedious 2/4 rhythms dominated attempts to play in a 'Western' style, it took less than a decade for Vietnamese drummers to master the poly-rhythms and feel of such genres as funk and swing.[27] This mastery, to a non-professional ear, draws upon innate sense. Yet no attempt has been made to develop a Vietnamese equivalent of Western 'electric folk', which adapted traditional folk music to modern instruments and rhythms influenced by R & B. Third, the fine (i.e. 1/32 or at least 1/16 beat 'misses') syncopations naturally used by non-professional Vietnamese singers while performing for friends are far ahead of what Westerners usually attain (especially the appallingly bad timing usually heard in Anglican churches).

Even finer manoeuvres are probably used by professionals in genres such as *Cai luong* or *Cheo*. Vietnamese folk music is heavily syncopated. Yet this is, so far as I can see, almost totally unexploited by those treading the interface between Vietnamese and foreign culture. This suggests that Vietnamese popular music is not able (unlike, say, black American musicians in the formative periods in Chicago or Soweto) to rely, when developing its own rhythms, upon an audience that draws upon local resources when it dances to its music. We shall see.

From an economic point of view, the most profitable and commercial areas for Vietnamese musicians are probably those that are aimed at domestic consumers. Their access to world music markets will of course depend upon their ability to devise a product that can compete with those already in existence. It will be interesting to see to what extent this is successful, and to what degree it manages to draw upon the distinct elements of Vietnamese music discussed above. Since many Vietnamese musicians are classically trained, the path will probably require technical proficiency, which is likely to result in a certain stifling of creativity.

Fragrance – am or duong?[28]

Fragrance is, so far as might be told, a distinctive element of certain aspects of Vietnamese culture. To give one striking example of personal observation, the main black market goods suited to deals made in Western aid projects in the late 1980s were cigarettes (unsurprising) and *shampoo*.[29]

Vietnamese markets for cosmetics and related goods exhibit a classic trajectory. With imported foreign brands so expensive and lacking Vietnamese-language labelling, joint ventures with major multinationals (Unilever, Colgate, Proctor & Gamble) are using standard packages of advertising and distribution to market to those with incomes sufficient to create viable levels of demand. There is little evidence that products are being adapted to specifically Vietnamese tastes. There is extensive smuggling of product, especially from Thailand. The market is large. According to one survey, the proportion of women's incomes in Ho Chi Minh City spent on perfumes, cosmetic, skincare, shampoo, etc. was around 1 per cent in 1991 and around 20 per cent by the end of the decade. In buying perfumes, 40 per cent reported that they bought foreign brands, 10 per cent Vietnamese and 50 per cent said that they used no perfume. According to another survey, around 70 per cent of women in the city spend between 300–400,000 dong on cosmetics.

At the same time there are a rather large number of Vietnamese companies who seek out various market niches: sales to low income groups, to the rural areas, and exports, particularly to China, Laos, Cambodia and the CIS (Commonwealth of Independent States). At the margin, they attempt to compete with the global brands coming from the joint ventures, but they lack funds for advertising and face steep entry costs in terms of brand recognition. As yet, they have not been able to offset this successfully through a specifically Vietnamese identification of their products. Whether they could prevent this niche from being bought by a foreign joint venture keen to preserve its market share would be interesting to see.

Food – from quantity to quality?

Perhaps the most striking aspect of Vietnamese food remains the strong regional differences in taste. One can no more get a northerner to like southern *pho* – noodle soup – than the reverse. I have already referred above to the adaptation process, yet who can tell me the origin of the custom of serving coffee in bowls of hot water?[30] Vietnamese opinion is vehement that it is not French.

In addition, attitudes towards foreign food remain very interesting. As a result of many foreign influences – Chinese, French, American, Eastern European – the Vietnamese diet, at least in urban areas, was penetrated early on by items such as breads, cakes, pâté, dairy products (especially yoghurt – see above) and, more recently, espresso coffee. Yet the basic diet and tastes appear fundamentally to have remained unchanged. Part of the explanation may be to do with the importance attached to 'balance' in diet, following traditional pre-scientific norms which do not sit well with Western cooking. Yet much also must be to do with indigenous 'taste' – even if this is normally expressed with the French loan word *gu* (*goût*).

An additional element to the economic impact of food is the legacy of the pre-1990 situation of poor nutrition and in many areas chronic malnutrition, especially among rural women in the north. The combination of a return to the normal open-air provision of food through stalls and street-side restaurants, with the corresponding far better access to food, led initially to a sharp rise in the quantity of food eaten. Later, in what is again a natural process, higher incomes and better supply has enabled a shift to better quality and an increase in the range of food eaten. in particular fast food

Conclusions

It would appear that localisation of foreign product is relatively well advanced in Vietnam. In the three case-studies discussed above change has either been rapid or, if not, there remains either clear potential or a rather long cosmopolitan history. Further, the technologies and prices associated with such products point to relatively cheap diversification and popularisation, and thus to what I would see as a better outcome than ersatz Western goods sold to the few.

Can development be fun? Conclusions: Merino Tigers?

The cultural elements of the arguments here have tended to reinforce the sense that Vietnam's particular 'development style' is likely to remain profoundly Vietnamese, as deep cultural elements exploit distinctly Vietnamese elements of social life there. Music, fragrance and food, all important parts of life, are part of creative negotiations of the 'localisation' of the global processes that now dominate the world economy. These are most obvious for music and food, less clear for fragrances.

In this sense, the 'New Men', unsurprisingly facing political opposition and contradictory incentives in their relationship with the state, are likely to remain inward-focused. This is of crucial importance: 'the "female" locates, the "male" negotiates'. It argues for a relative retention of an integrated domestic polity, and thus for the chance of better political outcomes. This is essential, as the hangover from the mid-1990s' 'boom', coupled with political pressure from rural areas and rising unemployment, forces a speedy divorce of these new commercial elements – the capitalists – from their origins in the state apparatus. And as such elements emerge, they will find, as they already have, that competition from foreign and domestic competitors is fierce.

If one wishes to be optimistic, then there is a strong argument that modern technology and market opportunities *must* enable a country such as Vietnam to grow fast and equitably. It is clear that the trends of the 1990s point in the opposite direction. It is also part of the World Bank's 'cookbook' – possibly now partly to be discarded – that with the right political solutions and mechanisms, better policies should be able to secure a change in Vietnam's development style that spreads the benefits of growth more widely. Getting there from here is an essentially Vietnamese opportunity.

Is it possible that Vietnam is a tiger in sheep's clothing ? They may yet surprise us. Effective use of state power based upon coherent, domestic, political processes may yet provide support for a reformed 'development style' that will realise Vietnam's potential.

Notes

1 Here see, for a position that leans towards the retention of a belief in the objective existence of a true development, Arndt (1981), and in greater depth Arndt (1987). For a contrary view that seeks to escape from the trap by stressing the doctrinal nature of concepts of development, see Cowen and Shenton (1996).

2 Thus the apocryphal proletarian saying that the only thing worse than being exploited by capitalists is the reverse – not being exploited by capitalists. This has dialectal significance.

3 See Fforde (1997).

4 For a contrary view, to the effect that it is not wise to refer to 'policy' even existing until the late 1990s, since only by then do the changes referred to by Thaveeporn (1996) imply a coherent basis for its existence, see my 'Light within the ASEAN gloom?' (Fforde 2002).

5 The history of this support remains to be written. See below on recent World Bank arguments about the overall correctness of the Vietnamese policy stance up to 1995.

6 See the November 1998 Newsletter from Aduki Pty. Ltd., available on our website, www.aduki.com.au.

7 His replacement by Nong Duc Many at the party conference of early 2001 was widely taken to show both concern with the direction in which politics was going, and a desire to further increase government (and this party) authority by legalisations, proceduralisation and other elements of what might, tongue in cheek, be taken as 'modernity'.

8 To quote Woodside (1997 74): 'Global capitalism, far from simply threatening the Vietnamese state, is supplying an arsenal of techniques by which state-directed cultural borrowing will salvage and refine a managerial regime whose previous policies had seriously tarnished it.'
9 The effects of this upon the relationship between central and local government (argued to be to the benefit of the latter) were discussed in IMF studies (see Tanzi 1998). But national governments, usually in control of the Army at least, will not go away.
10 See Fforde (2002) for a more up-to-date presentation.
11 See Fforde (2002).
12 The post-Crisis level of the Baht against the US$ was around 36, compared with 25 before the crisis – a 45 per cent change.
13 Other countries, for odd reasons, claim this crown. Here I follow the opinion of Taiwan's senior representative in Vietnam, who added in various investment flows by Taiwanese recorded as coming from other countries due to various multiple passports, companies, etc.
14 See the recent World Bank study of aid, *Aid: Where It Works, Where It Doesn't*. One of the authors, David Dollar, was a key figure in World Bank activities in Vietnam. It argues that policy, as objectively measured by a point system, was 'good' up until 1995 and was linked to a steep increase in aid. This is then taken to argue that Vietnam is an example of a country where aid and good policies are correlated. In fact, policies throughout the decade can easily be shown to be hostile to the development of the private sector, usually a major element of the World Bank's preferred development policy stance.
15 This was long taught to be revealed by the so-called 'pure' theory of world trade and economic relations in basic economics courses.
16 For an excellent piece of analysis and research in this area, see Per Ronnas (1998).
17 In the 1980s, managers of such businesses came from proletarian origins (Per Ronnas 1998:14, Table 10).
18 See work by Tuong Lai at the Institute of Sociology.
19 The gathering crisis of over-capacity in the sugar industry, for example, shows this clearly. The over-investment in capacity by a multitude of provincial SOEs was encouraged by their ready access to state bank credits.
20 An early and somewhat speculative attempt to place these strata into a category called the 'state business interest' can be found in my chapter in Ljunggren's *The Challenge of Reform in Indochina* (1993).
21 Whether the VCP should be compared with Cassandra's brother Hector is another issue; who, then, is Achilles? Note the perceptive quote from a student of another region with communist rulers: that for the Buddhist Buriats of Soviet Central Asia, the state appeared in many ways like the pre-modern Nature – distant, erratic, and possibly appeasible (see Humphrey 1983).
22 For me, any discussion should start with Veblen (see his classic works, especially his 1925 *The Theory of the Leisure Class*); see also Robison and Goodman (1996); Wong and Ahuvia (1998); Wee, Thomas Tan Tsu (1999); and, for a counter-intuitive conclusion, Chua Beng Huat (2000).
23 A defensive counter of '*Com Anh, Vo My, Luong Viet*' (English food, American wife, Vietnamese wages) was quickly modified to '*Com Anh, Vo My, Luong Nga*' (English food, American wife, Russian wages).
24 See Tran Huy Chuong *et al.* (1998).
25 I am not properly informed about foreign studies of Vietnamese music. Nor am I a qualified musician. An early endeavour is Fitchett (1984). Among other things, this discusses the innovative use of scalloped fret-boards on electric guitars. I recall seeing blind buskers around ferries on the way to Haiphong in the late 1980s using extreme lo-tech electric guitars, whose sound and rhythmic sense was for me reminiscent of a cross between Delta Blues and Captain Beefheart. See also the thesis by Ebbesen, for

which I do not have a proper reference, especially Chapter 7, 'An Essay on Music and Musical Life in the 1990s'. There is also a book by A. Reyes called *Songs of the Caged, Songs of the Free: Music of the Vietnamese Refugee Experience* (1999). I recall being told once by a Vietnamese friend, listening to songs played by a group of southerners up in Hanoi to refurbish a hotel, that the songs were sad because they were Cham songs, 'the songs of people who have lost their country'.

26 That is, in terms of dancing by people not seen as specialised 'dancers'.

27 This is my personal judgement as a somewhat over-serious electric bassist and is based upon personal observation.

28 This section draws heavily upon Tran Huy Chuong *et al.* (1998).

29 Why are the men so popular? – 'Because … and because they smell nice.' Reply to query regarding just what the reader can surmise for themselves, large aid project, north Vietnam, late 1980s.

30 Revenge is had in the fact that very few Vietnamese seem to know that the name of the excellent 'beef stew' sold as *sot vin* derives from 'wine sauce'.

Bibliography

Arndt, H.W. (1981) 'Economic Development: A Semantic History', *Economic Development and Cultural Change*, 29(3).

—— (1987) *Economic Development: The History of an Idea*, Chicago: University of Chicago Press.

Bray, F. (1983) 'Patterns of Evolution of Rice-growing Societies', *Journal of Peasant Studies*, October.

Chan, A. and Norlund, I. (1999) 'Chinese Labour Regimes: On the Road to Divergence' in Ben Kerkvliet, Anita Chan and Jonathan Unger (eds), *Transforming Asian Socialism. China and Vietnam Compared*, Canberra: Allen & Unwin.

Chua Beng Huat (2000) 'Singaporeans Ingesting McDonald's', in B.H. Chua (ed.), *Consumption in Asia: Lifestyles and Identities*, London: Routledge.

Cowen, M. and Shenton, R. (1996) *Doctrines of Development*, London: Routledge.

Fforde, A. (1997) 'The Vietnamese Economy in 1996 – Events and Trends – The Limits of Doi Moi?', in Adam Fforde (ed.), *Doi Moi – Ten Years after the 1986 Party Congress*, Political and Social Change Monograph 24, Canberra, Research School of Pacific and Asian Studies, Australian National University.

—— (2002) 'Light within the ASEAN Gloom? The Vietnamese Economy since the First Asian Economic Crisis (1997) and in the Light of the 2001 Downturn', *Southeast Asian Affairs*.

Fforde, A. and de Vylder, S. (1996) *From Plan to Market: The Economic Transition in Vietnam*, Boulder: Westview Press.

Fitchett, R. (1984) *Vietnamese Music in Britain*, unpublished Masters thesis, University of London, School of Oriental and African Studies.

Greenfield, G. (1993) *The Emergence of Capitalism in Vietnam*, York University: Socialist Register, online. Accessed: *http://www.yorku.ca/socreg/>http://www.yorku.ca/socreg/*.

Humphrey, C. (1983) *Karl Marx Collective: Economy, Society and Religion in a Siberian Collective Farm*, Cambridge: Cambridge University Press.

Kokko, A. and Zejan, M. (1996) *Vietnam – At the Next Stage of Reforms*, Stockholm School of Economics, 4/96.

Ljunggren, B. (ed.) (1993) *The Challenge of Reform in Indochina*, Cambridge: HIID.

Morris, C. (1955) *The Tudors*, London: Fontana/Collins.

Nguyen Manh Huan (1997) *A Socio-Economic Study of Agricultural Input and Output Prices and Exchange Relationships*, Hanoi: Mimeo.

Reyes, A. (1999) *Songs of the Caged, Songs of the Free: Music of the Vietnamese Refugee Experience*, Philadelphia: Temple University Press.

Robison, R. and Goodman, D.S. (1996) 'The New Rich in Asia: Economic Development, Social Status and Political Consciousness', in E.R. Robison and D.S. Goodman (eds), *The New Rich in Asia: Mobile Phones, McDonald's and Middle-Class Revolution*, London: Routledge.

Ronnas, P. (1998) *The Transformation of the Private Manufacturing Sector in Vietnam in the 1990s*, Stockholm School of Economics, Working Paper in Economics and Finance 241, May.

Tanzi, V. (1998) *The Demise of the Nation State*, IMF Working Paper 98/120.

Thaveeporn Vasavakul (1996) 'Politics of the Reform of State Institutions in Post-Socialist Vietnam', in S. Leung (ed.), *Vietnam Assessment: Creating a Sound Investment Climate*, Singapore: ISEAS.

Tran Huy Chuong *et al.* (1998) *Cosmetics Development Trends in Vietnam*, Ho Chi Minh City: Saigon Marketing Office.

Wee, Thomas Tan Tsu (1999) 'An Exploration of a Global Teenage Lifestyle in Asian Societies', *Journal of Consumer Marketing*, 16(4): 365–75.

Wong, N.Y. and Ahuvia, A.C. (1998) 'Personal Taste and Family Face: Luxury Consumption in Confucian and Western Societies', *Psychology and Marketing*, 15(5), August: 423–41.

Woodside, A. (1997) 'The Struggle to Rethink the Vietnamese State in the Era of Market Economies', in T. Brook and Hy V. Luong (eds), *Culture and Economy: The Shaping of Capitalism in East Asia*, Ann Arbor: University of Michigan Press.

Zebregs, H. (1998) *Can the Neo-classical Model Explain the Distribution of Foreign Direct Investment across Developing Countries?*, IMF Working Paper 98/159.

Chapter 4

The politics of the greenback

The interaction between the formal and black markets in Ho Chi Minh City

Martin Gainsborough

Introduction

This chapter seeks to shed light on political relations in Ho Chi Minh City as they relate to activities in the city's foreign exchange markets. It begins from the premise that access to and control over the US dollar, around which Vietnam's foreign exchange markets revolve, constitute a highly political matter. In Vietnam there are two foreign exchange markets: the formal market and the informal market. In the formal market, the currency is allowed to fluctuate 0.1 per cent a day either side of the previous day's closing rate on the foreign exchange interbank market. This so-called 'crawling peg' system, which was introduced in 1999, replaced a managed float system under which the currency was allowed to fluctuate in a narrow band either side of a fixed exchange rate set by the State Bank of Vietnam. The informal market is commonly referred to as the free market (*thi truong tu do*) or the black market (*cho den*). Naturally, the black market exchange rate is not administratively determined. It is also worth thinking of the black market not as a single market but as a series of markets or outlets spread across the city.

An important part of the research for this chapter involved getting to grips with the dynamics of the foreign exchange black market (i.e. how did it actually work) and particularly the nature of its relationship with the formal market. The chapter argues that the formal and the black market are much more closely linked than is officially depicted, notably in terms of who the key market players are. Once this is appreciated, it is suggested that some of the more puzzling aspects of the black market, and particularly state behaviour towards it, make more sense. In addition, it is suggested that a close look at the dynamics of Ho Chi Minh City's foreign exchange markets points to the need for us to think again about how we conceive of reform.

Research for this chapter was carried out in Ho Chi Minh City between 1996 and 1998. The principal sources were the Vietnamese press, interviews and informal conversations. The 1996–98 period proved a particularly apt time to study the city's foreign exchange markets. In October 1996, the dong broke out of the tight VND10,600–11,000 : US$1 nominal exchange rate band it had maintained over the previous five years. With the onset of the Asian financial crisis in July 1997, the dong entered a period of enhanced volatility notwithstanding the fact that it was not freely convertible. In 1997–98, the dong was devalued three times.[1] The 1996–98 period also witnessed increased black market activity and frequent foreign exchange shortages. All these factors contributed to a situation in which control over foreign exchange was highly contested, yielding rich insights about politics as a result.

The chapter is motivated by two further sets of ideas. The first has to do with Ho Chi Minh City's common identification with reformism. This is evident in relation to the city's post-1975 leaders – notably, Nguyen Van Linh, Vo Van Kiet, Phan Van Khai, Truong Tan Sang – who are regarded as having led the way with respect to their initiation of reform and the part they played in persuading the national leadership to follow suit (Porter 1990: 85; Sheehan 1992: 77–81; Stern 1993: 1; Thayer 1988: 190–1; Turley and Womack 1998: 95–6 and 108–15). By contrast, this chapter questions whether Ho Chi Minh City's common identification with the reformist label is valid. Indeed, much of the behaviour observed in the city and described here is arguably far removed from any conceivable definition of reformism. Second, rather than focusing on reform as a process of change, the chapter argues that it may in fact be appropriate to see reform more as the perpetuation of an existing system of domination and accumulation. With reference to the foreign exchange case, one certainly gains a sense of continuity in some respects rather than change. In addition, the chapter attempts to analyse politics by locating the activities of political and business elites within an informal context. Thus, rather than taking elites as the starting point, seeking to read between the lines of their public statements and writings – as is often done in political science literature on Vietnam – this chapter places the emphasis on studying the informal context first, in this case the foreign exchange black market, and letting this lead us to the elites. In my view this approach is particularly revealing.[2]

The US dollar in Vietnamese society

The dollar has long held a prominent place in Vietnamese society. In pre-1975 Saigon, the popularity of the dollar grew as the US currency flooded into south Vietnam as part of US aid programs and with GIs (Dacy 1986; Nguyen Huu Dinh 1996: 111). In the climate of shortage engendered by the central plan during the 1980s, hard currency was in extremely short supply and access to it highly restricted. Seeking to obtain it, whether companies or individuals, was a key locus of contest both within Ho Chi Minh City and between the centre and the city (Fforde and de Vylder 1996: 89, 135, 193–4, 290–1). Foreign exchange holdings enabled access to scarce resources, notably on international markets. Moreover, they also acted as a hedge against high inflation and the frequent devaluations of the dong, which characterised the 1980s and early 1990s.

Dollars continued to be similarly sought after during the 1990s for essentially the same reasons even if the nature of the restrictions regarding access to hard currency and the degree to which it was in short supply changed somewhat. With popular mistrust in the formal financial sector high, people commonly saved in dollars or gold during the 1990s. Goods from motorbikes to electrical items to household gas were usually quoted in dollars. The way in which people, including employees at state stores, were entirely at ease with dollars is summed up in the following extract:

> Keeping track of the dong dollar exchange rate is normal practice at state stores, trade centres and supermarkets. … Prices change daily. Ask a sales person, they'll reply with scarcely a thought: 'Today, the dollar is at 14,600 to the dong'.
>
> (*Nguoi Lao Dong*, 28 September 1998: 3)

Reform and the foreign exchange markets

Mainstream economic and policy literature, as well as international business, would typically emphasise the way in which the foreign exchange market, like other areas of the economy, is undergoing a process of reform. In an article in 1995, one foreign banker described the market as undergoing a 'process of incremental deregulation' (*Vietnam Business Journal* 1995: 28–9). In 1996, the International Monetary Fund highlighted what it referred to as a gradual loosening of foreign exchange controls on current account transactions over the preceding decade (IMF 1996: 46). Emphasis has tended to be placed on a number of key events, notably the abolition of the two-tier exchange rate system and the devaluation of the dong in 1989. The creation of a new institutional framework has also received attention. This includes the formation of the Currency Auction Centres in August 1991, leading to the establishment of an inter-bank foreign exchange market in October 1994. Other landmarks include the introduction of regulations on forwards and swaps in December 1997 and January 1998. Decree 63 issued in August 1998 also represented a turning point with its formal emphasis on giving individuals the right to store, carry, deposit and withdraw foreign currency (*Tuoi Tre*, 22 August 1998: 3).

Underpinning these developments is the idea that a greater role has been given to market forces in determining the exchange rate. Although the State Bank continued to set an official exchange rate on a daily basis until the introduction of the crawling peg system in 1999, commercial banks had in the course of the decade been given more leeway to buy and sell currency within a band either side of the official exchange rate. When the inter-bank market first opened in 1994 the band was just 0.1 per cent either side of the official rate. By February 1998, it had been widened to 10 per cent, although this was reduced to 7 per cent the following August. Nevertheless, it was generally felt that the State Bank had become more sensitive to market pressures. Thus, if the dollar fluctuated on international markets, it was not uncommon to see it making minor adjustments to the official rate. Abolition of the fixed exchange rate and its replacement with the crawling peg in 1999 represented a further step towards an, ultimately, fully market-determined exchange rate even though, with the currency only allowed to fluctuate by a maximum of 0.1 per cent either side of the previous day's exchange rate each day, the room for manoeuvre was limited.

The literature also tends to emphasise the extent to which during the 1990s the foreign exchange market remained highly regulated.[3] Aside from constraints on the setting of the exchange rate, only officially designated institutions were permitted to deal in foreign exchange. There were restrictions on the use of foreign exchange by companies and individuals. In terms of businesses, the restrictions on dollar use extended to who was permitted to charge in foreign currency. For most of the 1990s, organisations and individuals were permitted to have bank accounts denominated in dollars but often they were permitted only to withdraw dong.

Restrictions on dollar use could sometimes result in painfully contorted transactions. In one case, which occurred in 1998, the state-owned General Construction Corporation (COMA) borrowed dollars from the State Bank for Investment and Development (BIDV) to finance equipment imports it needed to undertake a project for a foreign client. When the work was completed, the client deposited dollars in COMA's account at Standard Chartered Bank in Hanoi. However, COMA was required by law to convert the dollars into dong at Standard Chartered. Standard Chartered in turn sold the dong to BIDV, which then required COMA to purchase foreign exchange from it in order to repay the debt. The whole procedure reportedly took some 15 days, during which time COMA was required to pay transaction costs and interest on the original loan amounting to 48 million dong (TBKTVN, 20 May 1998: 11).

Mainstream accounts have also tended to emphasise the way in which access to foreign exchange via the formal market continued to be tightly controlled throughout the 1990s. Officially, the State Bank guaranteed to supply foreign currency to so-called 'priority' projects only. This tended to be for companies importing materials or equipment for infrastructure development and key industries, notably export-oriented manufacturing. However, in times of shortage even priority projects had trouble obtaining foreign exchange. Against this backdrop, most of the economics and policy literature has taken the view that state-owned companies received preferential treatment in terms of access to foreign exchange compared with the private sector. In this regard, the state-owned Bank for Foreign Trade (Vietcombank) was still responsible for the lion's share of foreign exchange transactions in 1998 even though its monopoly position had been somewhat eroded with the formation of domestic shareholding banks (*ngan hang co phan*) and the opening up to foreign banks.

Against this backdrop, companies and individuals frequent the black market as a way of evading such restrictions in the formal market or because access via the formal market is denied to them. The black market is popular because formalities are kept to a minimum and it is largely anonymous. As one source said, you just have to make a phone call and they will come to your house.

How are the formal and black foreign exchange markets officially depicted?

According to official accounts, the foreign exchange black market is described as being considerably smaller than the formal market.[4] State Bank officials nearly always say that the black market accounts for no more than 10 per cent of formal foreign exchange transactions.[5] This is at best a guess. It does not change from year to year. It also does not increase when black market trade clearly picks up. Indeed, the 10 per cent figure is asserted with greater forcefulness the more active the black market becomes, and when it is almost certainly an underestimate. Official accounts also emphasise the separateness of the formal and informal markets. This applies both in the case of who frequents the respective markets and the capital within them.

Another feature of the way in which the informal market is referred to in official accounts relates to the vague way in which those who participate in the black market are talked about. References are usually no more specific than referring to black market participants as 'speculators' (*nguoi dau co*) or 'private money traders' (*nguoi chuyen vay*). The gold shops (*tiem vang*) which are found across Ho Chi Minh City are also cited as key black market outlets where people can buy and sell dollars. In addition, reference is occasionally made to *co* and *lo*, though the identity of who precisely these people are remains vague; these are slang words which refer to a broker on the one hand and a wealthy person who probably operates from home, on the other (*Tuoi Tre*, 7 March 1998: 11). This fits with the impression that some of the people who operate the black market are successful traders, seeking to get a return on the large sums of money passing through their hands. However in terms of the sources of dollars on the black market, official accounts commonly suggest that they derive from illegal activities such as smuggling or that they may possibly be under-the-table investment (*dau tu chui*). Although this is at least partly the case, such accounts still fail to say who precisely is engaging in such practices.

Emphasis is also placed on overseas remittances (*kieu hoi*) from Vietnamese abroad as a source of black market dollars. Some sources have suggested that 50 per cent of all black market dollars come from this source (*Thanh Nien*, 6 November 1998). Although the reliability of this estimate is doubtful, it is almost certainly the case that the majority of money remitted from overseas comes via informal channels, never entering the formal market. Aside from the lack of trust in the formal financial sector, changing dollars into dong at a bank would clearly result in a loss if the black market was buying dollars at a premium as it usually was during the 1990s. In 1996, the government introduced a 5 per cent tax on overseas remittances. This was quickly abolished as it resulted in a sudden and sharp fall in money coming through formal channels. However, it is far from clear that the lost custom was immediately won back. It is commonly suggested in the press that overseas remittances sent back, in total, US$1–1.2 billion a year, although the methodology used to obtain this figure is not clear. Estimates for Ho Chi Minh City suggest that informal remittances may account for three times the amount of formal ones (*Vietnam News*, 22 November 1998: 2).

A key source of demand for black market dollars derives from gold smuggling. In Ho Chi Minh City, which is the centre of Vietnam's gold market, this is evident when the international gold price falls below the price in Vietnam. This prompts increased gold smuggling, resulting in increased demand for black market dollars. A rise in the black market dollar price is usually perceptible as a result.

A further characteristic of the way in which black market activity is described in official accounts is that it is seen as being irrational. Most commonly, it is referred to as a problem of psychology (*van de tam ly*). Embodied in such references is the idea that people are creating an artificial shortage of dollars by hoarding them. Certainly, it is quite evident that this is self-fulfilling. However, any sense that people are holding on to dollars for quite rational reasons – namely that they anticipate a devaluation in the dong and want to protect themselves from it or make some money from it – is formally absent from official references to *tam ly*.

Black market puzzles

There are a number of aspects of the foreign exchange black market which on the face of it appear quite puzzling. Official assertions that the black market is small and consequently not worth worrying about are not credible. Quite frequently during 1996 to 1998, black market activity developed to such an extent that significant amounts of hard currency were drawn away from the formal market. This led to a shortage of dollars in the banking sector, severely undermining its ability to provide foreign exchange to business. Thus, despite the fact that the exchange rate is formally non-convertible, the authorities were unable to ignore market sentiment completely.

However, if one argues that black market activity is sometimes quite disruptive, why does the state not move to crush it? Furthermore, looking at foreign exchange policy throughout the 1990s, it is rare that it had anything more than a short-term impact on behaviour. A good example is provided by Decree 372 introduced in October 1994, ostensibly to stamp out the heavy use of the dollar in everyday transactions (so-called 'dollarisation'). However, the Decree was never properly enforced. Why was this?

The conventional answer would be that poor enforcement reflects weak state capacity. However, this is only part of the answer. A lack of capacity may be an appropriate explanation in certain situations but it is doubtful that it is the most important factor in the case of the foreign exchange markets.

What is most striking – and puzzling amid the common tendency in the literature on Vietnam to emphasise poor state capacity – is that the state sometimes shows quite remarkable capacity. Periodically, this includes implementation of its foreign exchange policy. Decree 37, which was introduced just before the devaluation of the dong in February 1998, was accompanied by a directive from the Central Cultural and Ideology Department (*Ban Van Hoa Tu Tuong trung uong*) instructing newspaper editors to stop reporting the black market dollar price (interview with Vietnamese journalist, 8 May 1998). Prior to this, black market exchange rates were quoted alongside official rates in daily newspapers. However, the authorities – probably rightly so – felt that this was fuelling the tendency of people at this time to hoard dollars. After Decree 37, press coverage of the black market changed dramatically. For a period, journalists stopped referring to the black market completely in their articles. References have gradually returned but coverage is still more cautious than it used to be.

Furthermore, regarding the common tendency of the state not to clamp down on the black market, it is not clear that it is primarily a question of weak capacity. Certainly it does not appear to be the case that the authorities are ignorant as to the identities of the main black market players. One of the black market's most striking characteristics is the way in which it is so blatant. One of the most overt black market centres in Ho Chi Minh City, although probably not the largest in terms of turnover, occurs outside the Intershop on *Nam Ky Khoi Nghia* in District One. Here women with small black bags loiter on the pavement ready to exchange money for passers-by who do not even have to get off their motorbikes to complete a transaction. Furthermore, two informants spoken to by the author prior to the issuing of Decree 37 in February 1998 separately made reference to a list of key black market traders apparently held by the Ho Chi Minh City party committee (*thanh uy*).

To reiterate, if it is not a question of capacity, why are clamp-downs on the black market rare and largely ineffective even though the market is capable of seriously disrupting activities in the formal sector? The next section attempts an explanation.

The close links between formal and black markets

In contrast to the way in which official accounts emphasise the separateness of the formal and black foreign exchange markets, the two are in fact closely linked. This can be observed in a variety of ways. First, capital moves easily between the two markets. At a time of rising expectation of a devaluation of the dong, both corporate and individual bank account holders commonly withdraw large quantities of dong to exchange into dollars on the black market in the hope of profiting on its rise. The amounts of money involved are often quite large relative to the size of the banks and can severely deplete their deposit bases. In August 1998, some banks saw withdrawals as high as 3.1 billion dong (US$221,000) in just one week, according to an official at the SBV branch in Ho Chi Minh City (TBKTSG, 27 August 1998: 34). Second, the formal and black markets are closely linked insofar as businesses and individuals readily frequent both markets if they are in a position to do so. Thus, a company which is able to satisfy only a portion of its foreign exchange requirement on the formal market will seek to make up the difference on the black market. The size of transactions which can be completed on the black market are significant. One source suggested '$1 million in an hour' (*Vietnam News*, 22 November 1998: 2). Another said that a $10 million transaction could be handled.

The most significant way in which the formal and the black markets are linked is that among the key black market makers are state-owned and share-holding commercial banks. Large companies, including state-owned exporting firms, also play a prominent part. Naturally, the evidence for such a heresy is sketchy.

However, it appears plausible based on a close reading of the Vietnamese press on this subject over a period of two years and backed up by interviews and informal conversations. One particularly bold journalist pointed the finger at the banks in early 1998: 'Where does dollar cash come from? From illegal activities, although this is just one part. In our view, commercial banks are the source of a rather large quantity of dollars in the market' (*Tuoi Tre*, 6 January 1998).

An article in October 1998 explored the question of who is best suited to be a speculator. This included a post-facto analysis of the events of 16 February 1998 when the dong was devalued. The article describes how the State Bank began the day as normal by announcing the same exchange rate as it had issued the day before. However, an hour or two later, it announced a new official exchange rate with the delay reputedly being designed to wrong-foot speculators. With the new rate announced, commercial banks reportedly stopped selling dollars but continued to buy. Meanwhile, the black market was silent (*yen ang*). Taking advantage of this, an unnamed speculator went to the black market with VND130 million, which he exchanged into US$10,000 at the old black market exchange rate of VND13,000 : US$1. This money was then deposited in the bank and a further US$9,000 was borrowed in dong using his deposit book as collateral. The 'speculator' then returned to the black market – which was still unaware of the morning's devaluation of the dong – and bought more dollars. This process continued for an additional third round until midday. By this stage, news of the devaluation had filtered through to the black market, which became animated (*nhon nhao*) and the dollar price shot up. The article's author then noted that not everyone was in a position to speculate in the way described:

> But not everyone can participate. If you to want speculate like this person did, you need to have the edge on others in two ways: you need to get information before others and you need to be able to borrow money from the bank quickly in order to be able to shift the dong into dollars in your hand.
> (*Tuoi Tre*, 8 October 1998: 11)

The timing of a devaluation is naturally kept secret. Only those in the banking sector – either the State Bank or commercial banks, or people connected to them, such as friends and family members – could be privy to such information. Moreover, it is also the case that you would need to be a particularly special customer to be able to withdraw VND130 million and borrow the dong equivalent of possibly as much as US$18,000 on the basis of your deposit book all in the course of a morning. This again suggests that people operating in this way came from within the banking sector or were closely connected to them.[6]

Exploiting the differential

Banks operating in both the formal and black markets can thus be seen to have a vested interest in the continued existence of an informal market. It is to their advantage that the dollars are sold at a premium in the black market since it enables them to charge customers who visit them in their formal capacity at a rate higher than the officially determined one. How much higher is largely conditioned by the size of the premium obtainable on the black market (TBKTSG, 29 October 1998: 36). The differential is then taken as a kickback by those overseeing the transaction process. Alternatively, if a bank wishes to reward a favoured customer, they can complete the transaction at the formal rather than the market rate. The gap between the formal and informal rate is never huge but it translates into significant amounts of money on the basis of a large transaction. During 1996–98, the differential varied between 0 and 1,200 dong; normally the differential was a few hundred dong.

Evidence for the existence of a variety of exchange rates in the formal system is widespread:

> In one bank, two or three exchange rates are operating: one exchange rate follows the system; one is determined according to the extent of State Bank intervention; one according to the reality of the market.
>
> (TBKTSG, 3 March 1998: 19)

At various times of dollar shortage during 1997 and 1998, banks complained that they could not obtain dollars if they kept within the officially determined band (*Tuoi Tre*, 9 December 1997: 2). When the government introduced Decree 173 on 12 September 1998, whereby companies were required to sell 80 per cent of their surplus foreign exchange holdings to banks within 15 days, companies actually refused to sell unless they were offered an exchange rate higher than the formal one. Most banks accepted this because they wanted the dollars (TBKTSG, 11 November 1998: 35). However, there were cases of prominent companies switching their accounts from less cooperative banks to more cooperative ones. Vietcombank seemed to lose some customers in this way (SGNR, 23–24 October 1998: 2). Competition for overseas remittances has also led banks to offer exchange rates more in line with the black market rate (SGNR, 5 November 1998: 3).[7] Furthermore, people interviewed by the author have even suggested that the State Bank in Ho Chi Minh City is party to such activity. In one case a company wishing to change US$1 million worth of dong into dollars was offered a price by the State Bank which was 500 dong per dollar over and above the official rate (interview with state enterprise official, 4 February 1998). It is worth noting, however, that banks are not able to behave in this way entirely with impunity. Every so often they are censured and ordered to return money to customers, but this is relatively rare.

Some puzzles explained

It can therefore be seen that the limited impact of official measures on black market activity is less a question of capacity and more one of insufficient will – namely that powerful forces exist which do not want to see the black market crushed. Once this is appreciated, some of the more puzzling aspects of the foreign exchange market begin to make more sense. The relative infrequency of clamp-downs can be explained with reference to these interests in the banking sector, as can the very limited impact of measures when they are introduced. Bankers are only prepared to go along with official policy insofar as it does not eliminate the differential between the formal and black market rates. Moreover, frequent complaints by commercial banks that they are unable to procure dollars – because the formal market is short of dollars – also become harder to take at face value. Overemphasising a climate of shortage is likely to result in increased hoarding, forcing more companies to turn to the black market. This will benefit the commercial banks as it likely to result in a continued healthy differential between the official and the market rate.

The interpretation offered in this chapter makes other aspects of the foreign exchange market more comprehensible too. The way in which official accounts stress the relative insignificance of the black market can be seen as an attempt to focus potentially awkward attention elsewhere. The vagueness of official accounts when they refer to participants in the black market simply as speculators or private money lenders equally takes on a different meaning when one argues that the key speculators are commercial banks and prominent companies.

It is also striking that on the relatively few occasions when black market traders are arrested, they tend to be depicted as being key players when other details suggest that they are in fact rather unimportant. This came across strongly in a description of one black market trader arrested in January 1998, who was depicted in the manner of the business tycoons (commonly referred to as 'kings') who dominated the south Vietnamese economy prior to 1975: 'Year of birth 1968, permanent resident in Hanoi, temporary resident in Ho Chi Minh City, of no fixed occupation … Pham Van Duc looked like a "king"' (*Tuoi Tre*, 20 January 1998).

In reality few people had heard of Mr Duc. Depicting people arrested in this way as being more important than they actually are creates the impression that the state has taken steps to clamp down on the speculators when in reality the more important black market players remain untouched.

Furthermore, the blatant way in which much black market activity is conducted makes more sense if one emphasises the importance of powerful local institutions in the trade. The Intershop on *Nam Ky Khoi Nghia* in District One, which is the location for blatant black market dealing, is linked to the prominent local state company, Saigon Jewellery Company (SJC), which has its office 25 metres away around the corner. SJC originally belonged to Ho Chi Minh City's Department of Trade (*so thuong mai*). In 1996 it was formally brought under the Saigon Trading Corporation (*tong cong ty thuong mai Sai Gon*, SATRA) banner but Department of Trade interests remained dominant.[8] One source described how, using SJC as its cover, the black market traders outside the Intershop have formed an informal co-operative to collectively bribe the police. Certainly, the police rarely make any effort to clamp down on trade.

Rethinking reform

At the beginning of this chapter, it was noted that the foreign exchange market is typically conceived of as undergoing a process of reform. As was emphasised this is understood in terms of a shift towards a greater use of the market in determining the exchange rate and a gradual lifting of controls governing access to foreign exchange. Particularly important is the sense that these changes are underpinned by a shift in thinking embodying a greater belief in the efficacy of markets. Conventional accounts also emphasise the continued prominence of state-imposed restrictions on activity involving foreign exchange.

This way of conceiving of change in the foreign exchange market is clearly helpful up to a point. Over the course of the 1990s, the market *has* begun to play a greater role. Reform measures *have* been introduced and ostensibly reformist sentiment expressed.

However, such an account ultimately fails to capture an important element of what is going on. On close examination of activity in Ho Chi Minh City foreign exchange markets – along the lines attempted in this chapter – one does not encounter many examples of what might be described as reformist behaviour underpinned by 'enlightened' thinking.

Rather, what one appears to see is the key players in the foreign exchange markets seeking to exploit the way in which the market is presently structured to their maximum advantage. To be more specific, one gains much less of a sense of change in a reformist direction and much more of a sense that those involved in the market have a vested interest in preserving the status quo. In the case of the foreign exchange market, this means the continued existence of the black market and the differential between the formal and the informal rate, enabling banks to manipulate the formal system. Also noteworthy is the way in which the State Bank – formally responsible for making the system work better and overseeing the implementation of reformist policies – seems also to be acting in this way.

In addition, the tendency in the literature to suggest that state companies receive preferential access to foreign exchange at the expense of the private sector does not entirely stand up to scrutiny. For small private companies, the scope for accessing foreign exchange via the formal market is limited. However, larger private companies or those with the right connections are more than able to secure foreign exchange through formal channels, as the cases of three (ultimately ill-fated) Ho Chi Minh City companies, Minh Phung, EPCO and Tan Truong Sanh illustrate.[9]

Equally, having a state sector label is no guarantee of access to foreign exchange via the formal markets. In 1998, one prominent Ho Chi Minh City company, Saigon Petro (*Cong ty Dau khi TPHCM*), was unable to satisfy its foreign exchange requirements on approaching Vietcombank (SGGP, 16 October 1998: 3). On the face of it, Saigon Petro was a well-connected company affiliated to the Financial Management Department of the Ho Chi Minh City party unit (*Ban Tai chinh Quan tri Thanh uy TPHCM*). It was also an important company insofar as it was one of five firms permitted to import refined petroleum products. What precisely precipitated Saigon Petro's difficulties is unclear, although the event caused a stir in Ho Chi Minh City in October 1998. Interestingly, Vietcombank appeared to successfully hold its ground despite strong criticism by Saigon Petro both in the press and in representations to party leaders in the city. Vietcombank said that Saigon Petro was not one of its major clients so that, while it was welcome to borrow dollars, it could not buy them. One informant suggested that Vietcombank might have suspected Saigon Petro wanted the dollars for speculation rather than for bona fide business reasons (interview with Vietnamese journalist, 26 October 1998).

In addition, state companies are just as liable as other companies to have to pay over and above the official rate if they wish to secure dollars. However, it would be quite wrong to interpret this as a reformist step on the part of the banks, moving to harden the credit constraint for state enterprises. Rather, it is once again a case of the banks seeking to manipulate the way in which the market is organised to their advantage.

As a result, rather than emphasising the foreign exchange market as undergoing a process of reform, its seems more appropriate to stress the way in which a situation had emerged by the late 1990s whereby measures designed to stamp out the black market or eliminate the differential were likely to be opposed by powerful forces within or connected to the formal banking sector. This seems to be the dominant dynamic much more than a process of reform. Most striking of all is that this was observed in Ho Chi Minh City, hitherto widely regarded as a bastion of reform.

Notes

1 The devaluations took place on 14 October 1997, 16 February and 7 August 1998. In terms of the maximum rate permitted on the inter-bank market, this resulted in a combined fall of 18.5 per cent.

2 For background on this method of analysing politics, see Dittmer, Fukui and Lee (2000).

3 I intend only to sketch the broad outlines here. Regulations on foreign exchange are actually extremely complicated and change frequently. For more details, see National Political Publishing House, *Cac Van Ban Phap Luat Ve Quan Ly Ngoai Hoi* [Regulations on Management of Foreign Exchange], Hanoi 1995.

4 Official accounts include statements by Vietnamese government and banking sector officials as well as the way in which these are reflected in journalistic writing.

5 Estimates of the extent of formal transactions are surprisingly difficult to come by. However, a figure of US$ twenty million per day, making an annualised US$ seven billion per year is commonly quoted.

6 The author would like to thank participants in the Vietnam Update meeting in Canberra in December 1998, where the ideas contained in this paper were first presented, for sharing their own insights regarding state involvement in the foreign exchange black market.

7 The banks were also competing with official remittance companies.

8 In 1998, plans were announced under which a number of SATRA companies, including Saigon Jewellery Company, would be hived off. The official reason given was that their strengths were not being fully exploited within SATRA. However, also at stake was a struggle between rival political–business interests in the city for control over some of the city's most lucrative assets (see *Saigon Times Daily*, 22 October 1998: 1).

9 These three companies became embroiled in major corruption cases. It is for this reason that we know so much about their activities.

Bibliography

Dacy, D.C. (1986) *Foreign Aid, War and Economic Development: South Vietnam 1955–75*, Cambridge: Cambridge University Press.

Dittmer, L., Fukui, H. and Lee, P.N.S. (eds) (2000) *Informal Politics in East Asia*, Cambridge: Cambridge University Press.

Fforde, A. and Goldstone, A. (1994) *Vietnam to 2005: Advancing on All Fronts*, London: Economist Intelligence Unit.

Fforde, A. and Vylder, S. de (1996) *From Plan to Market: The Economic Transition in Vietnam*, Boulder: Westview Press.

International Monetary Fund (1996) *Vietnam: Recent Economic Developments*, IMF Staff Country Report 96/145.

National Political Publishing House (1995) *Cac Van Ban Phap Luat Ve Quan Ly Ngoai Hoi* (Regulations on Management of Foreign Exchange), Hanoi: National Publishing House.

Nguyen Huu Dinh (1996) *Kinh Doanh Vang Tai Thanh Pho Ho Chi Minh: Chinh Sach Va Giai Phap* (The Gold Business in Ho Chi Minh City: Policies and Solutions), Ho Chi Minh City: Nha Xuat Ban: TPHCM (Ho Chi Minh City Publishing House).

Porter, G. (1990) 'The Politics of "Renovation" in Vietnam', *Problems of Communism*, 39(May–June): 72–88.

Saigon Times Daily.

SGGP, *Sai Gon Giai Phong.*

SGNR, *Saigon Newsreader.*

Sheehan, N. (1992) *Two Cities: Hanoi and Saigon*, London: Picador and Jonathan Cape.

Stern, L.M. (1993) *Renovating the Vietnamese Communist Party: Nguyen Van Linh and the Programme for Organisational Reform, 1987–91*, Singapore: Institute of Southeast Asian Studies.

TBKTSG, *Thoi Bao Kinh Te Sai Gon.*

TBKTVN, *Thoi Bao Kinh Te Viet Nam.*

Thanh Nien.

Thayer, C.A. (1988) 'The Regularization of Politics: Continuity and Change in the Party's Central Committee, 1951–86', in D.G. Marr and C.P. White (eds), *Postwar Vietnam: Dilemmas in Socialist Development*, Ithaca: Southeast Asian Program, Cornell University.

Tuoi Tre.

Turley, W.S. and Womack, B. (1998) 'Asian Socialism's Open Doors: Guangzhou and Ho Chi Minh City', *The China Journal*, 40(July): 95–119.

Vietnam Business Journal.

Vietnam News.

Part II

Everyday life and cultural change in contemporary Vietnam

Chapter 5

Footpath traders in a Hanoi neighbourhood

Peter Higgs

> The transition to the market economy has truly created great and rapid changes unseen before in the cities and towns of Vietnam. The events of the past 4–5 years have quickly and strongly penetrated the lifestyles of people living in the major urban centres. The crowded and bustling streets, the abundant displays of goods and the availability of services that people find today in cities and towns are only the easily identifiable outward changes. More profound are the changes in the structure of trades and professions among the populations, in their material and spiritual life and in the patterns of their behaviour
>
> (Trinh Duy Luan 1995: 135)

Urban Vietnam today is the juxtaposition of a village-based rural tradition and the creation of new opportunities within a government system which has been promoting a market economy since the mid-1980s. Since then, Vietnamese people, particularly those living in urban areas, have embraced the opportunity for economic reforms provided them by *doi moi*[1] and are an active part of the social changes taking place within their own neighbourhoods. Indeed, as one Vietnamese social scientist argues:

> [the Vietnamese] are not simply passively enjoying the achievements of *doi moi*; they are 'co-authors' of *doi moi* … [it] was welcomed broadly by the masses because it was they themselves who had created the motivation for the process of *doi moi* …
>
> (Tuong Lai 1997: 184).

One intention of the Vietnamese government's *doi moi* policy programme is to encourage flexible approaches to non-state-owned enterprises (SOEs). An example of this can be seen in the development of an increasingly active footpath economy. Local residents often conduct such trading, and Hanoi's footpath economy also combines trading by peasants from both the urban fringes of Hanoi and the nearby provinces, illegal lotto and other more underground activities, including an increasing amount of illicit drug distribution and street-based sex work.

While Vietnamese scholars have produced considerable research on social issues, social research by non-Vietnamese on Vietnam is a rapidly developing phenomena and it provides opportunities for comprehensive analysis of the change taking place in urban areas. Fforde and de Vylder (1996: 8) note that much of their most revealing and reliable data was collected at the informal and local level. Locality-based studies are a useful contribution to the broader study of urban social arrangements but they require intensive fieldwork and a clear framework on which to build a better understanding of the daily life experiences of Vietnamese people.

The data presented here was predominantly gathered between January 1993 and July 1995, within the district Hai Ba Trung in a neighbourhood fictitiously named Xuan Phuong. Most of the fieldwork used ethnographic approaches and relied heavily on participant observation techniques as well as semi-structured and unstructured interviews to elicit information from a number of key informants involved in footpath trading within the neighbourhood studied. However, it also includes a more recent trip to Hanoi between March and August 2001. Participatory observation and the use of both semi- and unstructured interviews provide an insight into footpath traders like those in the neighbourhood of Xuan Phuong which cannot be attained by looking at government-produced macro-economic statistics alone.

The Hanoi urban district of Hai Ba Trung, a part of which is the focus of this paper, is a mix of residential (public and private housing), light industrial and large numbers of small businesses. It also includes a large market, some Buddhist temples and a Catholic church, schools, other educational, training and research institutes, health clinics and hospitals, a number of SOEs and local factories. Xuan Phuong is towards the northeastern end of the district. It has more in common architecturally and socially with the smallest and oldest district Hoan Kiem than with some of the more remote parts of other Hanoi districts.

The locality of Xuan Phuong includes sections of two streets within the district Hai Ba Trung, one of the four central districts of Hanoi. It is a maze of different architectural structures. Like many other streets in the district, Xuan Phuong has an area of footpath between the road and the houses large enough to enable the operation of income-generating activities.

As Vietnam's administrative boundaries have been artificially drawn by state planners without regard for the localities themselves, our understanding of these urban neighbourhoods requires looking beyond what maps or electoral divisions construct. Interaction within Xuan Phuong occurs in the context of both social and economic relations. Some of these are based on an historical association with the area; others are determined purely by the emerging market economy.

Xuan Phuong borders on what Logan (1994) calls the French quarter of Hanoi. It is a complex locality which was largely unsettled until the 1920s. Xuan Phuong includes a number of larger art-deco-style French villa houses (circa 1925–45), but these are interspersed with both Soviet and more Western-style architectural influences. Two of the French villas upgraded since 1993 now house an internationally based consulting firm and a foreign-owned bank, and there are several examples of upmarket Western-style apartments rented to expatriates living in Hanoi. Of the street-fronting properties, the most noticeable are the large French villas. Many of the Vietnamese people living in these villas are long-term residents who were allocated the properties in the years following the liberation of Hanoi from French occupation and administrative control in October 1954.

This case-study documents the dynamics operating between those who live and those who work inside Xuan Phuong. It shows that, in the period since the introduction of *doi moi*, many of the social relationships evident on the footpaths are being transformed from above through policies of the state, and from below via initiatives taken by the participants in the footpath economy themselves. In discussing the blurred line between public and private in Vietnamese spatial practices, Drummond (2000) conceptualises this indistinctness as created from the 'inside out' and the 'outside in'. This 'blurring', then, also characterises the social relations of the footpath as traders, residents and the state negotiate the public and private commercial sectors.

When the initial research began in early 1993, trading was essentially small-scale (mainly food) and conducted by locals with street-fronting properties. By 1995, Xuan Phuong had at least forty people engaged in some form of income-generating activity based around the footpath. Some of them travelled from Hanoi's neighbouring provinces every day while others lived locally. Together they dominated the landscape and created the character of Xuan Phuong. On returning to Xuan Phuong for five months at the beginning of 2001, I found many of the footpath traders had remained the same. While the use of space had become more sophisticated and there was some change in the people who utilised the footpaths, on a superficial level Xuan Phuong was much as it had been when I first began collecting data in 1993.

Demolition, renewal and transformation

In 1995, the busiest section of the street was based around the latest building site. Workers, stall holders and those transporting materials to the site all added energy to the local area. Throughout the six months of fieldwork in 1995 a villa was demolished and rebuilt by hand. The demolition required the people who had previously been trading in fruit on the footpath to relocate, with no 'compensation' for the fact that they no longer had a prime footpath space from which to operate. What had been a small private library, simply a collection of books and magazines which people could borrow for a small fee, simply disappeared overnight and the fruit seller who had organised the library now had just enough space on the footpath to sell her produce.

This loss was just one example of the abruptness with which local residents experienced change. These members of the footpath economy had limited rights to the space they used, and many had to pay neighbourhood officials a fee for the chance to trade. There was an understanding that certain space 'belonged' to specific traders during core working hours (7 am–7 pm). After this, the footpath was used by any number of other traders passing through Xuan Phuong, but it was quiet in comparison with the daytime trade.

Demolition and reconstruction also required the labour of a number of people from outside Xuan Phuong. About a dozen *cuu van* (manual labourers) were involved in the project. The majority of them were males and they were paid daily for their work, often labouring for as long as fourteen hours. Described in Vietnamese as *cho nguoi* (literally, people market), the labourers also contributed to the footpath economy. One study showed that almost half of their daily earnings are spent on food and drink (Nguyen Van Chinh 1997). Inevitably, much of this income was spent in a locality like Xuan Phuong. By 2001, the site had been transformed into a number of Western-style, fully furnished, two-bedroom apartments that were rented for over US$1,000 per month. The people market had also gone and footpath trading had returned.

Given the premium which footpath space demanded, it was not unusual for the same territory to have multiple purposes. In June 1995 a street-fronting household stall, the *Hang Hoa Cat Toc*, added hairdressing to its small but busy general, mixed business shopfront. Within Xuan Phuong the local regulations which determine the sort of businesses that can be established are limited. In this case no permit was acquired, a newly painted sign was simply hung in front of the household stall to advertise the fact that they now cut and washed hair. Having the necessary space to carry out hairdressing close to home was considered one way to ensure the teenage daughter learnt some on-the-job skills. It also added to the income-earning potential of the family, who previously had relied solely on the income generated from a household stall.

Kinship

The family is a key social institution in Vietnamese culture (Freeman 1995: 87–92; Nguyen Xuan Thu 1990: 36) and this is clearly evident in the locality of Xuan Phuong. As described above, immediate family and extended kinship ties are also important for business and income-generating activities. Flourishing businesses were often based around family units or other small groups of people with a 'connection' to each other.

Many informants describe themselves in terms of kin relations within the neighbourhood and I consciously emphasised a type of kin relationship with my landlords (whom I referred to as uncle and auntie) so as to become less threatening to the footpath traders with whom I was talking. Indeed many of them also became my aunties, my older/younger sisters and even my nieces. Kin attachments in Xuan Phuong were evident among the footpath traders. These included Bich Hien (43 years old), who lives locally and who has been selling a variety of fruit since she stopped work with the state-owned rubber company in 1990. Her elder brother is married to the *bun* noodle soup seller Thu Hue, who also works from the footpath. Bich Hien used her lump sum payout of about one million dong (A$125) to establish herself as a fruit seller by purchasing enough fruit as capital to begin a business. Bich Hien restocks her supplies of fruit regularly, though not every day, from the market near the bus station at *Gia Lam* about eight kilometres away.

Thomas (1999: 164) notes that some scholars of Vietnamese social life describe women's power as limited to the family, while others suggest that women continue as the authority within both the domestic and trading sphere (Fahey 1998: 235; Zutt 1997; Hy Van Luong 1991: 751). This was clearly evident in Xuan Phuong where, of those participating in the footpath economy, very few were male. Men in the neighbourhood who worked often held positions in the state sector and hence were not always highly visible around the neighbourhood during working hours. It was also the case that limited opportunities for men in the footpath economy were dictated by social stereotypes of work. Men were, however, actively involved in social interactions with other underemployed males in the neighbourhood and hence occupied considerable space on the footpaths drinking beer or coffee. This use of space may also be seen as a reflection of the dominant role they played both within the family and as part of the broader society.

Drummond (2000) offers some insight into the distinction between 'Vietnamese' and 'Western' concepts of public and private space. She argues that in the post-colonial period the Vietnamese state has attempted to interfere in the private family space, previously 'a space of independent patriarchal authority in the same way as it has been idealised in the Western concept of private' (Drummond 2000: 2382).

Rural traders on urban footpaths

Since its origins, Hanoi has been a city of migrants whereby village identities historically existed within the city itself (Tana 1996: 15). Social ties are important for rural traders and workers who spend time in the city of Hanoi. In Xuan Phuong many of these people are from the provinces abutting Hanoi, some of whom spend hours every day just travelling to and from their home villages to sell their products in the city. These people are important in understanding the process of 'renewal' in urban Vietnam.

Inside Xuan Phuong there are two banana sellers who spend weeks at a time in Hanoi. They travel from the province Nam Dinh about a hundred kilometres to the south and they frequently occupy footpath space near a local resident, Thu Trang, whose family was also originally from that province. There was evidence that other members of the footpath economy in Xuan Phuong join together to behave like a family. For example:

> On returning home one afternoon in the pouring rain I found three young women, Tra My, Thu Hien and Nhu Hoa sheltering under the balcony of my house. They explained that they lived in Hanoi for short periods of time having come up from Nam Dinh (a small provincial city about one hundred kilometres south of Hanoi) to work. They collected paper and cardboard for resale and had a small part of Hai Ba Trung district which they regularly walked from door to door. Tra My, Thu Hien and Nhu Hoa were all about 17

> years of age and lived close to each other. While in Hanoi to collect recyclable goods they all stayed with Nhu Hoa's extended family in Hoan Kiem district.
>
> (Personal field notes, 13 March 1995)

Tana (1996) and Nguyen Van Chinh (1997) both outline the key role that rural migrants play in the footpath economy of Hanoi. Their research uncovers a growing trend in the urbanisation of Vietnam – that of urban–rural migration.

In Xuan Phuong the urban–rural interface also created some tension. For example, at new year (in 1995 before fireworks were banned by the state) some of the teenage males actually fired long whistling fireworks directly at people for their own entertainment. Those to suffer such harassment included the street cleaners, young, female traders and *cyclo* riders, all of whom were at some stage referred to by the somewhat derogatory Vietnamese term *nha que* ('from the countryside'). The phrase was used in a manner which inferred they were unsophisticated. Tana (1996: 53–4) notes that many migrants would rather keep their problems to themselves than report them to the police, because they did not have any residence papers and they believed the police would not act upon their reports.

As a direct result of changes in lifestyle due to the 'open door' economy, Hanoi has experienced a substantial influx of people (including significant numbers of young people) from the countryside for varying reasons and lengths of time. A newspaper article from *An Ninh Thu Do* (Capital City Security) states that there were 40,000 migrants from various areas in Hanoi in 1995, not including street children or those who worked in the city by day and returned to their village at night (cited in Nguyen Van Chinh 1997: 39). Xuan Phuong includes many people (generally under-employed rural farmers) who regularly move through the neighbourhood offering services such as shoe-shining, washing and cleaning, key-cutting and refilling disposable lighters. Others walked through the neighbourhood selling new and used clothing. There was also a constant stream of people, mainly women, who collect a range of products for recycling including plastic, rubber, metal, glass bottles and paper.

It was the rural peasants engaged in door-to-door trading through neighbourhoods such as Xuan Phuong who often sold the cheapest goods. One knew a real bargain was available when people from several parts of the neighbourhood came out to see what was being sold. This was especially common when seasonal fruits such as raspberries or more exotic seafood like crabs were being sold. It was not unusual to experience bargaining for up to fifteen minutes while local residents tried to get the best price possible.

Outsiders

The owners of the *Cafe Sua Tuoi* employed a domestic helper, Nhi Ngoc, from the province of Thai Binh (south of Hanoi) to cook and clean for the family. For this she received 150,000 dong (a little less than A$20) per month and food and lodging. She worked from early in the morning until late in the evening seven days a week. Even though she had lived in Hanoi for more than six months, she had only been home to her village once and had not even had the opportunity to go sight-seeing around Hanoi. Nhi Ngoc was very much an outsider. Her request for a day off over the Liberation Day and May Day holiday (30 April and 1 May) to visit, with a friend, several local pagodas southeast of the city was denied. To counter this, she rose at 3.30 am, cleaned and cooked for the day and then rode her bicycle for thirty kilometres to spend a day out of Hanoi.

Unlike Nhi Ngoc, not all the rural migrants living in Hanoi were able to find work. Many had moved to Hanoi in order to find more stable employment but ended up struggling. Several of the *pho* stalls were frequented by beggars, some of whom were long-term residents of the neighbourhood, who would wait until a customer had finished eating before pouring the remains of the soup into their own tin for consumption Whether the stall owner accepted this was generally determined by the number of customers: the fewer the customers, the more acceptable it was. If the stall was busy, then the beggars tended to be moved on as this was not considered good for business. Some of the begging was more sophisticated and included the presentation of a person's disability card from the Ministry of Labour, Invalids and Social Affairs or the singing of traditional folk songs.

Begging in the streets and from door to door had become a permanent income-raising activity for a number of individuals. A police study of Hai Ba Trung district in Hanoi found that 40 per cent of female migrants in Hanoi worked as petty vendors, prostitutes, garbage collectors, thieves and beggars (cited in Nguyen Van Chinh 1997: 43). While not being truly accepted as a part of Xuan Phuong, the beggars did appear to be tolerated more than other less socially acceptable groups or sectors of the neighbourhood; these included, for example, women rumoured to be involved in prostitution and young men who supported their heroin dependence by stealing within the locality.

The nature of work

In the 1992–93 *Vietnam Living Standards Survey* (VLSS) of 4,800 households throughout Vietnam, a job is defined in three ways. The first is working for cash or a salary; second, working for one's own benefit as a full or part-owner of the business or land; and third, where unpaid work was undertaken for one's household. The survey showed that more than 25 per cent of urban residents were *khong hoat dong kinh te* (not economically active), whereas less than 18 per cent of rural persons were considered in this way. By contrast, those considered unemployed were actually looking for work, were sick, waiting to start a new job or were on holidays. The unemployed population was less than 7 per cent of rural people interviewed and less than 10 per cent for those living in the city (State Planning Committee 1994: 119–25).

The activities of participants in the footpath economy in Xuan Phuong can be examined within three overlapping and interchanging categories. The first is work performed by people previously employed in the state sector who have continued to perform the same tasks in a different management structure. The second category involves the activities performed by rural people temporarily working in the area. Some of these people would come daily from their villages to Xuan Phuong, others were in Xuan Phuong more permanently, and some simply came for several weeks or months with the intention of returning home to their villages. The third category comprises local residents of Xuan Phuong who are now taking on employment in petty trading or small businesses. A number of these people have only ever worked under the new economic system which allows a diversity of family business, while others have a clear memory of working in a more centrally planned economy.

Fforde and de Vylder (1996: 309) conclude that many people found a better life outside the state sector: '[they] became independent and autonomous as workers and they had more control over their lives'. This explains why the government-imposed retrenchment programmes met with such little organised opposition. It is specific policies such as these which can be identified as benefiting many participants in the footpath economy.

In my interviews with people in the variety of work categories, I had detailed conversations trying to clarify what they understood by the noun 'employment' (*viec lam*) and the verb 'to work' (*lam viec*). It was clear that the definitions provided in surveys such as the VLSS were more general than people's own perceptions of what a job involved.

From state-owned enterprise to footpath trading

Fforde and de Vylder (1996) note that many state-owned enterprises simply became shells for profitable private enterprises, often without much change at all. There is certainly a group of people in Xuan Phuong who are benefiting more than others in urban Vietnam. Many of these are workers in the previous state system who are now able to utilise their networks to operate within a market economy. Quoc Tuan is one such example. He lives with his wife Hoai Huong and their young son in a narrow laneway of Xuan Phuong. During 1995, he was the director of a company which used a street-fronting property as a point for distributing green bean paste to some of Vietnam's northern provinces. Previously Quoc Tuan had been employed in a state company that was responsible for distributing the same green bean paste to provinces throughout the country. Thus, he was well placed to make use of contacts and to continue distributing across several provinces of northern Vietnam.

On my return in 2001, the shopfront had become a café and the bean paste business had been significantly scaled down. Some of those who had worked with state-owned enterprises prior to their new 'careers' on the footpath were forced to retire whereas others had done so voluntarily due to age or ill health. One who chose to retire from a state company about ten years ago is Thu Trang, who since then has operated a small business from inside the gate of her laneway. She explained her special privileges as follows:

> the only reason I was allowed to sell *che* (sweet bean soup) and *xoi* (sticky rice) when other people were not trading prior to 1990 was that I was doing so from inside my own house boundary and not on the street. In recent times I have crept out onto the footpath like everyone else.
>
> (Personal field notes, 27 February 1995)

Thu Trang believes that, prior to *doi moi*, people were allowed to sell goods but not as openly on the footpaths as they can now. Thu Trang feels that the footpath gives her more space and opportunity than she was able to utilise prior to the development of such an active footpath economy.

Itinerant occupations

Within Xuan Phuong there was a substantial mobile street market which the Vietnamese call *cho coc* (literally, frog market). The markets were so named because of their vulnerability to police attention and the fear of having goods confiscated. This required the vendors to be ready to move around, in the same way that a frog jumps around from place to place. The main traders in fresh vegetables in Xuan Phuong were peasants from the outskirts of Hanoi and the neighbouring provinces, especially Hai Duong. Xuan Phuong had up to twenty-five individuals selling fresh fruit, vegetables and herbs on the footpaths, often from the back of their bicycles.

An example of obvious government control in the informal sector was in relation to these mobile street traders. For these people the confiscation of goods was a regular occurrence even prior to the introduction of the government's Decree 36 (*nghi dinh 36 chinh phu*).[2] After the announcement of Decree 36 the local People's Committees, through the police, have aggressively implemented a small section of the decree which deals with trading on streets and footpaths. Of the seventy-four articles in the decree, only one (Article 62 comprising four paragraphs) relates to the control of trading on the streets and footpaths.

Several times a day the police could be seen riding their motorbikes past the *cho coc* in order to limit this type of trading. Despite regular police patrols and signposts throughout Xuan Phuong telling people not to trade in this manner, people persist. Onlookers barely react to the aggressiveness which is sometimes shown by police 'round ups', as if such a response is simply an occupational hazard for street traders. It is the chance to earn some money regardless of the consequences which encourages many of those who travel several hours per day to continue their footpath-based trade. Indeed two of my key informants, Minh Loan and Minh Hoa, commented that:

> the only way farmers could become wealthy was for them to travel to the city to sell their goods, as people living in rural areas do not pay (and cannot afford) the price which can be charged in the urban areas.
>
> (Personal field notes, 24 April 1995)

While there was some resentment towards the implementation of some government decisions, there was also a sense that little could be done to stop it. People would defy the rules by moving back to the edge of the street or footpath and continuing to trade almost immediately after the police had passed. The police were keeping the footpath traders constantly aware of their vulnerability – a form of social control which nonetheless failed to stop trading completely.

When discussing the implications of restricting this type of trading and the resultant harassment suffered by the traders, feedback from within Xuan Phuong was mixed. On one level, local residents enjoyed the convenience of shopping without leaving their motorbike and it was much quicker (and often cheaper) than shopping at the formalised markets. Others, however, felt the *cho coc* blocked the through flow of traffic too much and that these traders unfairly avoided paying local taxes levied on traders in the formal marketplace.

Some have argued that the people most affected by the strict control of footpath trading are those who are poor but from 'good socialist backgrounds' and who were merely supplementing their inadequate pensions (ADUKI Pty. Ltd. 1995: 15). In fact the former Prime Minister Vo Van Kiet was reported in the Vietnamese daily press as stating that the government deeply sympathised with the small section of the population who are using the streets as a marketplace for their livelihoods (*Vietnam News*, 21 August 1995: 1). However, he reiterated that the implementation of government decrees is essential to maintaining order in urban areas.

The beginnings of commercialisation

The footpath traders had a system of price negotiation for different customers and there appeared to be clear, unwritten rules about the prices charged for each. This was also the case in the formal market where non-Vietnamese were seen as rich foreign tourists by the market sellers. Even if one knew the local price of goods, it would not necessarily reduce the price. *Cho Hom* (the Day Market) is mentioned in several tourist guidebooks and is consequently regularly frequented by foreign tourists. Vendors may refuse a sale rather than be seen to be selling to a *tay* (Westerner) at the same price as they sold to Vietnamese locals. Alternatively, other customers would protest loudly if they saw a *tay* being charged the same price as they were.

Commercialisation could also be seen with the advent of Western-style advertising. This was a new concept for Vietnam, which had little experience of this prior to the socialist market economy. For example, a large billboard was placed just outside Xuan Phuong advertising a Western-brand milk drink. The style of the billboard was obviously Western but the advertising company had also incorporated the image of a young Vietnamese pioneer[3] hailing the advantages of drinking chocolate-flavoured milk. Again this emphasises the contradictions which the market economy has brought to urban areas.

Even as Vietnam hustles desperately for foreign investment, it has launched a campaign to obliterate one of the most visible indicators of its success. In an on-going campaign against what the government calls 'social evils', foreign advertising has been demonised along with prostitution, gambling and illicit drugs.

The seeming contradiction is the product of a watershed moment for Vietnamese leaders. They are engaged in a far-reaching debate as they pause to assess the effects of an economic and social transformation that they themselves unleashed. Their experiment in economic liberalisation is succeeding in textbook style, but it has brought with it unruly market forces and social changes that threaten the dominance of the Communist Party (Mydans 1996).

While the state itself (through the various apparatus responsible for each area) is not overly concerned with the daily occurrences in the footpath economy, there is evidence that it is at least aware of what is taking place even if only in a purely physical way. One example is the control which neighbourhood officials maintain over household registration. Recent changes in China may encourage Vietnam to lessen their hold in this area. According to China's powerful State Development and Planning Commission, the government is working on a plan that will do away with migration restrictions over the next five years and create a unified national labour market. In August 2001 the Chinese Ministry of Public Security, the main administrator of the household registration system, confirmed its support for the reforms (*The Economist*, 30 August 2001).

Conclusion

The aim of this paper has been to explore socio-economic change in urban Vietnam and the processes by which people can make the most of new opportunities which are both presented to and created by them. It is clear that some urban Vietnamese people are better positioned to do so than others. The first are those families who straddle the state and private sectors, as they are in the best position to utilise those advantages which still exist. Many participants in the footpath economy of Xuan Phuong were previously employed by the state. The development of their own small businesses has helped them to make *doi moi* a success.

Two themes emerge. The first concerns the vulnerability of working in the footpath economy and the flexibility demanded of traders. The second theme concerns the impact of policy reform developed by the Vietnamese government. This chapter argues that the gradual lessening of government control has major ramifications for the conduct of income-generating activities such as those which take place in the footpath economy of neighbourhoods like Xuan Phuong.

One of the principal findings centres on the transient but complex nature of footpath trading. For the forty individuals involved with the footpath economy, their lives and that of their families were often directly affected by the implementation of government policy, and more specifically by the manner in which government policies are interpreted at a local level. The implementation of decrees such as *nghi dinh 36 chinh phu* which controlled the flow of traffic through urban areas created a sense of order at the local level but at the same time it also restricted footpath-trading activity. This is a good example of the way in which state laws impact directly at the local level.

It is important to note that the implementation of these campaigns and the enforcement of these laws occur unevenly throughout urban neighbourhoods of Hanoi. The results show how far participants in the footpath economy are prepared to push the boundaries of policies that impact upon their daily lives. For example, while it was evident that non-compliance in regard to Decree 36 was common for traders in Xuan Phuong, in other localities footpath traders had been removed more permanently – compliance was simply not an issue. It was also the case that, while Decree 36 resulted in a 'cleaning up' of the streets of Xuan Phuong through the imposition of trading restrictions, within a few weeks certain traders had returned.

While opportunities for marked improvements in the quality of life have presented themselves for some groups of people, others are ill placed to take advantage of emerging markets. Those more vulnerable to market changes, including women overburdened by increasing work and family responsibilities, would previously have been protected by the safety nets of the co-operative system. The most vulnerable are evident on the footpaths of Xuan Phuong in occupations such as door-to-door trading.

Elements of contemporary Hanoi life identified include the changing social relations in the neighbourhood, the flexible yet vulnerable nature of work patterns, and the increasing international influences. People trading on the footpaths of Xuan Phuong conduct a diverse range of activities in order to generate income. However, much of it is exposed to the vagaries of the implementation of government policy. For those able to establish a regular income, there are now opportunities to achieve far more than would have been possible under the centrally planned economy. As part of its gradual transition to a market economy, the Vietnamese state has placed a substantial emphasis on restructuring the economic system while at the same time resisting political changes in order to maintain social and institutional stability. This 'socialist market economy with Vietnamese characteristics' is promoted so as to ensure that Vietnam makes this transition while not exposing its population to the dismantling of the political system.

At the same time the Vietnamese state is constantly reminding people to pay due attention to the law in everyday life. In one form the reminders are seen through the propaganda billboards which have been used for decades as a way of disseminating information. The 'campaigns' are one way of encouraging support from Vietnam's citizens. However, Thi Thao, one of my key informants, notes that for her 'they're blank messages. I don't think they fool anyone' (personal field notes, 3 June 1995), which suggests that at least some educated urban Vietnamese young people have become cynical of them.

Importantly for many who participate in the footpath economy, the state has become less directive in terms of its management of local populations. This has led to increased autonomy for the most economically disadvantaged citizens. For example, the establishment of food stalls on the footpath outside their own homes has allowed people to determine their own income-generating activities. It is clear that there is currently a vigorous footpath economy on the streets of Hanoi which has developed steadily over the past few years.

Notes

1 Translated as 'renovation' (Vo Nhan Tri 1990: 183) or 'renewal' (Fforde 1997: 1).
2 Decree 36 deals with traffic order and safety on the roads, which among other things limited trading on the foothpaths.
3 As a form of passage through the education system, any Vietnamese student who does well in their studies can become a young pioneer.

Bibiography

ADUKI Pty. Ltd. (1995) *Vietnam: Economic Commentary and Analysis*, no. 7.

Drummond, L.B.W. (2000) 'Street Scenes: Practices of Public and Private Spaces in Urban Vietnam', *Urban Studies*, 37(12): 2377–91.

Economist, The (2001) 'Mobility in China: Off to the City', 30 August.

Fahey, Stephanie (1998) 'Vietnam's Women in the Renovation Era', in K. Sen and M. Stivens (eds), *Gender and Power in Affluent Asia*, London: Routledge, 222–49.

Fforde, A. (ed.) (1997) *Doi Moi: Ten Years after the 1986 Party Congress*, Political and Social Change Monograph 24, Canberra, Research School of Pacific and Asian Studies, Australian National University.

Fforde, Adam and Vylder, Stefan de (1996) *From Plan to Market: The Economic Transition in Vietnam*, Boulder: Westview Press.

Freeman, James M. (1995) *Changing Identities: Vietnamese Americans 1975–1995*, Boston: Allyn & Bacon.

Higgs, P. (1993) Personal diary notes, January–December, unpublished.

—— (1995) Personal field notes, January–June, unpublished.

Hy Van Luong (1991) 'Vietnamese Kinship: Structural Principles and the Socialist Transformation in Northern Vietnam', *Journal of Asian Studies*, 48 (4): 741–56.

Logan, W.S. (1994) 'Hanoi Townscape: Symbolic Imagery in Vietnam's Capital,' in M. Askew and W.S. Logan (eds), *Cultural Identity and Urban Change in Southeast Asia. Interpretative Essays*, Geelong: Deakin University Press, 43–69.

Mydans, S. (1996) 'Hanoi Seeks Western Cash but Not Consequences', *The New York Times*, 8 April.

Nguyen Van Chinh (1997) *Social Change in Rural Vietnam: Children's Work and Seasonal Migration*, working paper number 13, Canberra, Department of Political and Social Change, Australian National University.

Nguyen Xuan Thu (1990) 'The Vietnamese Family Moral Code', *Journal of Vietnamese Studies*, 3: 30–6.

State Planning Committee – General Statistics Office (1994) *Vietnam Living Standards Survey 1992–3*, Hanoi.

Tana, Li (1996) *Peasants on the Move: Rural–Urban Migration in the Hanoi Region*, occasional paper number 91, Singapore: Institute of Southeast Asian Studies.

Templer, R. (1998) *Shadows and Wind: A View of Modern Vietnam*, London: Little Brown & Company.

Thomas, Mandy (1999) *Dreams in the Shadows: Vietnamese-Australian lives in transition*, St Leonards: Allen & Unwin.

Trinh Duy Luan (1995) 'Impact of Economic Reforms on Urban Society', in Vu Tuan Anh (ed.), *Economic Reform and Development in Vietnam*, Hanoi: Social Sciences Publishing House, 134–96.

Tuong Lai (1997) 'The Issues of Social Change after 10 Years of *Doi Moi* in Vietnam', in A. Fforde (ed.), '*Doi Moi*: Ten Years after the 1986 Party Congress', Political and Social Change Monograph 24, Canberra, Research School of Pacific and Asian Studies, Australian National University, 181–99.

Vietnam News, Vietnam News Agency, daily publication, various issues, Hanoi.

Vo Nhan Tri (1990) *Vietnam's Economic Policy since 1975*, Singapore: ASEAN Economic Research Institute, Institute of Southeast Asian Studies.

Zutt, S. (1997) 'Women's Activities in Vietnam: Female Fruit Traders in Hanoi', paper presented to *Euro Viet III*, bi-annual conference, 2–4 July, Amsterdam.

Chapter 6

Speaking pictures

Biem hoa or satirical cartoons on government corruption and popular political thought in contemporary Vietnam

Pham Thu Thuy

Introduction: speaking pictures

Iconology, or the study of visual representation, is derived from two Greek words meaning 'speaking pictures' or 'discourse of images'. Visual rhetoric involves the use of such speaking pictures to influence people's sentiments, beliefs and behaviour in certain ways. Accordingly, rhetorical iconology is the study of how advocates have used a society's representational and symbolic systems in attempts to enlist the will of an audience or different audiences.

As messages that employ symbolic forms in the creation of meaning, cartoons appear to possess rhetorical properties. They argue for a viewpoint, thereby engaging the hearts and minds of readers. The aim of cartoons as speaking pictures is thus to convey specific and persuasive meanings through the use of familiar images, metaphors and allusions, and to seek to expose hitherto unnoticed aspects of real life through the lens of a fantasy world. By recasting familiar or true events into imaginative – even fantastic – settings, cartoons often create a story, producing an unconventional viewpoint on the true nature of events. Since cartoonists must get their 'message' across to viewers as quickly as possible, they must invent imagery that is at once compelling and powerful, drawing frequently from potent symbols and imagery that make up the community's political and cultural mythology.

Owing to their rhetorical or persuasive aspects, cartoons qualify as important objects of study. They are cultural artefacts that employ symbolic constructions to communicate not only certain messages, but also beliefs, values and attitudes. By reducing complex current issues to simple metaphoric representations, the cartoonist is able to provide viewers with new insight and understanding. More often than not it is this newly gained insight and understanding that can serve as a basis for subsequent thought and action by the public, making cartoons a powerful tool in political communication in many societies. While the limited scope of this chapter does not allow a more in-depth scrutiny of the role of cartoons in political communication, we will examine how these pictures speak to their audiences, as well as the messages that they convey.

In recent years, satirical cartoons or *biem hoa* have become an indispensable feature of many daily newspapers in Vietnam, and have a wide following among a politically aware reading public. Yet this unique and popular form of visual entertainment and communication has so far failed to attract the attention of serious scholars, who may have considered them trivialities outside the scope of academic research. For some, cartoons usually evoke connotations of fun and entertainment. This chapter argues that Vietnamese *biem hoa* are not created solely for the purpose of generating comic laughter. As speaking pictures, each cartoon offers a view or an opinion on the myriad issues of everyday life. I have selected to focus on government corruption and bureaucracy because these issues are still regarded by the majority of the public as the most urgent problems confronting Vietnam as the country enters the twenty-first century. I will also argue that, due to their inherent capacity to produce simple but very potent images that impact upon popular perceptions of the country's political system, satirical cartoons can be an unconventional channel for political discourse and communication in Vietnam.

Cartoon or caricature?

The terms 'cartoon' and 'caricature' tend to generate a great deal of confusion, especially when many writers are in the habit of using them interchangeably. According to some scholars of cartoon communication, there is, however, a fine distinction between the two terms. The word 'cartoon' originates from the Italian expression *cartone* meaning thick paper. Originally referring to a full-scale sketch for murals and paintings, it gradually came to imply a humorous line drawing that could be mass-produced and transmitted to a wide audience. Nowadays, the term is used to describe a broad range of pictorial representations including the political or editorial cartoon, the comic book and the comic strip. Caricature, on the other hand, is derived from the word *caricatura,* to denote a likeness that has been grotesquely exaggerated and distorted. It is therefore a portrait loaded with expressive meaning through distortion and exaggeration of a person's most characteristic features (Harrison 1981; Langeveld 1981).

Lawrence Streicher, a well-known researcher in the field of political cartoons, believes cartoons to be basically value-neutral, humorous or witty drawings that could be used for both debunking and elevating purposes. In contrast, the sole function of caricature is to hold up an object or person to ridicule and scorn (Streicher 1967). Nowadays, a caricature no longer has to be a portrait. It may be a symbolic representation of a group of persons, a situation or event. What we call caricature today could be an allegorical or emblematic drawing, the purpose of which is not to make us laugh but to raise our awareness of salient issues. The aim of caricature, therefore, is essentially to lampoon the vices and follies of individuals and society at large through the use of satire, distortions and exaggerations. Indeed it is the caricature's strong affiliation with satire that distinguishes it from other types of visual art. For this reason, a brief examination of satire in literature at this point would afford some useful insights about the nature and function of caricature, especially as it relates to the Vietnamese *biem hoa.*

As a literary genre, satire typically deals with the exposure of human vices and follies to scorn and ridicule. It often involves the debunking or diminishment of powerful persons and institutions. Although the literature on the function and nature of satire is extensive and diverse, it is still possible to identify the two most essential ingredients of satire: humour and criticism.

It is important to point out that laughter provoked through satire is not the same as the innocent laughter at the comic. According to some theorists, pure comedy reveals to us what is generally regarded as harmless, whereas satire employs comic techniques of ridicule but also discovers harm and even evil in the ridiculous. Just as satirists debunk and humiliate through contemptuous laughter, cartoonists limit themselves to attack, satisfied that viewers will laugh or smile, not necessarily because the caricature is humorous but because someone has been cast as a fool or villain. Whereas authority figures are brought low by satiric humour, the weak and defenceless feel empowered by mocking laughter, and therein lies the mass appeal of satire and caricature.

In his incisive study on satire as a literary genre, Matthew Hodgart identifies two principal devices for achieving this mocking humour and laughter. The first is through irony, the second through a technique of reduction or degradation of the target. The latter is sometimes also referred to as a technique of 'downward conversion'[1] that basically aims at diminishing the target's dignity and stature. The result of such reduction is most acute when the subjects of ridicule are persons or ideals commonly held in high regard. According to Hodgart, the most severe form of downward conversion occurs when the target is depicted as an animal, for 'it reduces man's purposeful actions, the ambitious aims of which he is proud and his lusts of which he is ashamed, all to the level of brute instinct: hog in sloth, fox in stealth' (Hodgart 1969: 24). Another form of reductionism is stereotyping, in which individuals are reduced to a simple social type and as a result cannot step out of the role imposed on them or act freely.

Although it can generate laughter, many theorists view criticism or expression of a basic dissatisfaction with the state of things as satire's most important function. Its aim is to expose wickedness and folly, to express as well as provoke anger and indignation at some wrongdoing or injustice. Similarly, the caricature usually begins as an aggressive and critical idea in the artist's mind which is full of irritation at the latest example of human absurdity and wickedness. Thus both satire and caricature spring from a sense of moral outrage and indignation.

Behind satire's ridicule lies an implicit idealism and hope in its power to effect change. The aim is not only to steer audiences toward the desire for change, but also to induce a sense of shame in the persons targeted for ridicule and upon whom moral judgement is being made. This corrective function of satire becomes most obvious in cultures that rely on various forms of public disapproval to govern social behaviour. In such cultures, if a person's transgression becomes known, he or she will be subjected to ridicule and satirical abuse. According to some theorists, individuals usually desist from wrongdoing through fear of public derision and censure.

> In any society in which high value is placed upon the opinion of others, ridicule will clearly be a potent deterrent to deviant behaviour; the more a

> person dreads shame, the more he will avoid situations which might bring upon him the bad name conveyed by public mockery.
>
> (Elliott 1960: 69)

In traditional Vietnamese society, one of the chief means of punishing unacceptable social behaviour was by circulating satirical songs and verses (*vè*) which held the offender up to thinly disguised mockery. When individuals persistently violated customs or propriety, their actions were likely to be made the subject of prolonged ridicule and invective. The basic ingredients of satirical verses consist of wit, humour and sometimes even obscene scurrilities, all of which are designed to attack and revile the enemy, whether personal or public.

Anonymous verse invectives were not the only form of satire in traditional Vietnam. Other rich sources include proverbs, folk songs, allegorical tales, jokes and riddles, the majority of which tend to appear during periods of great social and political upheaval. Their aim was to target social injustices and to give expression to the suffering of the silent masses. From the view of Marxist scholars, such as the famous Xich Dieu,[2] satirical poems and verses composed during the traditional periods were progressive only insofar as they involved self-mockery by Confucian scholars, or exposed the follies and vices of the ruling classes. Thus the role of the people's satirist was to use humour and wit to speak out against abuses. Interestingly, this image of the satirist corresponds to the way in which journalist-cartoonists in contemporary Vietnam perceive their social role and function. For example, in a cartoon published in 1997, when the nationwide campaign against social evils was at its height, the journalist-cartoonist is depicted as a slightly built, office-type person who leans on his pen for strength and momentum, then angrily delivers a powerful kick straight in the face of a much larger person with a top hat labelled 'social evils' (Figure 6.1).

Figure 6.1 Saigon Giai Phong, 24 June 1997

As we have seen above, humour and wit play an important part in satire. However, according to Xich Dieu, humour is not always a requirement in traditional Vietnamese satire, which tends to concentrate more on the elements of criticism and attack (Vu Ngoc Khanh 1974: 21). This observation is also true in the case of modern satirical cartoons. The term *biem hoa* denotes a picture or drawing that exposes social vices and follies through satiric devices. Although seemingly unsophisticated in their appearance, *biem hoa* are very similar to social and political caricatures in Western societies in terms of their role and function. However, unlike caricature and satire in Western countries, the entertainment function of *biem hoa* is clearly secondary to its provision of political and social criticism.[3] Consequently, very few *biem hoa* manage to generate comic laughter; at times all they can do is extract a gentle nod or a knowing smile from viewers, which often indicates successful communication of the cartoonist's message.

In his 1967 article entitled 'On a Theory of Political Caricature', Streicher identifies two categories of caricature: the political and the social. According to him, political caricature usually deals with the debunking or exposure of persons, groups or organi-sations that engage in power struggles in society. Thus the targets of political caricature are almost invariably those who lay claim to some authority. Social satire, on the other hand, deals with non-political affairs and issues confronting those who do not possess the ability or desire to significantly alter their society's power structure. Furthermore, social caricatures often make use of stereotypically drawn figures representing various social types whose follies and vices invite the cartoonist's derision and ridicule.

As will be demonstrated below, *biem hoa* contain elements of both political and social caricature. However, unlike editorial or political cartoonists in Western countries that routinely portray politicians and other public figures in the most unflattering manner, Vietnamese cartoonists generally refrain from lampooning national leaders or criticising state policies. As a result, portrait caricatures of high-ranking state and party leaders are almost non-existent. On the rare occasions when criticism of political figures is tolerated, cartoonists would almost certainly be reminded not to depict them too realistically. With increasing press freedom in recent years, this taboo itself has become a subject of ridicule among cartoonists. One of the best examples is found in a 1999 issue of the *Youth Humour* magazine (*Tuoi Tre Cuoi*), in which an editor of a newspaper points to portraits of political leaders and celebrities on the wall, and orders the cartoonist to memorise them so as to avoid rendering these people too faithfully (Figure 6.2).

However, there seems to be little evidence of such restriction when it comes to the portrayal of government officials and company executives who are under investigation or have been convicted of some criminal offence. For example, in 1998, the cartoonist Choe[4] did not hesitate to depict in a relatively realistic fashion the deputy head of the anti-corruption task force of Long An province, who was at that time facing criminal prosecution for taking bribes (Figure 6.3).

Even more realistic is a cartoon which appeared on the cover of *Tuoi Tre Cuoi* magazine, showing plainly the faces of Phung Long That, the former chief anti-smuggling investigator in the Ho Chi Minh City customs department, and Tran

Figure 6.2 *Tuoi Tre Cuoi*, no. 185, June 1999

Trích Lao Động ngày 12.12.1998

Figure 6.3 *Lao Dong*, 12 December 1998

Figure 6.4 Tuoi Tre Cuoi, no. 183, April 1999

Dam, the owner of the private Tan Truong Sanh company (Figure 6.4). In 1999, these two men were sentenced to death for their part in one of the country's biggest smuggling scandals. Interestingly, even when their cartoons are debunking recognisable public figures, Vietnamese cartoonists still prefer to rely on the more simple method of labelling rather than that of physiognomy.

In his study of political cartoons on the Mexican revolution, Victor Alba argues that cartoonists who make use of verbal elements and symbols are often more popular in societies or groups of less social refinement. The low level of education or aesthetic appreciation means that cartoonists have to employ auxiliary markers to guide the viewers, to explain meaning, and to avoid the danger of erroneous interpretation. On the other hand, cartoons directed toward more intellectually refined audiences need few symbols (Alba 1967: 92). The classification of cartoon audiences into low- and highbrow categories, however, does not adequately address the inherent problems in viewing cartoons and caricatures as a form of visual communication.[5] In actual fact, the presence of accompanying verbal elements such as labels, speech balloons and captions can be useful in directing viewers to read the visual image and its intended message while minimising the risk of misunderstanding or misinterpretation.

Cartoons in Vietnam: a brief history

Some of the earliest forms of caricature in Vietnam are found in woodblock reproductions of traditional popular drawings, which often depict various scenes from everyday life, village celebrations, and traditional or religious festivals. A large number of these woodcuts are of a highly satirical nature, lampooning foolish behaviour by ordinary people and directing unveiled criticisms against what the artist perceived as social injustice. A popular debunking device is the depiction of animals in human roles. For example, the toad usually represents pompous and arrogant people, the cat oppressive village officials, while the mouse stands for the poor and the downtrodden in society. There are also humorous pictures showing scenes of domestic quarrel, jealous wives catching their unfaithful husbands in bed with other women and so on (Nguyen Khac Ngu 1988: 147).

By the early twentieth century, Vietnamese intellectuals, especially those who were educated under the new French or Franco-Vietnamese system, began to blend traditional satire with Western forms of humour including cartoons and drawings. In an effort to increase sales and subscriptions, Vietnamese language periodicals quickly underwent numerous changes in both format and content. At first, satire permeated nearly every aspect of the press, including reportage on current events and social commentary. Gradually, however, humour became a distinct and indispensable feature of newspapers and magazines of the 1920s and 1930s in an attempt to cater to growing popular demand for light entertainment. More newspapers and magazines began to supplement serious articles with illustrations, satirical drawings and cartoons in an attempt to capture the attention of readers. Almost every publication made an attempt to include jokes, cartoons and humorous stories among their pages. Some of the earliest satirical and humorous magazines to appear in colonial Vietnam included *Duy Tan*, *Phong Hoa*, *Con Ong*, *Vit Duc* and *Ngoi But*. Under the editorship of the writer Nhat Linh, the periodical *Phong Hoa*, which began publication in 1932, concentrated on attacking outmoded social customs and religious beliefs among villagers and less-educated urbanites, while at the same time promoting a certain paradigm of modernity and modernisation.

Owing to censorship and crackdowns by the French colonial government, explicit political caricatures were gradually replaced by representative or symbolic types that stood for recognisable categories of people in society. One version of this device was the 'emblematic type', a fictional character with a proper name and set of characteristics with whom the public could gradually develop familiarity. Once created and established in the public's imagination, such types were put through a variety of humorous situations with the aim of drawing attention to the practices and beliefs regarded as harmful by Vietnamese intellectuals of this period. The sources for these popular types were found in illustrations, popular literature, folk tales and popular songs. Inevitably, the depiction of such types tended to represent weaknesses and faults rather than merits.

Most notable were the three fictitious characters of Ly Toet, Xa Xe and Bang Banh. Created by the poet Tu Mo (1900–76), Ly Toet appeared first as a bare-footed village dignitary who became instantly recognisable by his vulgar grin and uncouth attire. He was soon joined by the pot-bellied Xa Xe, and together they symbolised the backwardness and ignorance of the rural population. The third character, Bang Banh, represented greed and corruption among mandarins and government officials. He was often depicted as a grotesquely obese man dressed in mandarin garb (Figure 6.5).

Despite numerous restrictions on the press, political cartoons flourished in southern Vietnam in the 1960s and early 1970s. One of the most well-known cartoonists of this period was Nguyen Hai Chi, popularly known as Choe, whose cartoons appeared in *Newsweek* and the *New York Times*. Born in 1944, Choe became famous for his grotesque depictions of American and south Vietnamese political leaders, and his scathing pictorial commentary on the savage war that was destroying so many lives. Choe's talent is demonstrated in a simple cartoon that in many ways exposes the true nature of US–Vietnamese relations at that time. Uncle Sam is depicted as a young hippie, complete with shaggy long hair and bell-bottoms, running away and leaving behind a heavily pregnant woman surrounded by her hungry brood – a poignant symbol for south Vietnam – while still doing up his pants (Figure 6.6). Despite his critical stance against the Saigon government and US policy in Vietnam, which eventually led to his arrest during the last months of the war, Choe was again imprisoned in April 1976, ironically for being a 'reactionary and counter-revolutionary element'. He is now a free-lance cartoonist for major newspapers in Vietnam including *Labour*.

With the renovation of the print media in the late 1980s, cartoons and comic strips now appear regularly in many daily newspapers and magazines,

Figure 6.5 *Tuoi Tre Cuoi*, special edition, spring 1999, p. 21

Figure 6.6 No source (private collection, David Marr)

enlivening their pages with witty commentary on a wide variety of issues salient to the public interest. The growing market for pictorial humour is evident in the appearance of numerous magazines specialising in satirical cartoons and humour, such as *Youth Humour* published by the Youth Union of Ho Chi Minh City, *Humour* published by the Fine Arts Association of Vietnam, and *Relaxation* published by the Labour Publishing House. Daily newspapers also carry cartoons or comic strips, sometimes both, on designated pages. *Labour*, for example, publishes satirical cartoons by the famous cartoonist Choe in addition to a regular comic strip, which appears at the bottom of page one. Its Saturday edition devotes an entire corner to humorous illustrations, satirical verses and modern parodies of traditional sayings and proverbs.[6] Corrupt government officials and wasteful bureaucrats are not the only groups pilloried in these cartoons. Ordinary people's vices are also held up to ridicule by the cartoonist. For the purposes of this chapter, however, only satirical cartoons dealing with government corruption and bureaucracy will be considered in any detail.

Cartoons and the anti-corruption drive

Before looking more closely at specific examples of *biem hoa*, it is useful to examine briefly the socio-political setting in which they appeared, namely the campaigns against government corruption and bureaucracy in the 1990s. Since the introduction of economic reforms and the open-door policy, the spectre of government corruption has overshadowed much of Vietnam's political landscape. Despite numerous official pronouncements on the need to root out graft and corruption, the government has so far failed to convince people that it is serious about doing so. In 1998, the weekly *Law* of Ho Chi Minh City published a survey of some 2,000 readers from which it obtained a 'top ten' of crimes or violations considered by the public to be the most urgent and serious problems facing the country today. At number one is corruption, garnering 26.82 per cent of all responses, followed by drug addiction and prostitution (Marshall 1998).

Communist Party and government officials have always maintained they are determined to combat the problems of corruption and bureaucracy. According to some of the country's top leaders, however, the fight against corruption and social evils represents 'a complicated and long-term project' which cannot be accomplished within a short period of time (Xinhua 1998). In 1998, Do Muoi, the former party Secretary General, said that widespread corruption and entrenched bureaucracy were posing a serious threat to the authority and legitimacy of the ruling party. In a speech given to party officials in the northern province of Hung Yen, Muoi said that red tape and corruption 'caused moral decay and sabotaged the close relationship between the party, state and people' and that 'the struggle against corruption and red tape had been inefficient'. According to Muoi, the reasons for growing public discontent lay in corruption, red tape and the undemocratic behaviour of local officials and party cadres (VN News Service 1998).

Nevertheless, national leaders continue to argue that, unlike in other countries, the scourge of corruption did not reach into the senior levels of Vietnamese political leadership. From the party's point of view, the problem of corruption is not systemic; rather, it arises from the greed and immoral behaviour of a few dishonest individuals. According to a translated article published in May 1999 in the theoretical journal of the Vietnamese People's Army,

> a number of typical cases of corruption and smuggling have shown that most of them were committed by individuals. They were people of position and power, people who worked in areas relating to material supplies, the budget and the market. With the exception of a number of people who erred because of poor managerial and professional standards or because they were deceived, most of the rest violated the law basically because of a decline in ideology, quality and morality. They also transgressed the law because of a lifestyle marked by deficiency in viewpoints, position, and political responsibility, as well as a sense of organisation and discipline. In addition, they erred because they were tempted by material things, a pragmatic lifestyle, individualism, parochialism, money and material interests in everyday life. The excuses often cited by people practising corruption and smuggling are that

> 'they were influenced by circumstances', that they acted to make just a meagre profit for themselves or for their 'small collectives', or that they 'could not resist the temptation' because 'others did the same thing'.
>
> (Man Ha Anh 1999)

In August 2000, the *Youth* newspaper also quoted Pham The Duyet as saying the party was determined to root out corruption, but that any anti-graft campaign must be carried out carefully to avoid misunderstandings. As Pham The Duyet stated, 'It's essential to remember that any issue always has its positive and negative sides. It would be dangerous if the anti-corruption drive led to the mistaken assumption that the entire party was corrupt' (Reuters 2000). Occasionally, some minor officials are sacrificed to public opinion but in reality, graft and corruption continue to erode the government's power base as ordinary citizens generally feel marginalised by the perception that government officials are unable to resist the temptation of profiting from their positions of power. Asset-stripping, for example, has become so widespread and rampant that newspapers routinely carry *biem hoa* depicting managers of state-run enterprises as rotund and paunchy middle-aged men. One particular *biem hoa* in the *Lao Dong* turns corrupt government officials and company executives into grotesquely obese rats exchanging witty comments in a prison cell. One of the rats is saying to the other that they could never fit through the small 'frame of punishment' (Figure 6.7).

Figure 6.7 Lao Dong, 21 October 1997

The Vietnamese government no doubt realises the extent of the damage wrought by rampant corruption, and has been pressing for harsher penalties even in the cases of officials at the very top of the power structure. Nevertheless, despite acknowledgment by party leaders that corruption is endemic and threatens to undermine the legitimacy of the state, few of the two million members of the Communist Party have fallen victim to the numerous anti-graft campaigns since the mid-1990s (Watkin 2000).

As part of the printed media, cartoon depictions of government corruption and bureaucracy are thus heavily influenced by official attitudes. Instead of exposing graft and corruption as a problem brought on by the lack of accountability and transparency in the current political system, cartoons tend to concentrate on a group of unnamed and faceless 'bad individuals' at whose door are laid most of the country's difficulties. Only a few real-life individuals accused and convicted of corruption and fraud are ever depicted in satirical cartoons. These include the chief executives of the moribund Nam Dinh Textile enterprise who were found guilty of embezzling millions of dong in 1998; Tang Minh Phung who was convicted of fraudulent business practices in the same year; and the former chief anti-smuggling investigator in HCM city customs department, Phung Long That, and owner of the private Tan Truong Sanh company, Tran Dam, both of whom received the death sentence for graft and smuggling.

Metaphors

Cartoons are like stories. These stories are satirical, humorous and short – as a rule only one scene is shown. They take us into an imaginary world, which may have much in common with our perception of the real world, but which also distorts it systematically through the use of readily recognised symbols and stereotypes. To understand cartoon messages, it is important to look more closely at the conventions through which they are communicated – conventions that are indispensable in an art form that aims for instant communication.

The major conventions of cartooning have been identified by the art critic E.H. Gombrich (1978) in his classic essay on political cartoons, 'The Cartoonist's Armoury', in which he delineates those references by which cartoonists make visible their ideas and associations. According to him, condensation and comparison are the essence of the cartoon's appeal, and therefore such literary forms as metaphors and personifications play a significant role in their message. Cartoon images regularly condense meaning through metaphors and symbols, creating new frameworks for understanding. Metaphor, in relation to the art of cartooning, is a structuring device by which new meanings are created. As the meaning generated by metaphors is greatly facilitated and assisted by the audience's recognition of metaphorical references, metaphors can transform a subject in such a way that we look at the subject in a new manner, one suggested by its referent. In so doing, metaphors invite particular constructions of the world in the course of communicating ideas.

Looking at specific examples of *biem hoa* on government corruption, one cannot help noticing that animals are frequently used as a metaphorical device.

There is a distinct trend in satirical cartoons to diminish officials and company executives who have been convicted of corruption by portraying them as rodents and worms destroying society from the inside out. For example, the people found responsible for the collapse of the famous Nam Dinh Textile corporation are depicted as rats poking through a piece of fabric (Figure 6.8). Similarly, corrupt local officials in the southern province of Long An become shifty-eyed worms eating their way out of an apple (Figure 6.9). In another cartoon, the abstract concept of corruption is made concrete through a succinct and potent image of a caterpillar with the face of a balding and bespectacled official eating away at a leaf labelled 'public fund' (Figure 6.10).

Figure 6.8 Lao Dong, 21 March 1998

Figure 6.9 Lao Dong, 6 May 1998

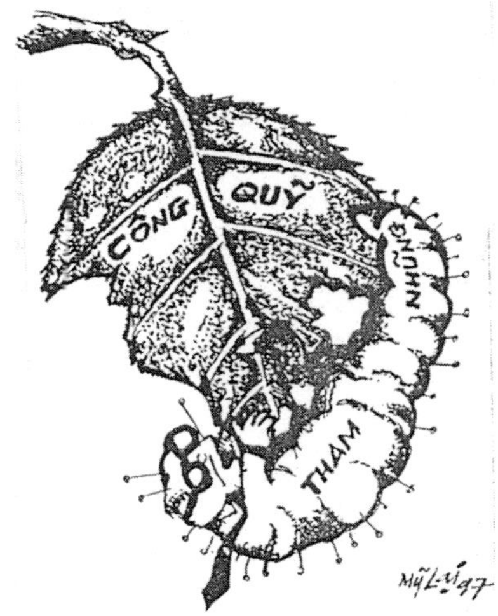

Figure 6.10 Saigon Giai Phong, 11 August 1997

Gombrich also identifies a class of potent metaphors which he terms as 'natural' in acknowledgement of their subversive power, for they are so universal that we rarely give second thought to how these metaphors construct our world. We consider them natural ways of perceiving, and respond to them with an immediacy that precludes close examination. Images, especially propaganda images, are thus capable of arousing our predilection for myth-making, such as the contrast between light and dark as symbol for the struggle between good and evil. Human beings tend to react to certain shapes and colours as they would to expressive features in the world. Huge, dark and sinister shapes therefore are often used to suggest evil intentions. According to Gombrich,

> [t]he cartoonist's armoury is always there in the workings of our mind. When perplexed or frustrated, we all like to fall back on a primitive, physiognomic picture of events which ignores the realities of human existence and conceives the world in terms of impersonal forces. The co-ordinate system in which we allocate a place to these forces and events exists, as it were, ready-made in our minds. Contrasts such as light and dark, beautiful and ugly, big and small, which form the co-ordinates of the cartoonist's mythical universe, would not be so effective if we all were not inclined to categorise the world around us in such basic emotional metaphors.
>
> (Gombrich 1978: 139)

Vietnamese cartoonists seem to understand quite well the potency of this weapon, and have used it quite frequently in their criticisms of government corruption and bureaucracy. In one of his more memorable *biem hoa* in recent years, the cartoonist Choe depicts the struggle against graft and bureaucracy as a dramatically unequal battle between a frail and diminutive figure of a man and a huge, evil-looking beast jealously guarding its hoard of treasure (Figure 6.11). As if to rule out any possibility of misunderstanding and misinterpretation, Choe then labels the dragon-like beast 'corruption and bureaucracy'.

Spatial syntax and stereotypes

Spatial syntax is another convention employed by the cartoonist to convey meaning. Cartoonists in Vietnam and other countries often employ this technique to signify inequality in social relationships: for instance, socially superior persons are invariable drawn larger, more centrally situated, or higher in the picture than their subordinates. Spatial syntax is often employed by Vietnamese cartoonists to draw the viewer's attention to the self-importance and condescending attitudes commonly associated with officialdom. It comes as no surprise, therefore, that in many *biem hoa* attacking the problems of red tape and bureaucracy, the frame is dominated by the corpulent figures of government offi-

Figure 6.11 Lao Dong, 10 July 1999

cers sitting behind a desk with arrogant, bored expressions on their faces. One particular *biem hoa* even shows the officer with his back to the public, reading a newspaper, while the person entering with an application is greeted by a mask which the officer wears on the back of his head (Figure 6.12). In contrast, members of the public seeking assistance with their applications are invariably depicted slightly off the centre of the frame or at the lower corners of the picture, looking up at the imposing figure of the government officer.

Popular imagery

One of the most striking characteristics of Vietnamese *biem hoa* is the frequent reference to the shared imagery embedded in popular thought and traditional folklore, especially that concerning corruption and officialdom. *Tham nhung*, the Vietnamese term for corruption and graft, combines two separate concepts: greed and official harassment. However, the concept of greed seems to play a more dominant role in cartoonists' visual depictions of government corruption. It is hardly a coincidence that corrupt officials and company executives are invariably shown as grotesquely obese individuals. The viewers are encouraged to believe that these officials have grown fat from 'eating' (*an*) an inordinate amount of funds and assets that do not belong to them.[7] In one *biem hoa*, a doctor advises his patient, who is apparently a senior official or company executive, to abstain from 'eating' public money and property (*cua cong*) as a perfect solution to his indigestion and high blood pressure problems (Figure 6.13).

In July 2001, the Sunday edition of *Youth Magazine* ran a satirical cartoon making explicit reference to the concept of greed in its depiction of government corruption. Alluding to the popular expression of *tui tham khong day*, which

Figure 6.12 Saigon Giai Phong, 16 July 1997

Figure 6.13 *Tuoi Tre Cuoi*, 22 July 2000

literally means bottomless greed, the cartoon featured a parade of different kinds of 'corruption bags' (*tui tham nhung*), from small to medium to the special size which has no bottom, an unveiled criticism against the greed of corrupt officials that knows no bounds (Figure 6.14).

Water is another important image and metaphorical concept employed by Vietnamese cartoonists in their visual depictions of corruption and bureaucracy. Since traditional times, water has symbolised prosperity, wealth and abundance, as is evident in popular sayings such as 'money flowing in like water' (*tien vo nhu nuoc*). Ironically, the image of water is often used by cartoonists to portray the wealth being stolen from the nation by corrupt government officials. In one *biem hoa*, state funds and capital, symbolised by water coursing through a main pipe, are diverted into small buckets labelled 'children', 'grandchildren', 'wife' and 'brothers', while the intended recipients, workers at a state-owned company, wait at the other end of the pipe with a forlorn expression on their faces. The thief is none other than the chief executive of that state company (Figure 6.15).

Conclusion

The psychological and social influence of cartoons and caricatures should not be underestimated. Rulers and politicians traditionally fear cartoons for three reasons: first, the cartoon's savage power to depict in unflattering caricature; second, its ability to crystallise complex issues into a simple but potent metaphor; and third, the cartoon's accessibility, even to those who may not be especially literate or politically aware. For these reasons, it is clear that the cartoon can be a powerful tool of mass communication and persuasion. There is no conclusive evidence to support this

Figure 6.14 *Tuoi Tre Cuoi*, 22 December 2001

Figure 6.15 *Saigon Giai Phong*, 24 July 1997

view however. Even now, we are not sure to what degree cartoons influence public opinion, if at all. The lack of consistent evidence for the propaganda value of satirical cartoons is compounded by the fact that little research has been done in Vietnam to gauge the effect of *biem hoa*, not only on viewers but also on the targets of satire and criticism. Despite this, one cannot deny that satirical cartoons, because of their capacity to generate and reinforce popular images of the socio-political system, can also be viewed as an unconventional channel for political communication in contemporary urban Vietnam. Through the process of attacking and lampooning the problems of government corruption and bureaucracy, whether intentionally or not, cartoonists have given rise to certain images about state officials and company executives that seem to match popular perceptions.

It has been observed that cartoons may affect political discourse in more indirect ways than by producing overt changes in public opinion. While they may not be very effective as direct agents of change, the power of satirical cartoons lies more in the ability to identify predominant themes, values and salient issues in society. They often serve to reinforce existing images of the body politic and sometimes even create new ones. As we have seen, existing images in popular political thought often provide a framework for understanding cartoons and are, in turn, affected by the contents of these cartoons. The relationship between cartoons and popular political thought therefore can be summed up as follows: cartoonists make use of existing political images embedded in popular perceptions to convey new messages regarding government corruption and social injustice in general. In turn, these messages reinforce widely held beliefs about the relationship between ordinary people and officialdom.

Notes

1 A term used by Janis Edwards (1997: 26) in her discussion about the use of irony and parody in political cartooning in the United States.

2 Born in 1913, Xich Dieu is the pen name of Tran Minh Tuoc, one of the most well-known social commentators and prolific writers in the history of Vietnamese journalism.

3 In my view, *biem hoa* should be differentiated from *tranh vui,* which are essentially humorous cartoons designed for entertainment and relaxation purposes only.

4 Choe whose real name is Nguyen Hai Chi passed away in the US in March 2003.

5 A major issue in the study of cartoons as a form of visual communication is that a cartoon message is not always clearly understood – at least in the sense intended by the cartoonist – even when words are included. Some scholars in this field argue that editorial or political cartoons are not like any other pictorial forms (photographs or paintings, for example), and therefore assumptions about pictures in general should not be made about this particular form of visual communication. The biggest problem lies with viewers who read their own subjective interpretations and meanings into cartoons. No two persons view a cartoon in exactly the same way. As meanings are relative to the individual, confusion, misinterpretation and the unintentional scrambling of the original 'message' may occur. Consequently, verbal markers such as captions, speech balloons and labels are often included to clarify meanings and to assist in general understanding and communication.

6 This corner is entitled *Xa xu bap*, which is the Vietnamese slang term for 'letting off steam'.

7 The Vietnamese expression for taking bribes is '*an hoi lo*', which literally means 'to eat bribes'.

Bibiography

Alba, Victor (1967) 'The Mexican Revolution and the Cartoon', *Comparative Studies in Society and History* 9 (January): 121–36.

Edwards, Janis (1997) *Political Cartoons in the 1988 Presidential Campaign*, New York: Garland Publishing.

Elliott, Robert (1960) *The Power of Satire: Magic, Ritual, Art*, Princeton, NJ: Princeton University Press.

Gombrich, E.H. (1978) 'The Cartoonist's Armoury', *Meditations on a Hobby Horse*, 3rd edn, London: Phaidon Press.

Harrison, Randall (1981) *The Cartoon: Communication to the Quick*, Beverly Hills, CA: Sage Publications.

Hodgart, Matthew (1969) *Satire*, London: Weidenfeld & Nicolson.

Langeveld, Willem (1981) 'Political Cartoons as a Medium of Political Communication', *International Journal of Political Education* 4: 343–71.

Man Ha Anh (1999) 'The Army Actively Joins the Entire People in the Struggle against Embezzlement, Corruption, and Smuggling, and Contributes to Making Social Relations Healthy', 1 May, FBIS Translated Text, Hanoi Tap Chi Quoc Phong Toan Dan, 20 July.

Marshall (1998) *Vietnam's Top Ten Vices*, listserver: owner-vnforum@vnforum.org [accessed 25 August 2000].

Nguyen Khac Ngu (1988) *The Art of Woodblock Printing in Vietnam*, Melbourne: Historical and Geographical Research Society.

Reuters (2000) 'Politburo Admits Vietnam Too Lenient on Corruption', 25 August.

Streicher, Lawrence H. (1967) 'On a Theory of Political Caricature', *Comparative Studies in Society and History* 9: 427–45.

Vu Ngoc Khanh (1974) *Tho Van Trao Phung Viet Nam* (Satirical Literature of Vietnam), Hanoi: Van Hoc Publishing House.

Watkin, Huw (2000) 'Corrupt Cadres Thrive despite Graft Campaign', *South China Morning Post*, 11 January.

Xinhua (1998) 'Vietnam to Fight Corruption and Bureaucracy', 12 June.

Chapter 7

Bia om and karaoke

HIV and everyday life in urban Vietnam

Stephen McNally

A cuddle at Pha Ni's Bar

'I'll take you to the "cuddle bar" that we went to last night' said my friend Mark Mark often takes friends on what he jokingly refers to as 'Cook's Sex Tours of Saigon'. It is a night 'on the town' where he gives his guests a glimpse of what the sex industry has to offer on the streets, in the small bars and clubs, and behind the facades of the karaoke bars and cafés. His guests get an opportunity to meet with some of the women who work the streets and bars that he has come to know over the years from his work with HIV/AIDS prevention. One of his regular tour stops is Pha Ni's bar in Thai Van Lung Street, just around the corner from the infamous Apocalypse Now bar. It is well placed to tap into the foreign tourist market and the local clientele who can afford it.

The previous night Mark had taken his friends Peter and Carol to meet the women at Pha Ni's. Tonight there were five of us heading off to Pha Ni's for a drink and a look. Peter and Carol, who joined us for a second night, were visiting Vietnam for a short time to make a documentary on the contradictions of HIV and AIDS in Vietnam. The night before had been a great success; Peter mentioned how they had spent over one million dong,[1] mainly on drinks but also on tips for the women so that they would get some good footage for their documentary. He said that 'the women performed wonderfully for the camera, they danced on the tables and flirted outrageously'.

We walked into the dimly lit bar at around 8.30 pm. Pha Ni's was clearly a space reserved for male clients. Young women lounged around the black lacquered bar, waiting and looking a little bored. My skin instantly responded to the cool of the air conditioner helping to bring me back in touch with my body. The air was 'sexed'. Perhaps half a dozen pairs of eyes were fixed upon me. I felt that the women saw me as a typical male customer looking for enjoyment. There was an overwhelming sense of opposites: male and female, first world and third world, although I knew it was not that simple. Behind the bar, the decision had been reached regarding who would be my hostess for what was to be our brief encounter with the libidinal economy. It was a decision I did not make.

I chose the stools against the bar instead of the chocolate-coloured, velour module pushed into the corner of the room behind the front door. The stools somehow seemed safer. It was still early; there was only one other customer in the bar being entertained by two of the women. Behind us, there was a narrow staircase leading to a room with a pool table and more velour seats that had somehow found their way here from the 1970s. I was told that upstairs was the place 'where the more serious cuddling was done'.

Pha Ni's was typical of a more 'up-market establishment'; there was nothing different about this place from the hundreds of others in Ho Chi Minh City. The bar ran down one side of the narrow room. Ricky Martin singing the theme song for the World Cup, 'La Copa de la Vida', drowned out a television perched up high behind the bar. The World Cup, it seemed, permeated every corner of Vietnamese life.

A Tiger beer was placed in front of me. Without hesitation, my hostess, Hien, set to work straight away on me. She gently laid claim to me by running a scented paper towel over my face and arms. She was confident and acted impressed with me as she wiped the heat and dirt of the summer night away. She asked if I would like her to massage me, perhaps noticing that I was a little tense. She didn't wait for an answer. Perhaps no one ever refuses. Her job was to relax me so I would drink more. She asked if she could also have a drink. A voice then came over my shoulder: 'Be careful where you put your hands, because the price goes up depending on what you touch'. We talked about nothing much. She asked the usual questions: What was I doing in Vietnam? Where was I staying and what did I think of Vietnam? Hien told me that she really wanted to work in an office for an international company, but jobs like that are hard to get. Her story was not uncommon. Nearly three years ago, she had left her family and come to the city to find work. She hasn't been back to visit them. I wondered how she sees herself – perhaps as the 'dutiful daughter' caught up in Vietnam's drive to modernise. Perhaps she sends money home as often as she can and works just for the moment to please men. She changed the topic as if she was tired of her story. 'If you like', she said, as she slowly worked her way down my body, making sure she didn't miss anything, 'I can get a day off work and we can spend it together'.

The night wasn't another million-dong night; we were soon off somewhere else. We, or perhaps Hien, had cuddled 50,000 dong's worth. The money for the drinks would go to the owner of the bar, but Hien would keep the 50,000 dong tip for her work at keeping me at Pha Ni's and keeping me drinking. Hien would have to work until at least 2 am. If she leaves with a customer at the end of the evening then that is her business. No sex takes place on the premises, which makes it much harder for authorities to control the sex industry, while also negating any responsibility on the part of the owner of the bar. It may be a busy night for Hien making men feel pleased with themselves or else she may have a night fixing her makeup. Tonight, however, would be different: the women will spend their time entertained by the World Cup game along with the rest of Vietnam.

We left the women at Pha Ni's to walk the streets again. If you wait your turn, 5,000 dong is all you need to buy yourself a few moments of pleasure on one of the benches in the park next to the cathedral. A woman sits there in the half-light with a roll of toilet paper displayed next to her, indicating that she is open for business. If it were not for the roll of toilet paper, you probably would not even notice her sitting there with her plastic basket. She is nothing special; a world away from the women at Pha Ni's. She has not put on any makeup or a short skirt for work tonight. She talks with another woman working one of the benches not far down the path. She smiles to her next customer as her last kicks up the stand of his bicycle, throws his leg over the rail and heads off into the noise of the city that he was momentarily taken away from. They sit close together, his arm wrapped around her. She reaches for the paper. It's over. Her capital outlay is negligible. Her operation was much easier to set up than a *pho* stand, but for the price of a bowl of *pho*, she will take you somewhere else. As we left the park, my friend Mark commented that once he counted fifteen pieces of toilet paper late one night once trading was over. A reasonable night's work, he thought.

The sex industry in Vietnam

Most people who have spent some time in Vietnam will have their own stories to tell about their encounter with the sex industry. The globalising forces that have accompanied Vietnam's industrialisation and modernisation have helped to increase the number of spaces where sex is bought and sold. Although prostitution is still neither recognised nor accepted in today's Vietnam, it has, argues Le Thi Quy, an historian at the Centre for Family and Women Studies in Hanoi, made a resurgence in Vietnam in the 1980s. It operates in 'a relatively open manner [and is] practised in almost all hotels, inns, restaurants, dancing halls, beauty and massage parlours, beer houses, cafeterias, public parks, street pavement, bus station, railway station and any other places such as dyke embankment or sea beach [sic]' (Le Thi Quy 1993: 4).

You could be forgiven for thinking that prostitution is legal in Vietnam. Recent economic and social changes throughout the country have made the booming sex economy, which some argue has always operated throughout all levels of society, more visible. For most men, a walk down 'General Uprising Street', the streets around the Reunification Palace, or up Pasture Street in District One on any night of the week will bring whistles from *cyclo* drivers or offers from female street vendors to find you a 'beautiful women' or perhaps an offer of a massage. You may be enticed by young women from doorways of small bars or karaoke cafés to come join them. Through representations from calendars and advertisements for cigarettes and alcohol in restaurants, to the early, government-sponsored, anti-social evils posters (which have a propensity to be recycled by local authorities), women's bodies are rendered as sexual, available, promiscuous and aplenty for the enjoyment or just for the gaze of men.

The increased visibility of the sex industry is in part due to the introduction of liberal policies associated with *doi moi*, along with the growing concern over HIV and AIDS. HIV entered Vietnam at an extraordinary time in the country's history; a time marked with promises of development and accompanied by temporal, spatial and cultural disjunctures. Drugs and prostitution assumed a new dimension within Vietnamese society. As Le Dien Hong, Director of the National AIDS Bureau, has stressed, these are new times in which drug use and prostitution have both increased the incidence of HIV and ultimately threatened the social fabric of society. He writes: Drug abuse and prostitution are the two social evils directly affecting the transmission of HIV infection in Vietnam and posing big problems to the Vietnamese society (Le Dien Hong 1992: 16).

Ho Chi Minh City authorities reported the arrival of the HIV pandemic with the detection of the first case of HIV in 1990. By August 2001, the government had identified 37,111 persons infected with HIV in all sixty-one of Vietnam's provinces. Over the decade, 4,728 people had been identified with AIDS and 3,020 people had died from an AIDS-related illness. By December 2000, the Ministry of Health estimated that there were about 120,000 people living with HIV throughout Vietnam and that the number would increase to 200,000 by 2005.[2] The government now estimates that over 50 per cent of new infections occur in young people aged between ten and twenty-four. Thereby, HIV has become one of the major problems threatening Vietnam's future. Lack of education, economic hardship and a range of social and cultural factors, including sexual conduct, are understood to be the main factors contributing to the increase of HIV among young people.[3]

In 1996, UNAIDS[4] estimated that only 10 per cent of people currently infected with HIV throughout the third world were aware of their status. The World Health Organisation (WHO) also estimated that only 11 per cent of all cases in Vietnam were reported in 1995 – this low level of reporting is thought to have significant consequences for social awareness of the issue.[5] Reasons given for such low awareness of HIV status relate to the paucity of reporting, limited confidentiality and people's limited knowledge about the virus and how it is transmitted. With Vietnam's HIV prevalence rate remaining at under 0.1 per cent, most Vietnamese have minimal, if any, direct experience with the virus and so HIV and AIDS has little meaning for the everyday lived experience of most Vietnamese people.

The reporting of the earliest HIV cases, which included only one Vietnamese national, contributed to a deceptive assumption of cultural immunity to HIV and AIDS among the Vietnamese public. Despite numerous HIV awareness campaigns to the contrary, many people in Vietnam accept that HIV is a danger to specific, often marginalised groups within society. Injecting drug users and sex workers have been identified as the two vectors of the epidemic – a view that is not necessarily unique to Vietnam. A widespread belief thus persists that HIV and AIDS are not a personal threat to 'good' people, but rather an affliction of those persons engaged in bad behaviour, labelled as 'social evils' in Vietnam. Through its association with the increased attention towards the state construction of 'social evils', the threat of HIV and AIDS has become a metaphor for many of the problems now facing a more open Vietnam.

The fight against 'social evils'

The struggle between what is understood as 'traditional values' and what Vietnam is allowing into the country from outside its increasingly porous borders can be seen through the government's campaigns that target 'social evils' (*Te nan xa hoi*). These 'social evils' cover a range of sins including prostitution, drug abuse, gambling, karaoke, pornography, fortune-telling, corruption, waste, and even at times Western music. The link between 'social evils' and HIV remains strong a decade into the Vietnamese HIV epidemic. At times even HIV appears on the list of 'social evils'.[6]

Although the fight is not simply against the decadence of the West, economic reform, and in particular globalising forces, are seen by some to be fuelling the flames of the rise of these 'social evils'. There is a constant struggle to find a balance between old and new. According to Le Thi Quy (1993: 5), it is important 'to preserve and to find a place whereby Vietnamese traditions can be in harmony with the country's modernisation and industrialisation'. She goes on to say:

> It is our view that we need to do much more to strengthen the traditional values in the family relations and increase the role of the community in the monitoring and surveillance of ethical actions of each individual.
>
> (Le Thi Quy 1993: 5)

Nowhere does this struggle with the devil appear to be so evident than in the attention given to reducing the number of sex workers and drug users. Despite the many economic and cultural changes ushered in by *doi moi*, Vietnam continues to be controlled by a one-party state that often remains intolerant of freedom and difference, and ambivalent towards change. The campaigns continually waged throughout the country to promote healthy cultural activities are campaigns of social control, reminders of the four decades in the north and two in the south of isolation and strict communist control. These campaigns aim to eliminate aspects of society considered unhealthy and thought to contribute to harmful and anti-social practices. The 1995 decree, referred to as 87/CP,[7] which was brought to life in February 1996 just before Tet, was the first of many campaigns targeting a range of 'social evils' and what are commonly referred to as poisonous cultures (*van hoa doc hai*). The timing of the campaign was not lost on some Vietnamese, as David Marr (1996: 40) comments: some saw the campaign as an attempt by the conservatives in the Communist Party to 'embarrass proponents of continued rapid economic transformation, in the lead-up to the 8th Party Congress scheduled for June 1996'. During the 1996 campaign, advertisements bearing Western brand names were either covered over with paper or removed by the police as they moved through the streets of Ho Chi Minh City and Hanoi. Raids took place on bookstores and other places thought to be selling illegal literature. Newspapers played their part by naming names and reporting on the unhealthy cultural phenomena discovered. Regulations were introduced for karaoke rooms whereby all rooms had to be more than twenty square metres in size with adequate lighting and clear glass in the doors to restrict privacy. Rules were also introduced for *bia om*,[8] such as adequate lighting, low partitions and the banning of waitresses from sitting, eating, drinking or singing with guests (Nguyen Van 1996).

With the fading of the campaigns, public billboards remain to provide a constant reminder of what to guard against. The three posters shown in Figure 7.1, which appeared in Hanoi in 1995 and again in 1997–98, are examples of large roadside billboards highlighting well-known evils. The first of the three depicts a giant red fist smashing a range of activities known to threaten society, such as karaoke, pornography, prostitutes, drugs and gambling, with the caption: *Prevent harmful culture. It's the responsibility of all society*. The next poster continues the theme with the message: *Determined to prevent and abolish all social evils*. The final in the series again shows a range of 'social evils', such as a prostitute, pornographic videotapes, a syringe and also refers to fortune-tellers (*boi toan*). The hand of the authorities, along with the accompanying message, is destroying all these vices: *Do not use or accept harmful cultural products: Do not [become] addicted to smoking or injecting drugs. Do not buy or sell prostitutes. Do not gamble or bet.*

Other billboards directly linking 'social evils' to the threat of HIV and AIDS play a major role in the government's HIV/AIDS prevention campaign. A 'social evils' poster from the northern province of Son La and a HIV prevention poster from the streets of Hanoi during 1997–98, are examples of a popular method of fighting the crusade against HIV and AIDS by targeting the two 'high-risk' groups (Figure 7.2). The caption on the right-hand poster reads: *To avoid SIDA [AIDS] do not have sex with prostitutes. Do no inject drugs.* These images reinforce the view that sex workers and drug users are at risk of contracting HIV and if you avoid going to a prostitute and using drugs then you are safe from HIV and AIDS.

Individualism has always been a threat to the socialist state and plays a pivotal role in the fight against the growing threat of 'social evils'. The battle against

Figure 7.1 Three 'social evils' posters displayed in Hanoi

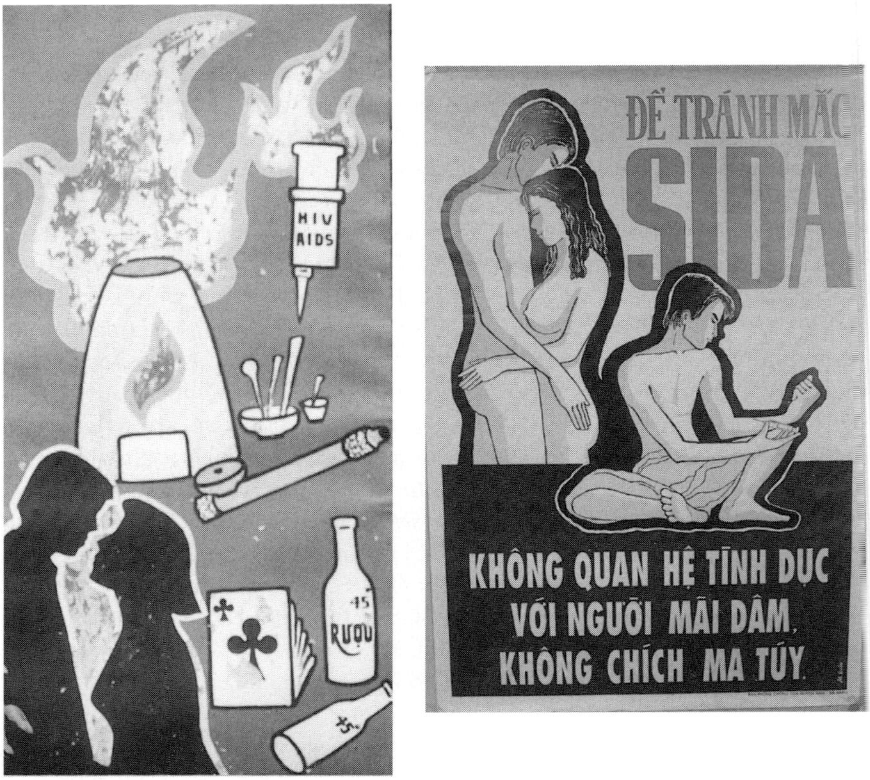

Figure 7.2 (a) A 'social evils' poster from Son La
(b) An HIV prevention poster displayed in Hanoi

individualism and the fight to save the family operate most notably under the banner of corruption, greed and even foreign lifestyles at times. As the government espouses and at times embraces the virtues of economic development, it is also forced to grapple with the effects of increased freedom and change upon people's everyday practices. The results are strains and contradictions within an abruptly changing society, which can be seen in the mismatch between the everyday intersections of informal state 'sponsoring' of the sex industry and the state's vision of the ideal modern family and female sex worker as a threat. Reports of government cadres promoting 'social evils' are becoming more common. These reports reveal a mismatch which is played out through state-owned business ventures which support the sex industry and the high number of government cadres who partake of the pleasures of the sex industry while also working on government policy to eradicate all 'social evils'. According to data from police records between 1995 and 1998, about two-thirds of known customers were state officials (Deutsche Presse-Agentur 1998). Nguyen Thi Hue, Director of the Bureau for Prevention and Control of Social Evils, comments on the need 'to change the basic awareness of a certain part of the population, especially state officials and main (Communist) party members' (Deutsche Presse-Agentur 1998).

Since 1992, the introduction of laws relating to HIV and AIDS has drawn heavily on notions of moral panic. The aim has been to protect society through strengthening the family and to protect the nation against the latest external threat. In 1995, two legal guidelines on HIV and AIDS were issued, along with a decree on 'social evils'. The first guideline, issued in March to all levels of the Party, had the title 'Instruction on the Guidance of the Prevention and Control of AIDS' and was an attempt to strengthen the Party's guidance on HIV/AIDS prevention and control. It stated: 'everyone maintains [a] clean, healthy and faithful lifestyle and self-conscious prevention of drug use and prostitution'.

Families have always played a strong role in traditional Vietnamese society and continue as the key to maintaining a high moral tone. The family came under renewed attention after the revolution when the socialist state directed its attention towards the family as the basic cell of society in its efforts to create 'the new society'. Today there is a search for a new family model as families find themselves facing new pressures that arise from their new role in a post-*doi moi* Vietnam. According to Vu Trong Thieu, a member of the AIDS Prevention Committee of the Ministry of Culture and Information, 'The question of "family" and "family culture" should be taken into account in AIDS prevention activities.' Addressing a conference on youth and AIDS in 1996, Vu Trong Thieu made the following comments:

> To stem the AIDS epidemic, it is first necessary to guide young people – especially young couples – to live, study and work in a healthy cultural environment. Young families are key components to build the "cultural family", an integral part of every family. The three criteria for achieving the title "cultural family" are: to practice family planning; lead a healthy, progressive and happy life; and, to maintain good neighbourliness with people nearby. Only when most families in Vietnam obtain the title of "cultural family" and all people in every family live in harmony with strict observation of disciplines and law will Vietnam be strong enough to push back the AIDS epidemic.

Nguyen Thi Hue cites the 'dark side of the market economy' as the main reason for the increased level of social evils. She concludes that these 'social evils' include 'the adoption of too pragmatic and luxurious living styles, departures from all the cultural and moral traditions of the nation, and the increasing discrimination between the rich and the poor in a society in which part of the people are still living in incredibly miserable conditions' (cited in Mai Huong 1996). Nguyen Thi Hue highlights the lack of emphasis placed by 'authorities of all levels' in educating young people:

> Carried away in moneymaking, families have reduced their important roles in education. The small number of the Communist Party members at the

> grass root level have deteriorated and joined hands with social evils. Not enough stern measures have been taken against these violations. Many district courts and at the commune level have judged the crime of holding and trading in prostitution so lightly, sometimes, their sentences are suspended, which is not equivalent to their violation.
>
> (Cited in Mai Huong 1996)

Faithful lifestyles

Paying for sex is a large part of Vietnam's growing leisure industry. A CARE study (Franklin 1993) of men and sex workers in urban areas found that 44 per cent of men interviewed claimed they had two or more sexual partners within a two-week period. Although this figure has alarming consequences, it is meant only to be representative of the 'categories of men who frequent the places where sex is sold, or where dates for sex can be made, such as cafes, restaurants, nightclubs, parks, streets, [and] bia oms' (Franklin 1993: 35). The study found that men report regularly going out to drink with friends and to seek prostitutes. They 'prefer to go looking for them in the company of their men friends'. As one respondent claimed: 'It's for fun if we go out for girls. So most often we go in a group, and we all share a girl' (Franklin 1993: 40). Women are the reason why men go to these bars. In a society with limited options for leisure *bia hoi*[9] and *bia om* offer relaxation, enjoyment and even adventure for people who find themselves with a little bit of money to spend on themselves, friends and work colleagues.

What happens in karaoke bars and *bia om* and what authorities are doing to control the rising incidence of social evils are increasingly reported throughout the media. While sex is often associated with karaoke, it must also be noted that for many people a night of karaoke 'is simply affordable entertainment' (Phuong Hoa 2000). One article which gives some insight into Vietnam's changing moral landscape appeared in the youth newspaper *Tuoi Tre*, titled 'Bia Oms are Just a Front' (Hoang Linh 1998).[10] *Bia hoi* and *bia om* are a growing industry, providing fun places for men to go. Unlike the opening story about Pha Ni's bar, an increasing number of restaurants and bars are allowing more than a cuddle in order to attract customers. In the past, *bia om* have been able to disguise prostitution but, with increased media coverage and greater efforts devoted towards controlling 'social evils', what goes on in *bia om* has become public knowledge. Although sex at a *bia om* is illegal and people do get caught, it is due to their growing popularity and competition that more sex takes place, even, as the article tells, 'with customers on the restaurant's tables'. In defence of these reports, the owners 'claimed that due to such stiff competition from many other *bia om* they had to turn to naughtiness and sex to attract customers (?!)' (Hoang Linh 1998: 5). No longer will the promise of just a cuddle attract a paying customer. Market forces are to blame, not only for introducing the spirit of competition but also for forcing young women into the sex industry.

The article is about two *bia om* in District 7 of Ho Chi Minh City: *Huong Lan* and *Huong Thao* restaurants. Both restaurants rely on sex to attract customers and a growing number of restaurants in other districts, most notably Binh Chanh District and Districts 5 and 6 have been 'upgraded' to simulate restaurants like Huong Lan and Huong Thao. In many ways it is a shocking article, reminding readers that sex at *bia om* is illegal, while also recounting the hardships faced by young women trapped in the industry. By drawing attention to the apparently increasing demand for *bia om*, the article fulfils its obligation in sounding alarm bells over the growing problem of 'social evils' in modern Vietnam. The article describes two *bia om*:

> Huong Lan Restaurant … is a large restaurant with hundreds of hostesses prepared to serve 'from start to finish'. The 'law' here is that after drinking half a slab [of beer] the customers can request the girls to striptease with prices at 50,000 dong for just a look before the girls put their clothes back on again; 100,000 for a feel and 200,000 for the girls to striptease and then sit down with the customer for the whole evening! The restaurant is designed like a battleground in order to avoid the attention of the police. Emergency exits are everywhere and some of the doors look like walls. When there is a raid the girls pick up their clothes and escape through the paddy fields and as a result, hooligans often give fake warnings of a police raid so they have a chance to see a free 'running striptease' …
>
> A nearby restaurant, Huong Thao … was even more reckless when the owner Le Thi Phuc, allowed the hostess and drinkers to go from A to Z right at the drinking tables. The restaurant was quite well organised. Waiters had the joint responsibility of standing guard, ushering customers into the restaurant and buying condoms if requested.
>
> (Hoang Linh 1998: 5)

With help from the accompanying cartoon (see Figure 7.3) and the lurid descriptions, such as the 'girls' providing a running striptease as they evade the authorities, the article flips between sensationalising the sex industry and the more serious tone of bringing these activities to the public's attention. The cornerstone of the government's social evils campaign consistently has been to stamp out prostitution and drug use. Articles such as this help not only to expose prostitution and the exploitation of young women but also to show the state regulating and controlling the moral conduct of its citizens by giving the names and addresses of restaurants, owners and managers who have been arrested for organising prostitution in their restaurants. As stated in the article:

> On 11 June 1998 investigators from the Ho Chi Minh City police caught five drinkers in the act of having sex with the hostesses right on the tables of this restaurant. On the same day, the police did a spot check on another unnamed restaurant … The owner, Nguyen Thi Dao, was arrested.
>
> (Hoang Linh 1998: 5)

Figure 7.3 Cartoon accompanying article by Hoang Linh (1988: 5)

The article reveals the commonly told, tragic story of innocent young 'girls' who have become victims due to limited choices. These women have been lured into the sex industry to become economically dependent upon the restaurant owners. As hostesses, they are not paid a wage and so are forced to rely on tips from customers.

> If they come late or leave early they will be fined 100,000 dong. Arguing will cost them a 50,000 dong fine and there is a 200,000 dong fine for going with customers outside of the restaurant's control … At Huong Lan Restaurant 70 to 80% of the hostesses were from far-flung provinces. Ms Tr. Th. P. told us that a woman from her village had suggested she come to Ho Chi Minh City to sell bia om. The pimp lent her 3 million dong to rent a house and buy a motorbike on credit. At first her life changed for the better, she was even able to buy a TV to send back to her home village. But after a while with compounding interest on the loan, the restaurant owner discovered the proposition of 'going with the customer'. If she agreed then the interest would be halved, if she didn't then her things would be repossessed and she would be thrown out, with the added 'present' of a few scars on her face. Ms. P. didn't have any way out.
>
> (Hoang Linh 1998: 5).

As is the case in many other countries under threat from HIV and AIDS, there is a homogenisation of identity implied in the aggregated statistics, studies and media reports conducted on sex workers in Vietnam. Due to the increased activities around HIV prevention, the female sex worker and her intimate activities are receiving more attention than ever before from experts across a range of disciplines. However, one-dimensional views tend to gloss over realities that are more complex. The male sex worker has still to receive attention from the expert in Vietnam.[11] Social research and the media construct the sex worker and other 'high risk groups' as what Porter (1997: 216) calls 'core transmitters' to the HIV epidemic. Prostitutes and drug users have become 'physically and socially discernible epicentres'. The realities have been forced to fit the model, whereby the subjectivities of sex workers are fixed through the variety of links made between 'poverty' and dominant representations of sex workers that promote the view of limited choices. Through articles such as that by Hoang Linh, discussed above, women remain at the epicentre of the HIV and AIDS threat along with drug users, women being easier to locate and to write about than the male customer. As Moodie (1997: 29) states, it is much easier to identify and test sex workers than clients, despite the fact that clients may be more likely to travel to other areas and spread the virus.

Conclusion

This chapter provides only a glimpse of Vietnam's growing sex industry, which, as Le Thi Quy notes, is all-pervasive. It is an industry that has grown at a unique time in Vietnam's history and, as the stories tell, it is a difficult industry to control. The state has depicted prostitution as one of the most serious 'social evils' which, the state believes, will provide the means for HIV to enter the 'general population'. However, there is no evidence of such a trend. While there have been attempts to promote faithful relationships as part of the government's and international development community's efforts at creating responsible subjects, the female sex worker rather than the client continues to be constructed as a threat to the social fabric of Vietnamese society. While social evil campaigns and the billboard messages are disseminated widely throughout Vietnam, instilling a consciousness of risk associated with a range of common practices, these very practices, which are outlawed, are at the same time being condoned by the state itself.

Notes

1 Nearly US$100.
2 All figures are from the Ministry of Health.
3 At this stage of the spread of HIV in Vietnam, intravenous drug users are the worst affected. According to official figures, intravenous drug users comprise 69 per cent of reported HIV infection. By the end of 1996, 6 per cent of all reported cases of HIV were labelled commercial sex workers (all figures are from the Ministry of Health). A 1998 paper by A. Chung, Vu Minh Quan and Timothy Dondero gives a detailed statistical account of the HIV epidemic until 1997.
4 Joint United Nations Programme on HIV/AIDS. Membership includes UNICEF, UNDP, UNFPA, UNDCP, ILO, UNESCO, WHO and the World Bank.
5 WHO, *STD/AIDS/HIV Surveillance Report*, July 1996, no. 7.
6 At times even HIV is labelled by the media as a social evil alongside prostitution and drug abuse.
7 'Enhancing the management of cultural activities and cultural services, increasing the elimination of serious social evils.'

8 *Bia om* literally means beer (*bia*) and a cuddle (*om*). There are variations on the *bia om* such as *karaoke om* and *café om*. *Bia om* officially do not exist in Vietnam. They are in fact *bia hoi* (see note 9); however individual bars are known as *bia om* because of the extra services they offer.

9 *Bia hoi* is a place where you can buy beer. Often they are bars that sell locally brewed cheap beer.

10 I would like to thank Lisa Drummond for bringing this article to my attention.

11 Save the Children Fund (UK) conducted a study in 1992, entitled *HIV/AIDS Programming with High Risk Behaviour Groups in Ho Chi Minh City*. This was the first and to date the only study addressing male sex workers in Vietnam.

Bibliography

Chung, A., Vu Minh Quan and Dondero, Timothy (1998) 'HIV Epidemiologic Situation in Vietnam: A Review of Available Data', *AIDS* 12(Suppl B): S43–S49.

Deutsche Presse-Agentur (1998) 'Vietnamese Government Officials Biggest Customer for Prostitutes', online. Available HTTP: *http://www.vinsight.org/1998news/0303.htm* [accessed 4 January 1998].

Franklin, Barbara (1993) *The Risk of AIDS in Vietnam: An Audience Analysis of Urban Men and Sexworkers with Guidelines for Prevention*, CARE International in Vietnam, Monograph no. 1

Hoang Linh (1998) '"Bia Om" lai bien tuong', *Tuoi Tre*, TPHCM, 11 August: 5.

Le Dien Hong (1992) 'HIV Infection and AIDS in Vietnam', paper presented at the *National Seminar on Social and Economic Implications of HIV/AIDS*, Hanoi, 3–4 December.

Le Thi Quy (1993) 'Some Ideas about Prostitution in Vietnam', paper presented at the conference, *Joining Forces to Further Shared Visions*, Washington, 20–24 October.

Mai Huong (1996) 'Te nan xa hoi co xoa duco khong?' (Is It Possible to Eliminate Social Evils), *Bao Suc Khoe* 3 (December).

Marr, David (1996) *Vietnamese Youth in the 1990s*, Working Paper Series, Australian-Vietnam Research Project, Canberra.

Moodie, R. (1997) 'The Situation Now and Possible Futures', in G. Linge and D. Porter (eds), *No Place for Borders: The HIV/AIDS Epidemic and Development in Asia and the Pacific*, St Leonards: Allen & Unwin, 24–40.

Nguyen Van (1996) 'Hugging a Beer Can Wreck a Marriage' *Vietnam News*, 23 July: 13.

Phuong Hoa (2000) 'Talk around Town', *Vietnam News*, 23 August.

Porter, Doug (1997) 'A Plague on the Borders: HIV, Development, and Travelling Identities in the Golden Triangle', in M. Manderson and M. Jolly (eds), *Sites of Desire/Economies of Pleasure: Sexualities in Asia and the Pacific*, Chicago: University of Chicago Press.

Vu Trong Thieu (1996) 'Strengthening Information, Education and Communication about AIDS Prevention for Youth', paper presented at conference on *The Threat of HIV/AIDS on Vietnam Youth: Meeting the Challenge of Prevention*, Hanoi.

WHO (1996) *STD/AIDS/HIV Surveillance Report*, July (7).

Part III

Vietnamese popular culture

Chapter 8

Pilgrims and pleasure-seekers

Alexander Soucy

On an early spring Sunday in the first month of the lunar new year (Tet) I went on a daytrip to a famous pagoda called Chua Thay with a group of young Vietnamese men and women from Hanoi. The pagoda was a popular destination for pilgrims at the beginning of Tet for a number of reasons. It was relatively close to Hanoi and could be reached by motorcycle in about an hour, making it appropriate for a day trip. The location of the pagoda, on a lake at the foot of a limestone mountain riddled with caves, added to its appeal as a destination for a picnic and a short walk. Its fame was also due to its history, the pagoda having been the residence of a renowned monk of the Ly dynasty. It was said also to be the location where water puppetry was invented, an art-form claimed to be uniquely Vietnamese. Chua Thay is considered to be an important example of traditional Vietnamese architecture, attested to by its inevitable inclusion in a number of coffee-table-style books about Vietnamese pagodas (for example, Ha Van Tan *et al.* 1993; Vo Van Tuong 1993, 1994; Vo Van Tuong and Huynh Nhu Phuong 1995).

When we reached the pagoda, the women promptly arranged the offerings of fruit onto a few of the plates that pagodas always supply for this purpose. The men of the group took a cursory look around the pagoda before settling down to smoke cigarettes and chat in the courtyard while the women went in and made offerings and wishes at the various altars in the pagoda complex. One of them prayed to get married, another wished for a son. By the time they made their rounds of all of the altars, enough time had passed for the offerings to be filled with the gods' and buddhas' blessings. The *loc*, the offerings infused with good luck from the gods or buddhas, were gathered up again and taken out to the men who were still smoking in the courtyard. The offerings were put back into the bags after some of the oranges were passed out and eaten immediately by the group. We then followed the stream of people up the mountain behind the pagoda and visited a few shrines and a large cave before finding a place to sit and have a picnic, consisting partly of the remainder of the offerings which had been transformed into 'lucky' food. After lunch, we went to visit Chua Tay Phuong, another famous pagoda nearby. At this pagoda a similar process took place. The young women made offerings of incense, while the men took a quick look around before sitting at a nearby drink-stand to order a pot of tea for the group. The men said that they did not want to go in and look as they had already been to this pagoda many times in the past.

Within this group, people had different reasons for visiting these particular pagodas. For the young women religion played a more central role in the desire to make such trips, and in this case, as in most, the trip was organised by the women. The men were invited partly for fun and partly for safety, but their motivation for going was entirely recreational. Even for the young women, entertainment was an important reason for embarking on the trip.

The tourist possibilities have not been lost on the local people who have taken free-market economics into their stride. There are entrance tickets for the pagoda, and entrance to the caves in the hills above the pagoda requires the purchase of another ticket. Flashlights can be obtained for a fee from boys who make money for their families from the tourists. Inside the biggest cave there is an altar at which people can pay for slips of paper that will tell them their fortune; always a popular activity amongst the Vietnamese who are ever-curious about what the future holds. In front of the pagoda, both inside and outside the entrance gate there are people selling souvenirs (either for themselves or for friends and family back in Hanoi). All these elements add to the entertainment value of the pagoda visit and contribute to the carnival-like atmosphere, to say nothing of the local economy. The character of the souvenirs is indicative of the dual religious/entertainment aspect of these visits. These souvenirs are usually described in religious terms as *loc*. *Loc* is considered to bring good luck to the person who possesses it and, when given to someone else, brings good luck both to the giver and receiver. As such, even the buying of souvenirs is fused with religious connotations.

Religion in Hanoi has seen a resurgence since the initiation of the 'renovation' (*doi moi*) period in the late 1980s. Pagoda (*chua*) and communal house (*dinh*) rituals are once again being performed as part of the religious lives of communities within the city (Malarney 1998: 7; Marr 1994: 15). Other officially prohibited religious activities such as shamanistic rituals (*len dong*) and seances (*goi hon*) have also become popular, although they are less prominent because of continued state disapproval. All of these rituals are attended mostly by people above the age of fifty, usually by women, and are mostly hidden behind closed doors. Young people have also come back to religious practice in a way that is a strikingly visible recognition of the importance they place on their tradition. However, the way that they approach it is an ambiguous mixture of entertainment and religion.

This chapter will deal with how young, urban men and women interact with religion, and thereby reify the value of Vietnamese 'tradition', but in ways that agree with the current articulation of the state. I will begin with a discussion of how religion plays a major part in the state's discourses of tradition, culture and nationalism. I will then look closer at quasi-pilgrimages undertaken by young Hanoians, paying special attention to the gender aspects of their practice.

Religion and the state: conflict and ambiguity

It is important to note when discussing religion in Vietnam, that there is a direct link with the state. Religion has played its part in both legitimising and reinforcing the state as well as in rebellion against it. For that reason, the state continues to monitor and tries to control religious activity. In turn, participation in religion is often imbued with political significance, whether intended or otherwise.

The renaissance of religious activity has not gone unnoticed by the Vietnamese press or the Vietnamese academy, whose views often reflect rather than influence the state.[1] In 1998 comments by the head of the Communist Party, Le Kha Phieu, regarding journalists made it clear what their expected role is: 'The citizen's duty requires the journalist to fight without compromise the dark plots and wrongful ideas of the hostile forces to protect the point of view of the party [and] policies and laws of the state' (Reuters 1998). Although there is no official censorship in Vietnam, journalists and editors who do not conform are punished (Reuters 1998).

In the discourse that surrounds religion, both scholarly works and the frequent reports in the press often distinguish between religion, as reflective of national culture, and superstition, which is regarded as a blight on the imagined Vietnamese tradition. Thus, 'they do not attack religious convictions directly, but rather condemn particular superstitions and religious practices, for example fortune-telling, faith-healing, monks seeking alms, bequests to churches or temples, and elaborate funeral ceremonies' (Marr 1986: 130). At a national conference held in Hanoi in March 1998, the Deputy Prime Minister gave a speech stating that, 'religious activities had contributed significantly to maintaining social stability', and that the government and the party 'always respect religious freedom, considering it a spiritual demand of the people and, at the same time, part of their democratic right'. However, in the same speech he made it clear that 'Outdated and harmful practices should be abolished' (*Vietnam News* 1997).

These words are echoed by Dang Nghiem Van, the director of the Institute for Religious Studies in the National Center for Social Sciences, and formerly the vice-director of the Institute of Ethnology, who wrote the following in his recent book, *Ethnological and Religious Problems in Vietnam*:

> Medium practitioners themselves confess that they have no need of educational qualification and that all they need is self-confidence and deceitfulness to make people believe in 'the teaching bestowed by the Saint'. All that is required for this business is prudence and craftiness. Soothsayers do not even need much 'capital'. What a pity! The credulous are numerous and do not even regret the money lost for this purpose; they are always telling themselves that they have to 'lose a penny to make a pound'. Fortune tellers are beginning to practice again, offering clients soothsaying services, practicing any form of divination wanted in deference to their clients' desires. This is a step backwards for both practitioners and clients.
>
> (Dang Nghiem Van 1998: 250–1)

This rhetoric is by no means new. Rather, the differentiation between religion and superstition is a continuation of Confucian discourses of the past.

The state's diatribes have been consistently against superstition in the latter half of the twentieth century, though they have changed in character. Pre-*doi moi*, the state's frequent focus was on 'superstitious' beliefs and practices as being reactionary or anti-revolutionary. For example, an article in the newspaper *Quan Doi Nhan Dan* (1983) stated: 'We must seek to thoroughly understand all the manifestations of superstition and devise measures to prevent the enemy from using them to their own advantage.' The way in which the press deals with superstition has since changed in character by typically combining mockery with an appeal to economics that stresses the material waste involved in these practices. Through the use of humour, the press highlights what it considers the absurdities of many practices, intending to show how superstition (as opposed to religion) is incompatible with Vietnam's drive towards modernity.

An example of this kind of mockery appeared in the newspaper *Lao Dong* in June 1997. The author relates an overheard conversation involving a young woman who wanted to have a petition to the gods (*so*) written for her and her American husband at Phu Tay Ho, one of the most popular shrines in Hanoi. The article plays on the mispronunciation of the husband's name, making the actors appear absurd. The story starts with the ritual specialist or scribe (*ong thay*) asking her husband's family name in order to write it on the petition:

> The young woman replied: 'Americans don't have surnames!' The scribe asked again: 'What's his name then?' The reply: 'Tron! (John)' [the Vietnamese pronunciation of 'John' and 'Tron' – meaning 'asshole' – are roughly the same]. The scribe listened, but didn't know what to do because he didn't know English, and in the depth of his stomach he thought that 'tron' meant 'dit' [asshole] – how Americans could have a name as ugly as that, he had no idea … If he wrote a petition with such a lack of respect, he was afraid that he would get in trouble with the gods, so he said to the woman: 'Perhaps I should write the name indirectly, OK?' The woman was really scared: 'Oh no, I gave you the name, why don't you write it? How will the gods know who it is? Why do you have to write it indirectly?' The scribe explained: 'If you offer up a petition to the gods with the name "asshole" [dit] on it, it isn't respectful!' The woman furiously shouted at him: 'That's stupid! Why would you write "asshole" [dit] on it?' The scribe angrily said: 'Because how are "dit" ['asshole'] and "tron" [also "asshole"] different?'
>
> (Nguyen Ha 1997; translation mine)

The incident ended with the woman refusing to pay him, leading to a noisy yelling match. The overall tenor of the story was comical, but the underlying message was that 'superstitious' practices are irrational and have no place in modern society; that they are ridiculous and backward. Thus, while the government has loosened some control over religious practice, and the line taken by the media is no longer as blunt, it has been replaced by a more subtle form of repression. This repression is aimed at practices which are considered embarrassingly backward by those who strive for 'modernity'. While desire for political control and a perceived need to rid Vietnam of 'backward' practices in order to modernise are strong forces, there is conflict with this impetus within the government and amongst individuals. This opposition arises out of the iconographic centrality which religion holds for Vietnamese nationalism.

Since the beginning of the twentieth century, a discourse has focused on 'tradition' and 'modernity'. The advent of *doi moi* has given 'modernity' a meaning synonymous with development and prosperity. However, in the minds of many Vietnamese politicians (as well as a significant segment of the population), the negative aspects of this modernisation process are associated with foreign (that is, Western) corrupting influences, termed 'social evils' in state parlance. Pornography, drugs and prostitution are the more prominently cited examples of this, but smuggling, AIDS, homosexuality and selfish materialism are all negatively attributed to modernisation and contact with the West. The frequent reaction of some officials has been a call to pull back from the open door policy, which has been perceived as allowing the influx of such evil influences. At the same time, there has been an appeal to Vietnamese traditional culture, believed to hold the power to stave off further encroachment from these 'evils'. This searching of the past has been attributed by Fahey to 'the demise of the communist moral code' (1998: 233), but is probably better understood as an assertion of nationalism meant to counter-balance influences from the West. This tactic is felt to be necessary due to the impossibility of closing the door to the outside world.

Religion often stands in the centre of this imagined tradition. So, despite the Party's routine reaffirmation of its 'commitment to materialism and its rejection of religious explanations of reality' (Marr 1987: 2), the state and Vietnamese scholars continue to recognise certain religious traditions as being foundational to their conception of Vietnamese culture and national identity.[2] Thus, Mac Duong, then Director of the Institute of Social Sciences, wrote:

> We must therefore wipe out unscientific prejudices on religions, overcoming one-sided, dogmatic views. Under socialism, religions have a bright future which can satisfy religious believers in their private lives and religious believers will become an active force for the building of socialism.
>
> (1993: 20)

More recently, the Deputy Prime Minister is reported to have stated that 'religious activities had contributed significantly to maintaining social stability in many areas' (*Vietnam News* 1998).

This conception of Vietnamese traditional culture is implicated in a nationalistic discourse that usually measures itself against China as the cultural 'Other' (Evans 1985: 127). Thus, claims are made in order to assert a distinction from China; for example, 'The numerous artefacts and linguistic vestiges witness that the autochthon inhabitants, the Viet [the ethnic group forming the majority of Vietnam's present-day population, comprised of fifty-three other nationalities] have had their own cosmology long before they were influenced by ancient Chinese and Indian cultures' (Thanh Huyen 1996: 5).

The construction of a monolithic tradition by Vietnamese academics is central to much contemporary social science work undertaken in Vietnam today. This was evident at the International Conference on Vietnamese Studies held in Hanoi in June 1998, about which Charles Keyes writes:

> The official scholarly establishment['s] … presentations together offered a view of Vietnamese history that has a single story, one that traces Vietnamese identity to a prehistoric culture and sees Vietnamese-ness as having persisted in essentially its original form despite the diversity of peoples living within the boundaries of Vietnam and despite foreign domination.
>
> (Keyes 1998: 6)

Examples of papers at that conference which expressed this are too numerous to mention, but some indicative paper titles were: 'Vietnamese Traditional Values – Endogenous Potential' (Nguyen Van Huyen 1998) and 'Vietnam's National Culture: Its Identity and Integration' (Thanh Duy A 1998).

Although not originating in Vietnam, Buddhism is often claimed to have reached Vietnam before China, despite the lack of evidence for this claim, and despite the dominant Buddhist tradition in Vietnam being undoubtedly of Chinese origin (for example, Minh Chi *et al.* 1993: 12; Nguyen Tai Thu 1992: 4). This view, regardless of its validity, is a valuable indicator of how Vietnamese tradition is constructed in relation to the Chinese 'Other', and in this case linked to religion. Pagodas, temples and community houses seem to become the principal material culture of Vietnamese tradition, their status reified by the conferment on many such structures of the title of *Di Tich Lich Su Van Hoa* (historical and cultural relic) by the Ministry of Culture.

In sum, there is a discourse against religion which stems from communist theories of religion, but which partly draws from Confucian discourses targeting competing belief systems and threatening ideologies as 'superstition'. However, there is a separate discourse which often contradicts the communist position: that religion is central to Vietnamese tradition and national identity. Religious practice has therefore lost many of the negative implications that it held prior to the Renovation period. The recognition of the value of, if not participation in, Vietnamese religion is an assertion of a distinct and strong national identity, and has come to symbolise values that are perceived to be under threat from foreign influence. We will assess below whether these concerns and reactions by the state are truly justified. But first we will consider how these pilgrimages impact upon the participants on a more personal level, for structures of gender play a role in the individual performance of these activities as much as political forces influence their social context.

Gendered institutions, gendered views

Generally women engage in religious practice, whereas men tend to dismiss publicly all religious activity as 'superstition'. The scepticism shown by young men parallels the portrayal of religion by the state, the media and the academy, all of which are male-dominated institutions and largely reflect a male world-view. Though one could attribute the state's negative attitude towards religion to Marxist or even Confucian influences, they are also attitudes that could be said to have a gender bias, inherent in the structures of Vietnam, that in some ways supersede these ideological imperatives. An illustration of how gender structures influence views and expectations on religion could be seen at the beginning of the twentieth century, when Vietnamese society was struggling to modernise itself. At this time, women were especially targeted by reformers because 'women were considered more prone to superstition than men' (Marr 1981: 345).

The way in which gender and belief are linked together make most men reluctant to take part in religious activities that may be perceived as superstitious (and therefore feminine). This could be seen in the way the young men waited in the courtyard rather than entering the pagoda and making offerings along with the women. Many of my informants, male and female, thought that religious activity indicated weakness and an inability to be self-reliant. The centrality of sexual desirability in structuring gender relations is particularly important for understanding attitudes towards religion.[3] Seeking supernatural help by making wishes at pagodas and temples is thought to indicate weakness and an inability to take care of one's own problems. Men who do this are therefore usually considered effeminate and unattractive. However, weakness and dependence are seen as sexually attractive in women, making religious practice by women 'sexy', albeit a tacit assertion of women's ultimate inferiority. Men strive to appear to be stronger than women, and this is a quality that women commonly seek in their prospective partners. These desires are significant in the production of hegemonic ideals that are important determinants in people's on-going gender projects, and play a significant role in the variant ways in which women and men approach religion. As a result, young men typically ridicule religious practice, whereas women tend to be religiously active.

Tradition, play and pilgrimage

In anthropological discourse, 'traditional culture' is recognised as being negotiated and constructed in a process.[4] Hanson writes: 'Tradition is now understood quite literally to be an invention designed to serve contemporary purposes' (1989: 890). In Vietnam as in other places, the use of the concept of 'tradition' is intrinsic to the production of national identity.

This constructed national identity in the form of tradition is seen as being compromised by young people, who are believed to be the most vulnerable to foreign influence. Of this, Marr writes:

> Angst about what it means to be Vietnamese goes back a long way, reflecting the love–hate relationship with China, the multitude of other influences from Southeast Asia and the West, and yet the deep felt need to be unique and to stand proud amidst all the cultures of the region, if not the world … However, amidst recent economic and social transformations, to include renewed widespread exposure to foreign culture, anxiety levels are rising, people ask once again if compatriots are 'losing roots' (*mat goc*), and even Party members loyal to the reform strategy sometimes wonder if Vietnam is losing its soul to Coca Cola, Madonna, and Hollywood.
>
> (Marr 1997: 339)

Youth, especially in urban areas, are in the spotlight when the state expresses concern about social evils, foreign influence and losing Vietnamese cultural roots. However, this concern over youth is unfounded. Vietnamese youth continue to take part in 'traditional' Vietnamese activities, and have a strong sense of their national and cultural identity. Furthermore, while the purpose of quasi-pilgrimages is often expressed in terms of entertainment, they are also part of a process by which culture, religion and tradition are negotiated. By their choice of destination they reaffirm that these religious sites are culturally significant and valuable. They discuss and internalise the importance of these places, remembering what they have learned about different locations within the sites, and their relevance to Vietnamese tradition and history.

Vietnamese religion is often idealised as the quintessential symbol of tradition. In this context, atheism is seen not so much as an acceptance of Marxist ideology (something positive) as a turning away from Vietnamese tradition and culture and an acceptance of Western values (something negative). For example, an illustration in the *Vietnam Investment Review* depicts a young woman praying, with the caption 'Today's youth have an eye on the past and a hand out towards the future' (Ngoc Anh 1995: 56). The accompanying story, 'Misguided, Selfish or Obedient? Who Are Today's Youth?' does not mention religion, but deals with attitudes of young people using the trope of modern versus traditional.

There are two kinds of religious practice in which young Hanoians typically participate.[5] The first is making offerings at pagodas or temples, especially on the first and fifteenth of every lunar month. In its most basic form, this practice consists of placing incense (*thap huong*) at the various altars of the pagoda or temple and making wishes. The wishes are usually directed towards desires such as general welfare for the family, passing exams, finding a marriage partner, having a child (hopefully a son), or succeeding in business. In a more complex form, additional offerings of fruit, flowers, *oan* (cones made of pressed sweet bean powder wrapped in coloured cellophane), immolative paper money and real money are made. The food items and the real money are then taken back; the money is saved and the food distributed to family and friends as edible charms which will bring good luck to those who consume them. The practice of distributing the offerings after they are taken back (after they have been transformed into *loc*) is usually performed only by women, which reflects their perceived roles as the caregivers of the family. If men go to pagodas to pray, they do not usually make offerings of anything other than incense.

Many of the pilgrimage sites have become more important recently for their perceived capacity to fulfil the wishes of devotees. It is partly in this capacity that places such as Den Ba Chua Kho, Chua Huong and Phu Tay Ho have become popular and are visited by crushing numbers of people in the first lunar month. The reasons people attend are more closely bound to religious practice than at other locations. These places are known to be particularly efficacious in fulfilling wishes for economic success or male progeny (Fahey 1998: 233). Making offerings at Den Ba Chua Kho, for example, is believed to bring success in business, and Chua Huong is known for bringing wealth and for curing barren women.

The second form of religious practice undertaken by Hanoian youths is the performance of quasi-pilgrimages during the first month of the lunar year (Tet), as described above, and to a lesser extent at the end of the lunar year. These pilgrimages are in some way related to those performed by more devout older women. Buses with flags tied to the front, usually filled with old women, can be seen in huge numbers in the first month, and have become increasingly popular in recent years (*Vietnam News* 1997: 4; Le Thi 1998: 78). Usually a bus is hired for the group, who travel to a number of religious sites in the Hanoi region. Prayers and offerings are thought to be more efficacious in the first month of the lunar new year than at any other time, which is reflected in the saying 'Praying all year does not equal praying on the fifteenth day of the first lunar month.'

While related in some ways, the excursions of young people are qualitatively different in character from the pilgrimages of older women. Young people's pilgrimages synthesise religious practice, entertainment in the form of sight-seeing and picnicking, and the communitas of embarking on a trip with a group of friends.

Trips are made to religious sites that are also scenic and of historical importance. Participants usually describe the goal of these day-trips as entertainment or *di choi*. That is not to say that the pilgrimages undertaken by the more devout are dour affairs. I took part in one pilgrimage with a monk, a nun and a number of devotees from the monk's pagoda. We visited a temple dedicated to Tran Hung Dao (Den Kiep Bac) and then climbed Yen Tu mountain – the tallest and one of the most famous pilgrim destinations in northern Vietnam. On the second day, we made offerings at a couple of other temples and then went on a boat trip around Halong Bay, purely for entertainment. On another pilgrimage tour with a group of old women, we stopped by a number of famous pagodas in Hanoi and then went to visit the Ho Chi Minh Mausoleum, his stilt house and the Ho Chi Minh Museum. Though 'pilgrimage' can be defined as 'any journey to a sacred place to perform some religious act' (Nanquin and Chun 1992: 3), such a definition does not accommodate the *jouissance* that is an intrinsic part of these pilgrimages. The difference between the pilgrimages of the truly devout and the quasi-pilgrimage made by the youths of Hanoi is in degree rather than type. There is certainly a religious element, particularly for the young women, but the element of entertainment figures much more prominently in the quasi-pilgrimages of youth.

While the purpose of their trips – entertainment or religion – is often ambiguous, the affirmation of the value of Vietnamese 'tradition' is not. Through their visits, youths participate in these symbols of Vietnamese-ness and, through that interaction, they actively affirm that certain architectural and artistic objects as well as locations are essential to Vietnamese culture. Youth plays an active role in the construction and perpetuation of these sites as symbols of Vietnamese tradition. When they discuss 'tradition' with foreign anthropologists, for instance, it is these architectural relics that are presented as visual examples of Vietnamese culture, along with other symbolic manifestations (for example, the Vietnamese family, Tet and Buddhism). In this way, urban Vietnamese youth take an active part in the re-creation of Vietnamese tradition.

Conclusion

Since the beginning of the Renovation period, there has been a bipolar attitude towards religion by the state, the academy and the press. On the one hand, religion is still addressed through Marxist/Confucian tropes of superstition, and seen as something which retards the progress of the country. On the other hand, religion is not entirely dismissed, because it is a cornerstone in the state's construction of nationalism. Its appeal to Vietnamese tradition is a way of combating the perceived threat that foreign influence represents to Vietnamese society. This contradiction is solved in part by the state's distinction between religion and superstition: the representation of 'religion' becomes sterilised and wiped clean of the polluting aspects that conflict with their construction of modernity. 'Superstitious' practices are denigrated as being feudal and backward; antithetical to the development and modernisation of Vietnam. This view of religion is part of a heavily gendered discourse that attributes superstition to women and influences the social practice of both men and women. The state is not the progenitor of this discourse, but has merely carried on earlier attitudes that remain within Vietnamese society.

Vietnamese youth are implicated in the debate about tradition because they are seen as the group most susceptible to the polluting influences of the West. They are the focus of a debate about Vietnamese tradition, and how one should behave in order to be both modern while at the same time retaining essential Vietnamese-ness. Youth in Hanoi have not turned their backs on Vietnamese tradition. They recognise certain elements as being essentially Vietnamese, and ratify them through their speech and their actions, as seen in their quasi-pilgrimages. They are not, therefore, simply receivers of the state's version of tradition, but are active in the process of its creation.

The quasi-pilgrimages made by urban youth from Hanoi, especially during the first month of the lunar year, provide a glimpse of the complicated role that religion plays in Vietnam today. Religion is heavily politicised and its practice holds ambiguous meanings concerning modernity, tradition and national identity. Gender structures play a large role in the way that religion is both viewed and practised. Because religious practices, such as pilgrimages, hold so many conflicting meanings, people often define their practices ambiguously. To some, visiting sacred sites has spiritual meaning, while others see their visit as entertainment. For all people, young and old, however, these pilgrimages out of the city every lunar new year are important events that reinforce their identity as Vietnamese.

Notes

1 For examples of recent Vietnamese scholars, see Dang Nghiem Van (1998: 232–3), Khanh Duyen (1994: 3), Nguyen Duy Hinh (1996: 5) and Nguyen Minh San (1994: 155).
2 For example: Tran Nho Thin (1991: 7), Nguyen The Long and Pham Mai Hung (1997: 5), Tran Lam Bien (1996: 5), Tran Hong Lien (1995: 5), Vo Van Tuong (1994: 15) and Ha Van Tan *et al.* (1993: 146).
3 Connell (1995: 74–5) calls this structure 'cathexis', and sees it as one of three important structures in the formation of gender, the other two being labour and power.
4 For examples of this literature, see Hobsbawm and Ranger (1983), Handler and Linnekin (1984), Hanson (1989), Anderson (1991) and Linnekin (1992), and for a review of the effects of this debate, see Briggs (1996).
5 By 'religious practice', I am not referring specifically to religious ritual, whether communal or individual in nature. Rather, I include all interaction with religious symbolism. Therefore, while strictly ritual activities would be included, so would such activities as reading books about Buddhism or visiting pagodas.

Bibliography

Anderson, Benedict (1991) [1983] *Imagined Communities: Reflections on the Origin and Spread of Nationalism*, revised edn, London: Verso.

Briggs, Charles L. (1996) 'The Politics of Discursive Authority in Research on the "Invention of Tradition"', *Cultural Anthropology*, 11(4): 435–69.

Connell, Robert (1995) *Masculinities: Knowledge, Power and Social Change*, Berkeley: University of California Press.

Dang Nghiem Van (1998) *Ethnological and Religious Problems in Vietnam*, Hanoi: Social Sciences Publishing House.

Evans, Grant (1985) 'Vietnamese Communist Anthropology', *Canberra Anthropology*, 3(1&2): 116–47.

Fahey, Stephanie (1998) 'Vietnam's Women in the Renovation Era', in Krishna Sen and Maila Stivens (eds), *Gender and Power in Affluent Asia*, London: Routledge, 222–49.

Ha Van Tan, Nguyen Va Ku and Pham Ngo Long (1993) *Chua Viet Nam – Buddhist Temples in Vietnam*, Hanoi: Social Sciences Publishing House.

Handler, Richard and Linnekin, Jocelyn (1984) 'Tradition, Genuine or Spurious', *Journal of American Folklore*, 97: 273–90.

Hanson, Alan (1989) 'The Making of the Maori: Cultural Invention and Its Logic', *American Anthropologist*, 91: 890–902.

Hobsbawm, Eric and Ranger, Terence (1983) *The Invention of Tradition*, Cambridge: Cambridge University Press.

Keyes, Charles (1998) 'The First International Vietnamese Studies Conference, Perspective #1: Scholarship as Politics', *SEASPAN*, Autumn, 12(1): 6–7.

Khanh Duyen (1994) *Tin nguong Ba Chua Kho* (Religious Beliefs of Ba Chua Kho), Ha Bac: So Van hoa Thong tin va The thao Ha Bac.

Le Thi (1998) 'Aged Women in the Vietnamese Family and Society, I. Position and Role of Aged Women', *Vietnamese Studies*, 128(2): 78–82.

Linnekin, Jocelyn (1992) 'On the Theory and Politics of Cultural Construction in the Pacific', *Oceania*, 62: 249–63.

Mac Duong (1993) 'Religion in Its Relation to the Development of Society', *Vietnam Social Sciences*, 2(36): 17–20.

Malarney, Shaun K. (1998) 'The Role of Women in the Reconstruction of Communal House Rites in the Outskirts of Hanoi', unpublished paper presented at the International Conference on Vietnamese Studies, Hanoi, 15–17 June.

Marr, David G. (1981) *Vietnamese Tradition on Trial, 1920–1945*, Berkeley: University of California Press.

—— (1986) 'Religion in Contemporary Vietnam', in R.F. Miller and T.H. Rigby (eds), *Religion and Politics in Communist States*, occasional paper no. 19. Canberra, Department of Political Science, Research School of Social Sciences, Australian National University, 123–33.

—— (1987) 'Church and State in Vietnam', *Indochina Issues*, 74(April): 1–4.

—— (1994) 'Religion and Money', *Vietnam Today*, 67(February–May): 14–15.

—— (1997) 'Vietnamese Youth in the 1990s', *The Vietnam Review*, Spring–Summer(2): 288–354.

Minh Chi, Ha Van Tan and Nguyen Tai Thu (1993) *Buddhism in Vietnam – From Its Origins to the 19th Century*, Hanoi: The Gioi Publishers.

Nanquin, Susan and Chun-fang Yu (1992) 'Pilgrimage in China', in Susan Nanquin and Chun-fang Yu (eds), *Pilgrims and Sacred Sites in China*, Taipei: SMC Publishers, 1–38.

Ngoc Anh (1995) 'Misguided, Selfish or Obedient? Who Are Today's Youth?' *Vietnam Investment Review*, January 16–22(170–1): 56.

Nguyen Duy Hinh (1996) *Tin nguong thanh hoang Viet Nam* (Religious Beliefs of Tutelary Gods in Vietnam), Ha Noi: Nha xuat ban Khoa hoc Xa hoi.

Nguyen Ha (1997) 'Thanh than ky su' (The Gods' Memoirs), *Lao Dong*, 7 June.

Nguyen Minh San (1994) *Tiep can tin nguong dan da Viet Nam (The Contiguous Beliefs of the Vietnamese People)*, Ha Noi: Nha xuat ban Van hoa Dan toc.

Nguyen Tai Thu (1992) *History of Buddhism in Vietnam*, Hanoi: Social Sciences Publishing House.

Nguyen The Long and Pham Mai Hung (1997) *Chua Ha Noi* (Pagodas of Hanoi), Ha Noi: Nha xuat ban Van hoa Thong tin.

Nguyen Van Huyen (1998) 'Vietnamese Traditional Values – Endogenous Potential', unpublished paper presented at the International Conference on Vietnamese Studies, *Vietnam's National Culture: Its Identity and Integration*, Hanoi, 1–17 July.

Quan Doi Nhan Dan (The People's Army newspaper) (1983) 'Need to Curb Superstition', 30 January: 2.

Reuters (1998) 'Vietnam Party Leader Warns Press to Toe the Line', 28 November.

Thanh Duy A. (1998) 'Vietnam's National Culture: Its Identity and Integration', unpublished paper presented at the International Conference on Vietnamese Studies, *Vietnam's National Culture: Its Identity and Integration*, Hanoi, 1–17 July.

Thanh Huyen (1996) 'An Overview of Beliefs and Religions in Vietnam', *Vietnamese Studies*, 121(3): 5–22.

Tran Hong Lien (1995) *Dao Phat trong cong dong nguoi Viet o Nam Bo – Viet Nam tu the ky XVII den 1975* (Buddhism Common to the Vietnamese in the Southern Region of Vietnam from the Seventeenth Century to 1975), Ha Noi: Nha xuat ban Khoa hoc Xa hoi.

Tran Lam Bien (1996) *Chua Viet Nam* (Vietnamese Pagodas), Ha Noi: Nha xuat ban Van hoa Thong tin.

Tran Nho Thin (1991) *Vao chua tham Phat* (Enter the Pagoda and Visit the Buddhas), Ha Noi: Nha xuat ban Cong an Nhan dan.

Vietnam News (1997) 'Religion Helps Beat Social Evils', 19 March, n.p.

—— (1998) 17 September: 4.

Vo Van Tuong (1993) *Viet Nam danh lam co tu* (Vietnam's Famous Ancient Pagodas), Ha Noi: Nha xuat ban Khoa hoc Xa hoi.

—— (1994) *Nhung ngoi chua noi tieng Viet Nam* (Vietnam's Famous Pagodas), Ha Noi: Nha xuat ban Van hoa Thong tin.

Vo Van Tuong and Huynh Nhu Phuong (1995) *Danh Lam Nuoc Viet Nam* (Vietnam's Famous Pagodas), Ho Chi Minh City: Nha xuat ban My thuat.

Chapter 9

Digesting reform

Opera and cultural identity in Ho Chi Minh City[1]

Philip Taylor

A defining moment

> *Cai luong* is famous for its capacity to digest the new, however in the contemporary situation it looks as if it is about to choke to death.
>
> (*Cai luong* opera enthusiast)

Writing as a critic for a Ho Chi Minh City newspaper, this *Cai luong* fan avidly followed developments in the Vietnamese musical theatre scene throughout the post-war era. However, by the mid-1990s when I spoke with him, his passion for the local opera form had considerably dimmed. When the economic reforms began in the mid-1980s, he said, '*Cai luong* met its nemesis with a flood of foreign films, videos and music coming through the open door'. He described the genre's plight as 'gasping for breath', in its struggle to compete for audiences' attention with these 'cheap and exciting' new imports. Pushed to the wall, he lamented, '*Cai luong* productions have increasingly resorted to cheap stunts, weird, inappropriate borrowings and spectacular fighting scenes.' Audience numbers were dwindling due to the genre's slide into the 'crude and melodramatic', not to mention the relatively high price of tickets compared with other forms of entertainment.

Cai luong, or 'reformed opera', is a variety of musical theatre originating in southern Vietnam in the early twentieth century. According to the musicologist Tran Van Khe the origins of *Cai luong* are in the largely rural Mekong delta (Tran Van Khe 2000b). The form's roots are said to be with the amateur musicians who combined spoken declamation and gestures with musical accompaniment. As it developed, *Cai luong* drew upon tales, musical influencesand performance styles from the court and from different regions of the country, and it borrowed music, instruments, themes, plots, forms and fashions from Chinese, French and other foreign sources. The opera form took off in the hands of impresarios based in urban centres drawing on diverse influences, from vaudeville to circuses, and introducing many innovations in terms of content, form and technology. Open to many sources, rapidly changing its appearance and its scope, and interpreted quite variously in different eras and places, *Cai luong*'s identity as an artistic form is remarkably hard to pin down (Dinh Quang *et al.* 1999). The genre courted controversy from the outset about its moral value vs entertainment quality, unacceptable mixings of disparate influences, degree of foreign-ness, class status and political tendency, and its dubious sponsorship by a succession of states, both colonial and post-colonial. Despite this, *Cai luong* became one of the major cultural and artistic movements in the urban areas of southern Vietnam in the twentieth century and its following and influence spread elsewhere in the nation and overseas.

Ho Chi Minh City has been one of the main sites of development for *Cai luong*: home to a substantial following and many important troupes, artists, impresarios, theatres and recording venues, and also serving as a centre for training and researching the form. In the 1990s, Ho Chi Minh City was itself undergoing immense social and cultural changes. As Vietnam's economic capital, Ho Chi Minh City led the rest of the country in terms of economic growth, foreign investment, industrialisation and commercial consumption. The influx of foreign investors and commodities was matched by an equally significant inflow of new ideas, cultural forms and technologies, and an increase in human movements, including visits by international and domestic tourists, return visits by overseas Vietnamese, migration from other parts of the country and the upward mobility of the city's large middle class. The dislocations entailed in these processes provoked heated discussion about the cultural consequences of the liberal reforms. Concerns about the impact of these changes on the *Cai luong* opera, which form the focus of this chapter, illustrate the kind of cultural anxieties found in Vietnam's cities in the 1990s. Yet, as reactions to the status of *Cai luong* were far from unanimous, debates about the form provide insight into the complex experience of life in Vietnam's cities and the different notions residents of Ho Chi Minh City have of the identity of their urban home.

The 'open door' as cultural crisis

At the time that the economic benefits of Vietnam's 'open door' (*mo cua*) policy were just becoming noticeable, in the early 1990s, this reform began to be linked to a perceived crisis in the country's cultural and artistic traditions. Among the adverse effects identified by concerned commentators of opening the nation's doors to the non-socialist world were a '*cult* of exotic taste', the dizzying pace of borrowing, the resurgence of a cultural inferiority complex (*mac cam van hoa*) (Nguyen Sinh Huy 1996: 86) and the emergence of consumerism (Dang Canh Khanh 1996: 71). According to a 1990 report in the Ho Chi Minh City newspaper *Saigon Giai Phong* to gain audience attention, 'quite a few artistic groups had to discard song and dance numbers full of folkloric and ethnic values and replace them with "new and exciting" ones' (*Saigon Giai Phong* 1990: 2). The report warned that traditional, folk, cultural (*van hoa gian dan*) and ethnic minority (*dan toc thieu so*) performances were facing 'a great and alarming danger of becoming hybridised or lost' (*Saigon Giai Phong* 1990: 2).[2] The influx of foreign music was blamed for undermining the local music scene, which many considered derivative. Economic liberalisation forced culture houses and artists to adjust their activities from high-minded social reform to an increasingly lower common denominator and incorporate the flood of cheap and profitable cultural imports. Stripped of subsidies and forced to operate as commercial ventures, theatres, musicians and artists lost their capacity to provide social commentary and forge new paths. Meanwhile critics linked the crisis in the nation's arts to insufficient controls on the flood of 'depraved cultural products' (*van pham doi truy*)[3] entering the country through its newly opened doors. Ho Chi Minh City, the bridgehead of foreign trade and investment in Vietnam, represented the epicentre of this crisis in the nation's traditional culture.

Tran Van Khe was speaking for many when he expressed the fear that foreign music, new fashions and technology would cause the folk arts to fade out and lose their appeal to subsequent generations (Tran Van Khe 2000a: 25). In particular, *Cai luong*, formerly a live, staged genre, was defenceless against new technologies such as video, tapes, cassettes, CDs and karaoke laser discs which satisfied the demands of the huge youth market and provided cheap access to high-quality productions from the United States, Hong Kong and Japan. Theatres were suffering in competition with videos – the price of a theatre ticket was many times the rental cost of a video and people commented on the added insecurity and inconvenience of going out to watch a film compared with staying at home. In consequence, performance companies were forced to rush through rehearsals in order to cut costs and to play for increasingly short seasons to fill theatres.

Many of the *Cai luong* performers, scriptwriters, choreographers and followers with whom I spoke in the 1990s labelled the genre 'repetitive and boring', 'catering to the lowest denominator' or 'bereft of artistic value' (*thieu gia tri my thuat*). The number of *Cai luong* troupes was said to have shrunk from around fifty in the late 1970s to five or ten in the whole south in the 1990s. Rehearsal times had dwindled, and performance companies lost their *esprit de corps*, with a handful of stars flitting from troupe to troupe. According to one disaffected *Cai luong* buff: 'The only thing keeping the industry alive is the cult of a few *Cai luong* superstars. Now it seems their personal lives are the only magnet still attracting audiences. People talk more about their affairs and holidays than their skill at performing.'

Although they were caught up in and benefited from the commercialisation of the urban cultural field, it was nevertheless not rare to hear those who worked in the arts in Ho Chi Minh City criticise the lack of intellectual substance, morality or aesthetic value of the chaotic field of production in which they were involved. However, they also expressed powerlessness to change their predicament, considering it an evil of life in a completely commercialised world. Some told me they felt helpless in the grip of a cultural crisis, facing a possibly fatal 'assault' on Vietnam's culture and traditional morality caused by 'opening the door' to the world. These concerns linked Vietnam's urban residents with those of China, the former Soviet Union and Eastern Europe, where a reduction in state support for cultural institutions and artistic forms has been relentless. Defensive measures such as conferences, competitions and consultations were implemented to identify and resolve the problem of *Cai luong*'s perceived decline but few considered that these actions had been successful at reversing its fortunes.[4]

Déjà vu

Not all the residents of Ho Chi Minh City viewed the incursions of capitalism and the opening up of the cultural world in such bleak terms. Many young people welcomed the arrival of foreign investors, discotheques and video culture with enthusiasm. Evidence of southern Vietnam's earlier brushes with capitalist culture, many of their parents greeted the return of foreign investors and tourists by polishing up English-language skills acquired while working for the Americans in the 1955–75 Republican (RVN) era and metamorphosed from down-at-heel accountants or *cyclo* drivers into professional English teachers. In the 1990s, Ho Chi Minh City was being described as the locomotive pulling the rest of the country into reform. Some residents, filled with hubris, believed that their irrepressibly free-wheeling city had ultimately triumphed over the socialist structures imported by its northern 'liberators', in an economic sequel to the Vietnam War. According to them, the market economy was an arena in which Saigonese had traditionally excelled, outperforming other Southeast Asian cities, until their advance had been rudely interrupted in 1975 by the city's take-over by unpolished peasant-soldiers and mandarin-cadres posted from Hanoi.

Among those residents who held the view that Ho Chi Minh City was experiencing a return to a more cosmopolitan identity, *Cai luong* itself was sometimes viewed as a relic of a rural past which urban Vietnam had long left behind. Viewed as nostalgic, out-of-touch or unrealistic, the operatic form was on occasion described to me as a pursuit for uneducated people, old women and country bumpkins, an outmoded morality genre at odds with the actively changing state of society, and it was for this reason that it was losing its mass appeal. Indicative of this loss in standing, the term '*Cai luong*' has become a descriptor connoting affectation, melodrama, impracticality and over-reaction. Alternatively, it signifies an inappropriate combination of elements. For instance, a representative of the nouveau riche might tastelessly mix their clothes in a '*Cai luong*' fashion.

However, others pointed out to me that even in the cosmopolitan environment of pre-1975 Saigon, to which many urbanites look back with nostalgia and pride, *Cai luong* had had a substantial following. Some long-time city residents recalled that pre-1975 *Cai luong* had been so good that it could make people cry. In this 'golden age' (*thoi vang*), the form had been highly inclusive, with a more equal distribution of males and females, educated and illiterate, and rural and urban people in attendance at performances. Many people looked back to the 1955–75 period as a time of unprecedented richness and development in other forms of music as well. Simultaneous innovations in fashion, education, eating habits, literature and the arts had occurred during the Republican regime that represented alternative expressions of Vietnamese culture to those unfolding in the Democratic Republic of Vietnam, the northern half of the then-divided nation. Some locals suggested that their city's intense encounter with the United States at this time had helped to foster among southerners a more flexible and discriminating cultural orientation. Not a few considered themselves consequently more at home with foreign influences than the residents of Hanoi. As one Ho Chi Minh City journalist who held this view told me: 'Southerners know how to tell good ideas from garbage due to twenty years of experience dealing with the Americans. Northerners risk losing their traditions or committing the worst kind of aesthetic gaffes due to inexperience, as they have been closed for so long.'[5]

The earliest academic studies of *Cai luong*, penned during the Republican era, located the emergence of this reformed genre of opera in the context of fundamental, colonial-era breaks with traditional Vietnamese culture (Hauch 1972: 20). *Cai luong*'s historical emergence in a capitalist and urbanist environment has led some to consider the form more at home with renovation and social change than the older theatrical genres of *Hat boi* and *Cheo* (Dinh Quang *et al.* 1999: 74). Tran Van Khe situated the genesis of the form in a 'gust of renovation' (*luong gio canh tan*) sweeping Indochina in the early twentieth century (2000a: 47). Its development was driven forward by relatively wealthy, urban-based figures, whose fascination with the new was apparent in their voracious consumption of foreign ideas, forms, fashions and technological gizmos of every hue (Pham Duy 1975: 146). According to Tran Van Khai, *Cai luong*'s beginnings as the first modern musical form in Vietnam, can be traced to a performance by musicians recently returned from France, in a hotel near the My Tho train station in 1911. 'Never before had music been played on a stage to a mass audience' (Tran Van Khai 1966: 81). *Cai luong*'s melodies were also more up-to-date than those of the much older *Hat boi* opera, he argued (1966: 81). Others noted that *Cai luong* productions stressed themes of individualism and freedom rather than the Confucian obedience and loyalty celebrated in the *Cheo* and *Hat boi* musical theatres (Addiss 1971: 144). Similarly, it has been argued that *Cai luong*, with its larger number of tunes and tempos to select from and its frequent scene changes, more easily depicts the inner feelings of its characters than these other operatic forms (VDC 2000).

The story of *Cai luong*'s relationship with modernity is, however, further complicated by many references to the cultural legacy of the Republican era that are less favourable. For instance, the *Cai luong* aficionado mentioned at the beginning of this chapter compared the crisis of the form in the 1990s with the challenges of the late 1960s, 'when it looked as if *Cai luong* was going to be crushed to death under the boots of an occupying army and its accompanying baggage of foreign films, music and fashions, Elvis, Brigitte Bardot and Hippies'. Musicians directed me to the work of Pham Duy, who had penned *Cai luong*'s eulogy in the early 1970s, foreshadowing contemporary concerns by two decades and using very similar words:

> During the period 1954–61, [a] major change occurred in *Cai luong*: almost all the traditional characteristics were lost due to the influence of movies. After WWII and especially after the Geneva agreement, transportation with other countries was rebuilt and a flow of foreign films poured into Vietnam, bringing a new form of entertainment to the people. *Cai luong* was influenced readily by these foreign products. Films like *Samson and Delilah* and *Rashomon* were shown on the *Cai luong* stage. Crossbred plays predominated

> at this time. The troupe Thuy Nga began its career with the presentation of Japanese plays and Indian films also influenced the genre. Later, plays with Mongolian, Egyptian and Montagnard origins also climbed onto the *Cai luong* stage and led this theatrical genre to a disordered period.
>
> (Pham Duy 1975: 148)

At the end of the century, this critic's fears about cultural hybridisation still haunted Saigon's cultural circles. Competition with foreign influences was still considered a threat to the survival of the *Cai luong* form. True to both periods is a perception of what Peter Manuel calls 'cultural glitter-out': the challenge to local ethnic styles 'when faced with the raucous competition of pop and modernity in general' (1988: v). Even a form such as *Cai luong*, which Tran Van Khe calls 'modern music with Vietnamese characteristics' (2000a: 25), has not been considered immune to this process.

Purging 'neo-colonial poisons'

In the aftermath of war in 1975, the communist liberators of the south viewed the cultural landscape of the southern cities in even bleaker terms. A Marxist-inspired critique of *Cai luong*'s 'comprador bourgeoisie' and 'reactionary' tendencies had been in evidence since the 1940s (Hoang Nhu Mai 1990: 133). Yet after 1975, critics of *Cai luong* also attacked the use to which the theatre had been put as a tool of pacification by the US military as well as the form's urban bias. Official spokespersons for the new regime described a telling blow that had been struck against the *Cai luong* opera by RVN-era commercialisation and censorship:

> *Cai luong*, the most popular theatrical form in the south, had not only to abandon current social themes [bowing to official regulations], but also to be satisfied with a stage direction adapted to the lower tastes. To satisfy the public, the artists no more thought of personifying the characters, of illuminating their personality but rather of 'bewitching' the audience by their voice and preening posture; they tried to enliven them with vulgar jokes and charm them with intrigues in which the unusual and wonderful prevailed, or give them a cold sweat with terrifying scenes, to dazzle them with sumptuous costumes and stage effects and brilliant footlights.
>
> (Nguyen Khac Vien and Phong Hien 1982: 119)

The identity of Saigon, the former enemy capital, was also thought to have been compromised by US 'neo-colonialist' (*thuc dan moi*) ideologies and 'poisonous' (*noc doc*) cultural forms that were deliberately introduced by the enemy to obscure its aggressive intent and to weaken people's revolutionary resolve (Taylor 2000). South Vietnam's wartime urban lifestyles were disparaged as corrupt, artificial and dependent on foreigners. Decrying the degradation of Saigon's stage and screen under the former regime, one critic noted that post-war

Cai luong audiences still had a taste for transient pleasures and were afflicted by the short-attention spans characteristic of the city's neo-colonial period:

> In neo-colonial society, human values are reversed and discredited, people live at an hysterical tempo, art aims only at giving them transient pleasure as they follow, for instance, the intricacies of a hopeless love affair, or watch a scene of swordsmanship or some act of robbery and murder in a far-off land.
>
> (Nguyen Vinh Long 1978: 125

In the new socialist era, the harmful 'vestiges' (*di tich*) of this socio-cultural orientation, among urbanites in particular, were thought to pose a serious impediment to the socialist 'modernisation' of the south. Addicted to love songs, nostalgic musical refrains and sorrowful laments, the urban populace was left unresponsive to exhortations to make 'sacrifices' (*hy sinh*) to achieve future collective economic advancement (Taylor 2001).[6]

According to some supporters of the new regime's cultural policies, the period of relative isolation during the 1970s and 1980s provided the opportunity to repair and restore southern Vietnam's much-compromised cultural integrity. This indeed was the self-image promoted by leaders and spokespersons of the unifying regime. For example, in 1981 Ho Chi Minh City Party President Vo Van Kiet spoke of the revolutionary artist's role as 'to light up dark and confused souls'. Socialist transformation in the south was aimed at sweeping away the dross of corruption, 'poison' or 'conditioning' inflicted on Vietnamese under the RVN and reminding the erstwhile 'puppet' (*nguy*) population of their heroic identity. Even 'reformed' genres such as *Cai luong* opera needed to be reformed anew, according to some who argued that, despite its 'good digestion', the form had exceeded the limits of its ability to assimilate the new in the late Republican era.

From this perspective, one observer described to me the 1975–86 period as 'a return to the golden age' of *Cai luong*. The official clampdown on foreign music, banning of many Western films and plays and reduction of the influence of the urban Chinese, he argued, allowed this indigenous folk form to thrive for the first time in two decades. The return to the south of several *Cai luong* troops that had been located in the north during the war injected new energy into the southern *Cai luong* scene. He argued that Soviet-trained directors had introduced fresh and imaginative innovations into the staging of performances, in a way that responded to the form's appetite for the new.[7] Admittedly, the new regime's post-war crackdown on urban lifestyles had indeed caused disaffection and led to a mass flight of intellectuals and artists overseas, but this he felt had not affected *Cai luong* artists to the same extent as those in other genres, for in his view *Cai luong* had a predominantly rural-based following. Furthermore, the termination of hostilities had enabled rural areas to be re-populated, allowing more favourable opportunities for touring and giving an enormous stimulus to the re-invigoration of the form. The number of *Cai luong* troupes had mushroomed and the genre's following greatly expanded.

Socialist reform as cultural threat

Despite such positive views of this period of supposed rehabilitation, I encountered little confidence in the late 1990s that *Cai luong*'s health had been restored. Many residents of Ho Chi Minh City attributed blame not to the operation of market forces, nor to the 'vestigial' influences of the neo-colonial era, but to the harm done by socialist policies themselves. Critics charged that the post-war regime's policy of 'building of a new life' (*xay dung cuoc song moi*) had been carried out at the expense of cultural traditions and had led to the neglect of a rich heritage in pursuit of an overly narrow conception of tradition as 'anti-foreign resistance'.[8] According to some *Cai luong* fans, this represented a severe breach with the genre's tradition of eclecticism and sensual stimulation. According to them, this had greatly impoverished the form, making performances monotonous and predictable. Another criticism, based on a less inclusive notion of the genre, saw the new regime's campaign to eradicate the 'vestiges of neo-colonial culture' to have sapped *Cai luong*'s indigenous cultural characteristics, replacing them with unacceptably 'foreign' East European or Chinese Communist contents and forms.

Indeed post-war *Cai luong* drew new influences from 'revolutionary music' (*nhac cach mang*), comprising songs from the resistance wars and the period of building socialism in the north as well as music from other socialist countries. In some circles this music was derisively referred to as 'red' music (*nhac do*). One music critic told me its repertoire had been restricted to three themes: 'productive labour (*lao dong san xuat*), struggle (*chien dau*) and love of the country/party/Uncle Ho (*yeu nuoc/dang/Bac Ho*)'. He argued that the expression of love in this music had also been limited to love for compatriots, the building of socialism and the fight against the Americans: 'Never did red music speak of love between two people or for one's family. Neither did it refer to disappointments in love, nor to feelings of sorrow or loneliness.'

A socialist-realist aesthetic of optimism prevailed. Compositions had to be 'positive' (*tich cuc*) and take a 'definite' (*quyet dinh*) emotional stance. Emotions such as sadness, bitterness and nostalgia were not addressed, nor could the music contain nuances of emotion that signified 'indeterminacy'. One of the worst consequences of this policy, according to another critic, had been misuse of the sorrowful and nostalgic melody called *vong co* (lament for the past) – *Cai luong*'s central melody. Representing an emotional register proscribed by socialist realism:

> There was initially suggestion that this component of *Cai luong* be dropped as the melody was 'weak', destroyed one's will and drove one into solitude. However, it was concluded the *vong co* melody was too popular and central to the *Cai luong* tradition to be dropped. Next an attempt was made to set lyrics

> expressing positive feelings of struggle to the melody, yet the result was so jarring that it was quickly dropped. Ultimately it was used for certain characters to express sorrow or desperation at some predicament, providing the opportunity for the hero of the play to counter such emotions with a martial melody full of optimism and resolution to overcome the problem. For example on seeing her son sent to prison, a mother would express sorrow in a melancholy *vong co* refrain, but her son, a communist militant, would reply expressing his optimism for eventual victory and even encouraging his mother to feel joyful!

This critic contrasted the socialist-realist heroes of post-1975 *Cai luong* with those of the former period. Formerly, heroes had expressed a range of emotions: doubt before going into battle, sorrow at separation from loved ones, fear for their survival, joy at being reunited with their family and tenderness at rejoining their wives. By contrast, the emotional register of post-unification heroes had been improbably limited to fearlessness and optimism:

> In one play, a cadre even rejoiced when his own daughter – a beautiful girl leading a debauched life – was sent to prison. She sang using *vong co* – 'you are not my father you are so cruel'. Her mother agreed. But the cadre-father would not bend. He was so full of revolutionary morality that even the most sad and beautiful *vong co* melody couldn't shake him. He replied, 'I would rather lose a daughter than society lose its purity'. She was sent to jail. Then, her formerly criminal lover would come to his senses and visit her in jail encouraging her to appreciate re-education and admire her father's actions.

Not only were these characters impossible to relate to but the enemies against whom they fought were caricatured in crude ways: 'Americans were depicted by big actors who used white make-up, hairy beards, spoke Vietnamese badly, walked awkwardly, but mysteriously sang *vong co* beautifully! They were portrayed as lecherous, aggressive, sinister and unfeeling.'[9]

These critics rejected the notion that that the unifying regime had engineered the restoration of a more 'wholesome' and 'vital' culture in the south. Instead, they implicated the new regime itself in the erosion of traditions and cultural impoverishment. On the other hand, while endorsing a notion of the genre's inherent inclusiveness, these critics rejected the innovations imported from the north, viewing them as inconsistent with the form's 'Vietnamese' identity. Yet despite a recent easing and broadening in the regime's cultural policies, few of them believed that the genre would make a comeback in the *doi moi* era. One *Cai luong* performer thought the damage was irremediable: '*Cai luong* became irrelevant, therefore people lost interest. Now they prefer to follow foreign music and fashions.'

As Vietnam stepped into new global engagements, some former antagonists in these debates moved into unexpected alignment. One of the critics who deplored the impact of 'Stalinism' on musical forms such as *Cai luong* told me in late 1993 that he hoped the US embargo on trade with Vietnam would not be lifted anytime soon. This was because of the poor preparation of youth for the 'foreign cultural invasion' (*xam luoc van hoa nuoc ngoai*) which, he said, would undoubtedly be unleashed by normalisation. He feared that young people would not be able to distinguish good from bad, as for many years they had been subject to a cultural invasion from the Soviet bloc. He hoped teachers, musicians and critics such as himself would have a period of respite in which to reawaken young people's interest in Vietnamese traditions and help them be more discriminating when the floodgates were eventually opened.

The city's indigenous hybridity

An alternative perspective eschews the language of purity, vulnerability and subversion and embraces the condition of mutability and inclusion as defining characteristics of the *Cai luong* form. Some see the alchemical preoccupations of *Cai luong* not merely as a reflection of colonial or post-colonial influences but of southern Vietnam's long history as a place of exceptional cultural ferment. This view was articulated by folklorist, Huynh Ngoc Trang, student of a wide range of popular southern Vietnamese folk forms. According to Trang, this region possesses a distinctive indigenous identity; that from the earliest days of Vietnamese settlement it has been a melting pot, a place of cultural exchanges and of constant transformation (Huynh Ngoc Trang 1992).

Trang found the eclectic spirit of southern Vietnam most evident in popular cultural forms such as *Cai luong* opera (Huynh Ngoc Trang 1992: 69). *Cai luong* typified southern Vietnamese culture in its absorption of diverse musical and theatrical genres, costume styles, plots drawn from all eras and all quarters of the globe, as well as its central characteristic of constant transformation. The significance of this genre for understanding the spirit of *Nam Bo* (southern Vietnam) was underlined in (appropriately) mixed metaphors:

> *Cai luong*'s quality of acceptance on no fixed principles could possibly be viewed as mere mixture yet from a different, more open and positive perspective, this characteristic signifies what is typical about Southern Vietnam – a crossroads with doors always open to waves from all the four corners of the earth from the time of its first settlement to today.
>
> (Huynh Ngoc Trang 1992: 69).

Throughout its development, *Cai luong*'s orientation towards the new was indeed marked by a voracious appetite. Its creators borrowed stories, songs, dances, costumes, staging conventions and musical instruments from both European and Chinese sources, as well as props such as the trapeze, real weapons and live ammunition, while genres such as spoken theatre, film, circus, ballet, popular dance and martial arts were incorporated into its performances. In consequence, *Cai luong* was to rapidly metamorphose and branch out (Pham

Duy 1975; Hauch 1972). Another distinctive feature was its catholicity. Kin to the Mekong delta's highly syncretic *Cao Dai* and 'Coconut' religions, *Cai luong* seemed able to reconcile the most diverse elements within its apparently infinitely accommodating structure. After all, *Cai luong* is the tradition which can boast Roman-swashbuckler operas (*Tuong kiem hiep la ma*) among its sub-genres which had characters dressed in Western medieval costumes doing kung-fu somersaults through windows and masked Chinese bullies fighting with *poignards* (Pham Duy 1975: 146). The marrying of Chinese and European mythical, philosophical and aesthetic traditions with Vietnamese folk tunes and stories was central to the genre's alchemical preoccupations, and around this core restless experimentation occurred with a host of other influences which washed up in southern Vietnam throughout the course of the twentieth century. The disputes one encounters about the extent to which the genre is consistent with southern Chinese, French, US, Soviet or other foreign influences are tribute to this history of borrowing. Suffice it to say that, in picking up this baggage, *Cai luong* has been one of the most important vehicles for the localisation of new ideas and forms, whatever their provenance.

Cai luong's 'good digestion' is taken by some as emblematic of the accommodating nature of southern Vietnam's cultural identity. Views of this region as a place with no stable or fragile traditions at stake would appear to exempt Ho Chi Minh City, along with the rest of southern Vietnam, from the cultural crisis which critics of the reform policies identified as facing the country in the *doi moi* era. Considering the south's supposedly long history of constant assimilation, the cultural traffic through Vietnam's 'open door' does not necessarily pose a threat to its residents' identity or traditions. This perspective meshes with a view of southern Vietnam as a major commercial entrepôt, of hundreds or thousands of years standing (Le Xuan Diem 1990; Nguyen Cong Binh *et al.* 1990). In such a reading, the transformation, hybridisation and commercialisation of culture have been taking place for a very long time and are not recent problems. These perspectives cast attention on the rest of the country, where a cultural crisis might reasonably be expected in the wake of the recent reforms, but from which Ho Chi Minh City is by nature immune.

Whether they saw *Cai luong* as exemplifying a defined tradition, a new genre that emerged in the early twentieth century or a moving nexus of cultural experimentation, many residents of Ho Chi Minh City, at century's end, could agree that this hitherto inclusive and dynamic local cultural form was running out of relevance. The challenges of the moment appeared to unite those celebrating the form's essential mutability and those critical of its decline in a shared sense of crisis, although they still might disagree whether the new technological, social and cultural relations of the period indeed presented an unprecedented dilemma or, alternatively, that the genre's potential for new adaptations had simply not yet been realised. Furthermore, while those who feared for the form's survival might share little common ground with proponents of an all-accommodating southern cultural scene, both of these views, in the energy with which they were put forward, challenged the stereotype of southern Vietnamese as characteristically laissez faire in matters cultural and the assumption that as modernised, 'neo-colonised' or rootless urban people, such questions of identity might not be of concern to them.

Reformed opera and moral reform

> The main reason *Cai luong* is so boring these days is because the content is controlled. If able to address real social issues, it would regain its popularity.
>
> (35-year-old male former *Cai luong* fan)

According to music buffs with whom I spoke in Bac Lieu, one of several contenders in the Mekong delta for having been the birthplace of the form, the name *Cai luong* refers to its underlying moral project: to renew (*doi moi*) and reform (*cai cach*) traditional culture and morality. *Cai luong*'s role as a vehicle of social renewal and commentary might be seen as resonant with the moral and educative concerns of the traditional literati. The first *Cai luong* performance drew upon the tale 'Luc Van Tien', a poem composed by Confucian scholar and anti-colonialist poet Nguyen Dinh Chieu. According to historians of the genre, rural-based intellectuals guided its early development and figured prominently in its audiences (Pham Duy 1975: 140). While *Cai luong* was an important clearing house for foreign musical forms, staging innovations, instruments and stories, Vietnamese classics such as the *Tale of Kieu* and other tales of moral education and rehabilitation remained at the forefront of popular demand into the Republican era (Hess 1979: 164). In the 1960s, urban *Cai luong* reportedly retained a role as an upholder of traditional Vietnamese values, with productions that celebrated filial devotion or criticised such contemporary aspects of Saigon life as mini skirts and bar girls who married Americans (Hess 1979: 229).

One of the most salient distinctions drawn between the present parlous state of *Cai luong* and its perceived former social centrality was the view that this opera form had formerly occupied a vital role as a vehicle for critically assessing the socio-cultural trends of the day. A commonly encountered view was that *Cai luong*'s decline came when it lost its following among intellectuals, who had once enthusiastically patronised the genre as a popular and vibrant medium of social commentary. According to some critics, the state's appropriation of the moralising voice of the form had choked its capacity to act as a moral counterweight. State control, which some saw as a legacy of the post-war 'Stalinist' era, was held reponsible for casting the survival of *Cai luong* in doubt.[10] This control, duplicated in all other sectors of the arts, the press, in schools, universities and research institutes, was held to restrict greatly the ability of those working in these areas to criticise senior political figures, the nation's orientation and the regime's sacred cows, as well as to explore ideas and models not authorised by the Communist Party. In the economically liberal 1990s, writers, musicians and artists were expressing themselves as never before, but with the question of the party's authority to govern off-limits, perceptions were that 'liberty' under *doi moi* meant only 'freedom to make money'.

Another explanation for this purported loss of relevance was that *Cai luong* had forsaken its moral role to become mere 'entertainment' and froth. One attempt to counter the perceived deterioration of the form into glitziness was 'Social *Cai luong*' (*Cai luong xa hoi*), which focused on social commentary and employed staging that placed more emphasis on speech than songs, discussions rather than fights, and everyday clothing rather than elaborate or fanciful costumes. Yet this innovation had only qualified success. Some critics of this sub-genre associated it with a northern Vietnamese orientation and mentioned the preponderance of socialist themes, unrelenting references to war and revolution and generalised drabness.[11] Others complained that, after 1975, the moralising message of most *Cai luong* was directed at urging youth to give up 'decadent, harmful, foreign' urban culture, follow in the footsteps of resistance fighters and cadres and embrace a 'new life' of simplicity, purity and sacrifice. According to one disaffected former *Cai luong* enthusiast, *Cai luong* was used primarily to mobilise people to fight Pol Pot and the Chinese or to attack the old way of life. A contemporary critic of *Cai luong* went further, dismissing all operas since 1975 as 'just government lies and propaganda'. As both victim and vehicle of post-unification cultural reform, *Cai luong* became didactic and unappealing. Today, a disparaging pun for particularly tedious *Cai luong* is to call it not 'social' but 'socialist' opera (*Cai luong xa hoi chu nghia*).

Yet one wonders whether it is the content of the message that is responsible for the limited success of such initiatives or rather the attempt to reduce *Cai luong* to a morality genre. Certainly, plays featuring the legendary Chinese anti-corruption fighter Bao Cung have received strong support because they take on a moral theme with clear contemporary relevance. As some critics told me, if social issues such as corruption, the legitimacy of leaders, the value of policies or the mistakes of the past could be discussed more explicitly through the vehicle of *Cai luong*, its popularity, especially to intellectuals, would return overnight. On the other hand, it is significant that *Cai luong* has remained a staple form of music in the karaoke and waitress bars in the penumbra of the city's sex industry, which are patronised heavily by male cadres, professionals and corporate directors. *Cai luong* cabarets also appeared in the late 1990s in which wealthy patrons, most of whom were men, could drink and watch performances and ostentatiously present large denomination bills to the largely female performers. This raises a question about *Cai luong*'s role in society as primarily a vehicle for moral reform. Critics during the late 1980s noted that, historically, *Cai luong* drew a following from the 'comprador bourgeoisie' (Hoang Nhu Mai 1990). Many of the party elite, indistinguishable from compradors of the past with monopoly access to foreign investment capital, were simply following in the footsteps of some of the most important early patrons of *Cai luong*, who also were privileged members of the urban bourgeoisie. Given its following as a form of light entertainment and conspicuous consumption among the moneyed classes of the city, has it not in some way remained faithful to its roots?

The story of the social eclipse of folk cultural forms due to the impact of modernity also needs to be examined for its gender bias. The oft-stated observation that *Cai luong* as an art form is dying as it no longer attracts men or 'intellectuals' overlooks the continuing relevance of the form to women, who comprise the majority of its followers and viewers. Among the main patrons of the *Cai luong* form were the women who operated the majority of the private trade and market outlets in Ho Chi Minh City, as well as those who worked in its enormous service sector. While as a group not regarded as prestigious or highly rated for their intellectual attainments, their labour undoubtedly was a key to Ho Chi Minh City's economic successes in the 1990s. Filling the city's large theatres and glued to TV screens, many of these women found *Cai luong* spoke to them, notwithstanding exaggerated rumours of its demise. *Cai luong*'s enduring themes of family, loyalty, moral integrity, punishment, loss, separation and love addressed real dilemmas in their lives, as the social dislocations that accompanied urbanisation and rapid economic change placed families and gender expectations under stress. Adding to their sense of marginalisation, the government's modernisation rhetoric gave undue weight to professional and technical development and industrialisation, undervaluing the contribution of these female-dominated occupations in Vietnam's economy. One has to be equally cautious of schemas that prematurely thrust the cultural and aesthetic preferences of this socially pivotal group into the 'regretfully' superseded past. The notion that *Cai luong* is 'outmoded' or in decline tends to place men's 'serious' public preoccupations in the vanguard of modernity, just as the idea that the form has become frivolous follows them into the city's bars and brothels.

Conclusion

During Vietnam's recent policy shifts, local commentators focused on the impacts to emblematic cultural forms such as *Cai luong* opera. Their sense of crisis in this genre can be linked to the intense transformations that have swept Vietnam in the wake of the 'renovation' and 'open door' reforms. However, *Cai luong* opera is a form that has attracted the attention of cultural commentators at various other historic junctures as well: during the south's transition to socialism, through the wars of decolonisation, in the years of late colonial cultural fragmentation or during the period of cultural ferment in the early twentieth century. Yet not all represented these turning points as crises. Some thought *Cai luong* able to thrive in cultural flux and capable of adapting to technological change, while others considered its decline a normal or even desirable event. Similarly, the idea that *Cai luong* had its own 'golden age' was common enough, but there was no agreement as to when this had occurred.

Divergent opinions as to the historical fate of this form highlight the different assumptions about its identity. One view considers it a traditional form under threat. Yet whose 'tradition' is it? Its lineage has been variously traced to different parts of rural Vietnam, urban centres, regions and even countries. Local cultural forms such as *Cai luong* have alternatively been described as inherently hybrid and flexible. Nevertheless, if most critics agree that *Cai luong* is remarkably synthetic and have equated it with change and reform, few seemed to think it capable of infinite development. Some have associated it intimately with modernity and foreign cultural borrowing. Yet there is disagreement over whether the different paths that the genre took in the north and south during the division of the country constitute acceptable 'modernisations'. Neither has there been consensus on which foreign sources are legitimate and indeed which of these are to be associated with modernity at all. One alternative view is that *Cai luong* is a young form, still trying to sort out its identity (Dinh Quang *et al.* 1999: 75). Little wonder then that there has been so much debate over the question.

Journeying in the Mekong delta countryside one hears the strains of *Cai luong* almost incessantly. From this rural perspective, the form hardly seems in crisis. Debates about its predicament have been far more salient and fierce in urban Vietnam and particularly in Ho Chi Minh City. This dissension can be taken as an indication that this city has experienced more societal dislocation and cultural turbulence than any other part of the country. Debates about *Cai luong* in Ho Chi Minh City are interesting for they open a valuable window onto the complexity of urban experience during Vietnam's recent re-engagements with the non-socialist world. As commentators have tussled over the meaning of this operatic form, they have mapped out the parameters of their own identity as national and global citizens, as local southern Vietnamese, and as urban dwellers. By identifying with the fate of the form, they have oriented themselves historically and charted the limits of acceptable change.

Notes

1 This chapter was written while a visiting fellow at the Research School of Pacific and Asian Studies, Australian National University, and was revised at the University of Western Australia. Some research funding was provided by the Department of Anthropology, RSPAS, Australian National University. I am grateful to the writers, artists and *Cai luong* fans and observers in Ho Chi Minh City who generously shared their thoughts about music and theatre with me. Their comments, reported anonymously in the text, were made to me during my visits to Vietnam between 1992 and 2000.

2 Fears about cultural hybridity feature in many of the reactions to the increased cultural flows of recent years. In the late 1990s, a spokesperson for the arts in Ho Chi Minh City lamented: 'lacking the ethos of national music, many new *Cai luong* plays pursue novelty and thus bring forth "hybrids" alien to our traditional theatre' (Le Duy Hanh 1998: 34).

3 This term designated 'degenerate' (*doi truy*) or culturally 'inappropriate' (*khong thich hop*) items, including pornographic or violent movies, sex manuals, playing cards, 'outmoded feudal romances', occult manuals and music videos.

4 A national *Cai luong* festival was held in the city in June 2000 with the declared hope of giving the form a new lease on life. However, audience members with whom I spoke complained about boring costumes, an excess of speaking, strange, stylised props, uninteresting stories and wooden adherence to the government's line on the war and revolution. One was surprised to hear that the performance she watched was considered by organisers to be the best of the festival. If so, she thought *Cai luong* must be in serious trouble. The play was prefaced by speeches including one by the director of the city's office of culture consisting of a list of the decrees promulgating the festival. The speeches were televised. One viewer complained: 'Those guys talk too much!' While commercialisation is sometimes blamed as undermining the form,

one viewer said he thought the reason the play he watched was so boring was that half the audience was there for free.

5 Whether or not reflective of the supposedly robust nature of southern Vietnamese cultural forms, the circulation of *Cai luong* in video and karaoke laser disc forms and its popularity among overseas Vietnamese in live, video and CD formats are indications that the form has adapted to major recent geographical dislocations, social transformations and technological shifts.

6 This critical view of urban areas was matched by the new regime's view of the rehabilitating value to culturally 'depraved' urbanites, of migration to rural areas in order to open 'New Economic Zones' and the 'heroic' nature of doing hard work on the new 'front' of the agricultural economy.

7 Spoken dramas and staging influences from Stanislavski to Brecht were also introduced.

8 Advocates of the regime's post-war policies argued that the purging of many Chinese costumes, stories, melodies and choreographic items that took place in the late 1970s was 'a good thing, for they were not *Cai luong* – they were very Chinese-looking'. Also purged were Western melodies, musical genres from the tango to love songs, eclectic foreign costumes, stories and motifs drawn from sources as varied as ancient Rome, Egypt, India and the American Wild West.

9 According to some long-time followers of the genre, the heavy hand of the government was all too evident in these new productions. I was told that some pre-1975 personnel such as actors, artistic directors and costume and makeup specialists continued on in the new troupes but each troupe had its own political cadre – either a northerner or a southern party member who had regrouped to the north in 1954.

10 It should be recalled, however, that state control and censorship existed during the colonial and republican eras as well.

11 This perception of the northern or communist origins of 'social *Cai luong*' runs counter to accounts dating this innovation to the 1920s (Hauch 1972: 41). In 1960s' Saigon, similar criticisms of the overly serious nature of 'social *Cai luong*' were already in circulation (Hauch 1972: 47).

Bibliography

Addiss, S. (1971) 'Theatre Music of Vietnam', *Southeast Asia Quarterly*, 1: 1–2.

Dang Canh Khanh (1996) 'Some Views about the Prevention of the Influence of Pornographic Cultural Products on Teenagers and Adolescents', *Social Sciences*, 6: 70–8.

Dinh Quang, Le Anh, Ha Van Cau, Nguyen Huy Hong, Tran Viet Ngu, Tat Thang and Ho Ngoc (1999) *Vietnamese Theatre*, Hanoi: The Gioi Publishers.

Hauch, D. (1972) *The Cai Luong Theatre of Vietnam, 1915–1970*, PhD thesis, Southern Illinois University.

Hess, D.L. (1979) *The Educated Vietnamese Middle Class of Metropolitan Saigon and their Legacy of Confucian Authority, 1954–1975*, PhD thesis, New York University.

Hoang Nhu Mai (1987) 'Cai luong', *Vietnamese Studies*, 17: 17–32.

—— (1990) 'The Cai Luong Stage', in T.V. Giau and T.B. Dang (eds), *Dia Chi Van Hoa TP Ho Chi Minh III* (Ho Chi Minh City Cultural monograph No 3), Ho Chi Minh City: Ho Chi Minh City Publishing House.

Huynh Ngoc Trang (1992) 'Tong quan ve van hoa Nam Bo' (A Synopsis of Nam Bo Culture), *Social Sciences Review*, 11: 59–70.

Le Duy Hanh (1998) 'Cai Luong: Its National Identity and Modernisation', *Vietnamese Studies*, 130: 32–5.

Le Xuan Diem (1990) 'Mien Nam Viet Nam, mot vung van hoa-lich su song dong' (South Vietnam, A Lively Cultural-Historical Region), in Nguyen Quang Vinh, Phan

Xuan Bien, Tran Du Lich and Nguyen Quoi (eds), *Mien Nam Trong Su Nghiep Doi Moi Cua Ca Nuoc*, Ho Chi Minh City: Social Sciences Publishing House.

Manuel, P. (1988) *Popular Musics of the Western World: An Introductory Survey*, Oxford: Oxford University Press.

Nguyen Cong Binh, Le Xuan Diem and Mac Duong (eds) (1990) *Van hoa va Cu Dan Dong Bang Song Cuu Long* (The Culture and Population of the Mekong Delta), Ho Chi Minh City: Social Sciences Publishing House.

Nguyen Khac Vien and Phong Hien (1982) 'American Neo-Colonialism in South Vietnam 1954–1975: Socio-Cultural Aspects', *Vietnamese Studies*, 69: 1–122.

Nguyen Sinh Huy (1996) 'Some Manifestations of the Conflict of Values in the Areas of Ethics and Social Life', *Social Sciences*, 4: 87–92.

Nguyen Vinh Long (1978) 'Changes in Saigon's Stage and Cinema', *Vietnamese Studies*, 52: 120–8.

Pham Duy (1975) *Musics of Vietnam*, Carbondale: Southern Illinois University Press.

Saigon Giai Phong.

—— (1990) 'Efforts Needed to Improve Ethnic Cultural Life', 30 August: 2, Joint Publications Research Service, South East Asia 1990 (31): 39–40.

Taylor, Philip (2000) 'Music as a "Neocolonial Poison" in Post-War Southern Vietnam', *Crossroads, An Interdisciplinary Journal of Southeast Asian Studies*, 14(1): 99–131.

—— (2001) *Fragments of the Present: Searching for Modernity in Vietnam's South*, St Leonards, NSW: Allen & Unwin.

Tran Van Khai (1966) *Nghe Thuat San Khau Viet Nam* (Vietnamese Stage Arts), Saigon: Khai Tri Publishers.

Tran Van Khe (2000a) *Tran Van Khe va Am Nhac Dan Toc* (Tran Van Khe and National Music), Ho Chi Minh City: Young Publishers.

—— (2000b) *Van Hoa voi Am Nhac Dan Toc* (Culture and National Music), Ho Chi Minh City: Youth Publishers.

VDC (Vietnam Datacommunications Company) (2000) 'Cai luong' (Renovated Opera), *VietnamStyle*, online. Available: http://www.vnstyle.vdc.com.vn [accessed 20 September 2001].

Vo Van Kiet (1981) 'The Cultural and Ideological Front in Ho Chi Minh City', *Vietnamese Studies*, 69: 130–50.

Chapter 10

Popular television and images of urban life

Lisa B.W. Drummond

Introduction

In addition to a wide literature on television and soap operas in general (see, for example, Abercrombie 1996; Allen 1995; Ang 1991, 1996; Brunsdon 1997; Drummond and Paterson 1988; Livingstone 1998; Williams 1992a, 1992b), there is a growing literature on soap operas and television serials in developing country societies and the non-Western world, particularly Egypt, China and Latin America (see, for example, Abu-Lughod 1995; Allen 1995; Biltereyst and Meers 2000; Chu *et al.* 1991; Das 1995; Flores-Gutierrez 2000; Lopez 1995; Martin-Barbero 1995; Phillips n.d.; Rofel 1994a, 1994b, 1995; Sun 2001; Zha 1995). The general literature on soap operas sees them as primarily a women's genre, though prime-time soaps such as *Dallas* are/were intended for and watched by men as well as women. This view of soaps as a 'feminine genre' stems from their reliance on plots which feature everyday life, domestic situations and personal social relations. These are highly personal stories. The action may be more wide-ranging than the literal domestic situation, but is always referred back to the impact of that action on the central domestic or personal relations in the story-line.

In television studies in developing countries, the role of these wildly popular shows as 'nation-builders', purveyors of a particular view of history, and as social mobilisation tools, is highlighted. In China, for example, Rofel discusses the role of popular culture as the means by which Chinese people are constituted as 'subjects of the nation'; a role necessitated by the 'bankrupt' state of 'official methods of ideological dissemination' (Rofel 1995: 303). Keane notes the efforts by 'Chinese propagandists ... to use television to "mould and shape" new standards of ethical behaviour appropriate to a modern commodity economy' (Keane 1998: 479). Sun (2001: 82), writing about Chinese television serials, argues that the serials are 'important cultural texts, in which Chinese identities are written to negotiate the new intersections of class, race, and gender brought about by world-wide migrations'. The Brazilian *telenovelas*, Lopez (1995) argues, were used by the Brazilian military state to portray a particular 'imagined' construction of the Brazilian state, obliterating any lingering 'differences' between regions and groups. The potential for references to the Vietnamese situation is clear.

This chapter highlights the images of urban social life portrayed in a four-part, soap-opera-style series, *12A and 4H* and will consider, briefly, the role of a romanticised rural setting in the urban cultural imagination.

12A and 4H was produced by VTV3, one of three national broadcasting stations, in the first year of its weekly *Van Nghe Chu Nhat* (Sunday Arts; hereafter VNCN) programme in 1995. VNCN airs approximately 150 hours of locally produced serials per year, most of which run from two to four episodes in length and have a budget of approximately US$10,000.

While the quality may differ from one to the other, and there are occasional (and apparently not very popular) series with historical settings, most deal with aspects of contemporary society. Some deal specifically with rural–urban differences, depicting, for the most part, rural people who move to the city and their experience of trying to adjust to urban ways (for example, the 1997 serial *Doi Nha Len Pho*). A few have dealt with heroin addiction, and these have generated considerable response from viewers, often parents or relatives of drug addicts who understand the serials as pedagogical tools which teach them how to recognise what is happening to them and their families and what they might do about it. In the words of the editor of the VNCN series (who is also one of its serial directors), its overall objective is:

> to discuss and resolve [*giai quyet*] all sorts of issues in ordinary people's daily lives, family life, society, etc. It aims to educate and contribute to the intellectual life of the people. Life as shown in the films should be like average people's lives, and the films should cater to all classes and stations in life: poor, rich, urban, rural, farmers, office workers, etc.
>
> (Nguyen Khai Hung, producer, VNCN, interviewed February 1998)

This explication of the 'serious' nature of the show may sound predictably pat to cynical Western ears, but that should not detract from the seriousness with which this responsibility is taken by those involved. In other words, the editor of a series of locally produced, soap-opera serials clearly sees the role of his or her programme as social education as much as, if not more than, entertainment.

When considering the 'message' of *12A and 4H*, and the various other serials made by VTV3, it is important to remember that even if the producers see themselves as independent, the fact is that all media in Vietnam are state-controlled. It may be a case of pre-emptive self-censorship, but all programming is vetted and censored at some level before it gets to air. Therefore, it is highly unlikely that any truly subversive ideas will make their way into locally produced shows. *12A and 4H*, more than many of the other serials produced in Vietnam, is surprisingly effective in blurring some of the black/white, good/bad conclusions about human motivation and how viewers should understand their world.[1] The serials which deal with heroin addiction are starkly pedagogical, as are many which depict the experiences of rural people in the city and which try to discourage rural residents from moving to urban areas (as in the serial noted above, *Doi Nha Len Pho*).

The conventions of soap opera and of melodrama are well understood. A central feature is the opposition of good and evil, each type of character being clearly drawn and easy to recognise and identify. Coincidences of fate also play a strong role, as do romance and tragedy, or, preferably, in the Vietnamese case, the tragic romance as epitomised by the *Tale of Kieu*.[2] Also very important is the location of the story in domestic space – the characters are mainly family members, neighbours, work colleagues, people whose relationships to each other are likely to mirror the web of relationships in which the viewer would be situated. This web of relationships on which the story-line is based requires the viewer to follow the serial from one episode to the next. The story might not appear to advance quickly and the 'action' consists mainly of conversations between characters about their relationships and those with others in the story, much as viewers might discuss their relationships in real life, and such that viewers can discuss the relationships between the characters. While soap operas generally mean open-ended story-lines which might, and do, continue for years, the Latin American *telenovelas*, for example, and some Chinese serials like the Vietnamese serials which are considered here, use closed story-lines. Nevertheless, the Vietnamese, the Latin American and the Chinese serials are clearly of the soap-opera genre, and unabashedly follow in the melodramatic tradition of romance and tragedy.

Melodrama, of course, is by no means new to Vietnam, and nor is soap opera. Arriving in Hanoi in 1991, I found a city (and by report, a nation) enthralled in the nightly exploits of Maria, the eponymous heroine of a 1970s' (possibly early 1980s') Mexican soap opera which had been dubbed over in Russian before being dubbed into Vietnamese (snatches of the original Spanish were also audible beneath the layers of dubbing, making it almost unintelligible). When *Maria* had run its course (to the intense regret of the viewing public), another Mexican soap was procured. *The Rich Also Cry* (*Nguoi Giau Cung Khoc*) was another smash hit. Both soaps depicted lifestyles of over-the-top luxury, much like *Dynasty*. Both also were shown every evening until the episodes ran out.[3] And both attracted huge audiences (not that there was much choice on Vietnamese television). Hanoi, certainly, seemed to slow down perceptibly every evening at 9 pm as people settled in for their nightly dose of *Maria* or *The Rich Also Cry*. In other words, the soap opera format is well established with viewing audiences in Vietnam, and the showing of foreign serials continues: in the 1995–97 period, the 1970s' US series *Little House on the Prairie* was shown nightly at 6 pm, replaced when it ran out in 1998 with the Canadian series set on a turn-of-the-century Prince Edward Island, *Road to Avonlea*. Although not soap operas generally speaking, both of these highly popular shows (both to their original audiences and to their Vietnamese audience) are primarily concerned with social relations and domestic life.

12A and 4H: portraying contemporary social relationships

The major social issues confronting Vietnam today, as they are reflected in these serials, particularly in the one discussed here, *12A and 4H*, generally concern social relations and lifestyles. The issue of the changing form of social, particularly family, relationships, is perhaps most pressing. This change often pits older generations, who have a clear nationalist image because of their involvement and sacrifices for the national liberation movement, against the younger generation, who now constitute the majority of the population, who were born late in or after the war with the United States, have experienced only the hardships of post-war, isolationist Vietnam, and have, in many cases, little such ideological clarity. The young are often perceived to be disrespectful of their elders, and often they are. Specifically, domestic relationships, family relationships, are portrayed as in transition in these serials; there is conflict in the domestic sphere over decision-making, such as over the 'appropriate' level of parental involvement in decisions affecting the child's life-course, i.e. education, jobs, marriage; the general sense of 'what's right' for the child. Understandings regarding the marital relationship appear to be changing and the serials appear to be asking what husbands and wives demand of each other, how they expect to relate to each other, what level of importance should be accorded to 'love', or even to 'personal happiness', and what significance should be attached to 'sacrifice'.

A panegyric to VNCN appeared in 1995 in the *Thanh Nien* (*Youth*) newspaper, praising the accuracy of the VTV3 serials in depicting family life in contemporary Vietnam, with all the trials and tribulations that are involved. The writer compared Vietnamese cinema films unfavourably with the television programme, saying that too often films that are made in Vietnam in Vietnamese with Vietnamese actors show Western lifestyles which are luxurious and strange to the Vietnamese viewers. In contrast, television shows, according to the reporter, portray the realities of social relations in the 1990s:

> 'Family' – is a topic which is shot through more than 70 episodes and passed on to the viewers [...] Everyday life in ordinary, common families in Vietnam: cheerfulness and sadness; happiness and unhappiness; harmony and falling apart; giving up and competing, etc. [these things] tie down and control the members [of a family]. Everything in these films is close [to reality], plain and unvarnished. Watching the films is like watching one's own household, like witnessing the neighbours' stories. Not a few of the films and scenes from the films make the viewers cry because they are moved, to the extreme of [our] common humanity. And people secretly thank VNCN for showing them meaningful Vietnamese films [literally: films which bring out the soul, the body].
>
> (Dao Mai Trang 1995)

Such an effusive tribute is clearly hyperbole, yet the series is indisputably popular and this popularity is no doubt attributable in large part to the type of material it presents, just as this reporter notes. In an interview, the editor of the series told me that the show receives a great deal of viewer mail, as do the actors. Overall, such mail indicated that the subjects of the serials appeared not only to be enjoyed but taken seriously.[4]

The serial *12A and 4H* deals extensively with relationships and with the changing articulation of social relationships in the 1990s.[5] Focusing on the friendship of four girls in their Grade Twelve year, the serial examines their relationships with their parents, with the adults and authority figures around them, with their peers, and with each other. In particular, the serial reflects various takes on the adult–youth relationship, whether it be parent–child, teacher–student, or transgressions of these, such as the sexual relationship between Hang and her teacher, Mr Minh.

Hang, who is the central figure in the serial, is an only child of wealthy parents, both of whom work outside the home; the father is the director of a state-owned enterprise. Early on, the audience is *shown* that there are tensions between the husband and wife of which their daughter is oblivious. Hang is indulged and lives a privileged lifestyle in a huge new house; she has her own room (very unusual in crowded Hanoi where per-person living space averages as little as four square metres) with modern furniture and an en-suite bathroom, an extensive wardrobe of Western-style clothing, a piano on which to practise her music, and is offered expensive presents by her parents, such as the latest Walkman, which they give her on her first day back at school 'to help her study foreign languages'. Her father is generous with pocket money, concerned only that she might not have enough to spend.

Ha, the second main character, is also an only child, as are all the characters about whom the audience is shown anything of their home life,[6] and the child of well-off parents. She also has her *own* room and a large wardrobe of 'stylish', Western clothes. Ha's father does not appear in the serial, but to the extent that her mother appears, she seems to be a full-time home-maker who is actively involved to the point of interference in Ha's life.

Hang and Ha, along with Hoa and Han, make up the '4H' group. They, in general, are studious, do well in school, are polite and respectful (even if Hoa is a bit of a 'tomboy') and are popular among their classmates. Hang is the class monitor and Ha is the Youth Union secretary, both positions of some responsibility.

The other students who figure more-or-less prominently in the serial include Ngon, the bad-boy student who heads up the 'Four Seasons' gang of delinquents-in-training who drink beer in the Queen Bar after school. Thien is a new kid from the south who is initially drawn into Ngon's gang but later realises how irresponsible and alienated they are and withdraws. Long is a former street-kid who has returned to school to finish his education after a long drop-out period of drinking and drug use. Both Long and Thien are attracted to Ha but, although the southern boy is good-looking and well placed in an influential family, it is to Long, the 'underdog', that she is drawn, much to her mother's dismay.

One of the most challenging aspects of the serial is the way in which it reflects on parent–child relationships. The parents here are portrayed as either 'traditional' or 'modern'. The traditional model is represented by the southern boy, Thien, and his father; theirs is the only relatively successful parent–child relationship shown. Thien speaks to his father deferentially, not in the familiar terms that Hang uses with her parents, and the father seems to lecture rather than talk to his son. The boy's more formal upbringing is noted in one of the earliest scenes when bad-boy Ngon tells him not to speak so politely but to use more casual forms of address, and Thien replies that he is not used to that style. It is interesting that it is the southerner who is portrayed in this fashion, as the south is often, it seems, portrayed as clinging to the more archaic forms of Vietnamese culture, the more Confucian, the more patriarchal, than the north, which is portrayed as more egalitarian and more progressive.

In contrast, Hang's mother and father give her considerable independence, shower her with gifts, and allow her to 'talk back' to them, and question them about their circumstances, as Hang does when she asks her father why he gives her so much money, where he gets the money from, and why they have so much while some of her friends are still relatively poor.

A clear challenge to the Confucian and therefore 'traditional' parent model is portrayed in the final episodes, when the parents, Hang's and Ha's in particular, are shown apologising to their children. Hang's parents split up, under the pressure of both of them carrying on extra-marital affairs and the lack of any real affection between them. They then apologise to her for the emotional burden their break-up places on her and demonstrate that their 'happy family' was all a fabrication and never really existed. Also, Hang's father apologises to her for the shame incurred by his corrupt business practices which have underpinned the lifestyle she has enjoyed (in the last episode he is found out and denounced in the press).

Ha's mother's apologises for not respecting Ha's privacy (in itself an unusual concept to highlight in Vietnamese culture). The mother reads Ha's diary, finds out about Ha's romantic feelings for Long, the former street-kid, and warns Long to stay away from her daughter. When Ha, who has been devastated by the sudden and seemingly meaningless termination of her friendship with Long, catches her mother red-handed reading the diary, figures out what her mother has done and confronts her, her mother apologises. In both cases, the parents plead that whatever they have done, however misguided or unsuccessful it might have proved, they did it 'for their children' (*vi con*). In both cases, the children retort that they didn't ask for these sacrifices or these interventions, and would much rather have dealt with the truth or made decisions themselves about their own circumstances. In Long's case, the split-up of his family is blamed for his turning to the streets, abuse of alcohol and, possibly, drugs, and that whole mixed-up, dropped-out period in his life.[7]

All the major adult characters, in fact, except southern boy's father and the physics teacher, are shown as lacking in morality (*thieu dao duc*). Another important exception is Hung, the pseudo-ethnic, semi-rural character who will be discussed below. The important point is that the adults are generally portrayed as morally corrupt in some way, or, possibly therefore, brutally misguided about what is best for these young people.

One of the early youth–adult relationships highlighted was the authority relationship between the physics teacher, Mr Tung, and the bad-boy student, Ngon.

This relationship, and the root of its breakdown, is clearly shown to be money, specifically, Ngon's family's money and the role of money in the family's social world-view: too much money, too early, and money used as a substitute for good parental supervision, the inference being that the father is more concerned with making money than with bringing up his son properly. Another youth–adult relationship highlighted throughout the serial is the sexual relationship between Hang and Mr Minh, the poet-teacher. This relationship probably caused the most controversy of any aspect of the serial because it cut so deep into the heart of the Confucian education ethic that Vietnamese society clings to so fervently, part of the oft touted 'love of learning'. The Vietnamese discourse on education and on Vietnamese intellectual traditions constantly reiterates the stereotype that the Vietnamese revere education and revere teachers.[8] This, and the matter of Ngon's misconduct and how it was handled, prompted a series of articles condemning the serial in the Ministry of Education newspaper (see, for example, Hoang Huy 1995).

The serial also deals with the matter of relationships between people of ostensibly different 'classes', in particular the relationship between Ha and Long, the former street-kid. Ha's mother tries to put a stop to the relationship because his family is 'not like ours' as she says to him, and although that 'isn't fair', he 'can't change anything', as that is the way society is. In this way, Ha's mother phrases her explanation of why he must not interfere with the plans she has made for her daughter's life. Such an expression of inequality is a powerful statement in a progressive, socialist society, especially as it seems she is positioning her family within an elite that is intellectual and economic, not revolutionary.

Marital relationships are dealt with harshly in the serial. Neither of the two marriages which are shown in most detail – Hang's parents and the teacher Minh and his wife – are shown to be happy. Hang's mother describes her marriage as having been brokered between her parents with Hang's father, and says that they were parted so long by the war that when they were finally married they had already grown into different people with little in common except their child. Hang's father had affairs, and her mother also started an affair. They stayed together not because of any affection between them but because it seemed appropriate and best for Hang. Teacher Minh and his wife are shown to be constantly bickering; she lacks any appreciation of his artistic nature or his non-remunerative poetry (he is teaching only in order to earn a living), and he seems almost repulsed by her brash, avaricious manner. In the end, however, he is shown as being perhaps no better than his wife, and certainly he elects to stay with her. For much of the serial, Minh is the most enigmatic character (in soap-opera terms), for while his treatment of Hang – he abandons her – clearly makes him a Bad Character, he himself is shown to be pitiable, misunderstood, a failure in all aspects of his life except with Hang, who appreciates him for the poet he considers himself to be.

Throughout the serial, a recurrent theme is the modern but immoral use of money to smooth over or to take the place of real, emotion-based relationships. Hang's father, for instance, uses money in every situation in which he finds himself – when he forgets his wife's birthday, he simply gives her money; when Hang starts a new school year, he tries to bribe her with money to do well, and wants to take her out to an expensive restaurant meal when she clearly feels it would be more fun, 'warmer', to eat together at home, something it appears they do infrequently. When Ngon gets in trouble, his father expects the splashing about of presents to dissolve any difficulties, and mentions his 'philanthropic' gifts to the school as a way of leveraging repayment in the form of lenience towards his son. Ngon does not stop when he knocks an old man off his bicycle while recklessly speeding through a red light on his Honda motorbike because he doesn't want to have to pay the old man compensation. His main concern is that the old man might have damaged his motorbike, and he is relieved to find only a headlight is broken. Monetary relations and monetary considerations replace relations of respect, particularly respect for one's elders.

The lifestyles depicted in the serial quite strikingly reflect perceptions of the affluent emptiness and idle corruption of urban life: witness bad-boy Ngon's worry about the state of his headlight after knocking over the old man; Hang's family life is based on lies and their comfortable existence is built on the proceeds of corruption; the Four Seasons skip school to hang out drinking beer at a bar where they are obviously regulars. One theme running through the serial is of the loneliness and isolation of urban lifestyles: the girls, Hang and Ha at least, have their own bedrooms, a physical symbol not only of their affluence but of their emotional estrangement from their families – Hang has had no idea of the true nature of her parents' relationship; Ha's mother routinely transgresses Ha's territory, her privacy, her personal relations, in a way the audience might be expected to assume would not be necessary in rural communities, where everyone's business would be known to all as a matter of course.

The soap-opera genre works by engaging viewers in a discussion about the relationships portrayed in the story-line. As the viewer identifies with a character, s/he is drawn into thinking about the web of relationships around that character, the things that happen to the character, and how s/he reacts. In the case of Hang, for example, the viewer may identify with her as the bright student, the responsible class monitor, the favoured, maybe spoiled, only child … but then is confronted by Hang's shocking relationship with Mr Minh, a relationship Hang clearly advances if not initiates. The viewer, already sympathetic to Hang, is likely to see this not as an act of wanton promiscuity, but as the product of her pitiable family situation, the heavy emotional burden her family places on her, her sense of having been abandoned by them. Thus the viewer is drawn into a consideration of how divorce, and more subtly, how marital unhappiness, affect the children of the family. Is this a declaration that divorce is wrong, which is the general existing consensus? Or is it a declaration that marriages arranged without affection between the partners are recipes for disaster? Or is it 'simply' a challenge to the viewer to think about his/her moral stand on these and related issues?

Certainly, the serial was successful in provoking this sense of dialogue in terms of generating enormous public discussion. The station received sackfuls of letters from viewers, many of them discussing various aspects of the story. There were dozens of newspaper articles, some – particularly in the Ministry of Education newspaper, as noted – discussing in detail certain aspects of the story and their relevance to contemporary society. According to VTV3, *12A and 4H* generated more mail than any other series ever shown during the programme's five years on air. In general, students who wrote in were positive about it and identified with it; parents and journalists tended not to like it and to take issue with aspects of the story-line which they felt 'couldn't really happen'.[9]

Romanticising nature: images of Vietnamese culture in popular culture

The gap between urban and rural lifestyles has seemed, particularly over the last five to six years, to be widening almost daily, with urbanites leading progressively more luxurious and modern lifestyles compared with the constrained access to facilities which is only slowly improving in the rural areas. Yet, it is a recurrent cultural theme in Vietnam, and one which is often reiterated in popular culture, that urban almost always equals bad, and rural equals good. Urban society is cold, modern and stressful; rural society is warm, traditional and timeless, and peaceful. This characterisation intersects with the perception of urban life as spiritually or morally bankrupt, as lacking a spiritual or ideological centre that would hold urban society together as a civilised entity. Rural life, with its close contact with nature, is seen as much more spiritual, more balanced, morally richer and stronger in community feeling. This is a theme which is ubiquitous in Vietnamese literature and culture – the good peasant, the romantic countryside, and the yearning affiliation with one's rural homeland, regardless of the fact that one may never have set foot in it.

The romanticisation of nature is by no means uniquely Asian, the English Romantics being an excellent Western case in point.[10] However, as Bruun and Kalland (1995: 10–11) point out, nature often takes on a religious or philosophical importance in Asian cultures which is unlike its conceptualisation in Western cultures: 'Nature and morality are closely linked in many Asian cultures, man and environment forming a moral unity' (see also Tu Wei-Ming 1989; Tellenback and Kimura 1989). In Vietnamese society in particular, rural society is considered the only purveyor of legitimate Vietnamese culture; urbanites therefore tend to have a rather disjointed relationship with the countryside which is both remote and antithetical, yet their own reality is perceived to be devoid of the characteristic Vietnameseness which constitutes their culture.

While other serials produced by VNCN deal more explicitly and much less subtly with rural–urban relations, *12A and 4H* eloquently expresses the urbanites' romantic view of rural life and the counterpoint role that the countryside plays to the shallow, spiritually and morally bereft lifestyles of the city.[11] The role of rural life and nature in modern, urban society is a major sub-theme in the serial. Their presence is manifest in ways which reveal, to some extent unwittingly, how urbanites idealise the countryside.[12]

One of the early scenes, in which the class is given an afternoon off and the students go to someone's house just outside the city for a picnic, symbolises much of the mystique and the romantic role of the countryside in Vietnamese culture. Here, the young people are pictured in an idyllic setting, by a lake, fishing, roasting corn on the cob or potatoes over a fire, singing … But the scene is also a foreshadowing of the crises to come; never again will these kids be able to be so innocent and therefore so happy and without taint. The note of melancholic consideration that this is their last year together only highlights the poignancy of their transitory happiness. At this moment, in this communion with and in nature, they are harmonious; future difficulties must be overcome by striving to recreate this moment of pure pastoral bliss.

However, after that brief location in romantic nature, Hung, a pseudo-ethnic semi-rural character, comprises the main 'nature' figure in the serial. Hung is a poet, friend of the teacher Minh, who has spent most of his adult life in the mountainous areas living with ethnic minorities who are widely perceived to be more 'native', more 'primitive', and therefore in closer contact with nature. He now dresses in ethnic minority dress, even in the city, and appears to have learned the minorities' secrets of healing. Hung is a pivotal figure in the plot because it is through his ethnic, healing process, his vicariously achieved connection to nature, that Long, prior to the start of the events of the serial, has been cured of his drug and alcohol addiction and has been able to re-integrate himself into mainstream society, albeit with a few bumps along the way courtesy of the moribund attitudes of the less progressive around him. In a similar fashion, at the moment of Hang's crisis, when she is about to throw herself off a bridge, distraught about her family situation and having failed to rouse any support from teacher Minh, who now regrets his involvement with her and wants to get as far away as possible, Long rescues her from herself, and eventually persuades her to go with Hung up to the highlands to experience the restful, healing properties of closeness with the ethnic groups and with nature.

Long is a minor 'nature' figure in the serial, or rather a 'rural' figure, in that he and his father pedal a *cyclo* (bicycle rickshaw) to make money; the kindly *cyclo* driver is a common stereotype in Vietnamese culture, where rich people are often portrayed as greedy and poor people as generous. Long can also be seen in the role of the poor student-hero whose hard work and careful study is rewarded in the end.[13] Long himself still finds it necessary to retreat to that spot by the river under the bridge where he can be in closest solitary communion with nature. Only nature, it seems, is able to rescue the troubled, disenchanted, urban youth. Those, particularly the adults, who do not or cannot experience this spiritual refreshment through nature are portrayed as having 'lost their way', as having become involved with 'social evils', including corruption and adultery.[14]

Conclusion

One of the most interesting things about the Vietnamese television serials is the fact that the local producers have taken a foreign genre, the soap opera, melded it with the foreign and local tradition of melodrama (as evident, for instance, in *The Tale of Kieu* and *Cai luong* (reformed theatre), both examples of the Vietnamese melodramatic tradition), and bent it to convey Vietnamese messages about how the social world should be understood and enacted (see, for example, the discussion of the Cantonese film industry in Ang 1996: 154–5). While using conventions of soap opera – the focus on relationships, on domestic space and domestic situations, on romance, and on coincidences of fate – the serial manages to evoke a range of Vietnamese motifs which call upon notions of 'traditional Vietnamese culture' while at the same time challenging some of the inconsistencies and hypocrisies of modern urban life.[15] Many of the themes which are utilised in the serials were also common themes in earlier literature; it is the persistent Vietnamese practice and ability to infuse foreign genres with local meaning which is the point here.[16]

The central issue in this serial is the attempt by Ha, Hang and their classmates to formulate identities for themselves in a complex social world of modernity and uncertainty. They are not willing to accept unquestioningly the structure of the relationships and identity that their parents force upon them, and often find those relationships to be lacking in substance. Although the serial does not come down firmly on the side of modernity by any means, indeed it shows up plainly the darker side of modern society, it also does not wholeheartedly endorse the firm or blind imposition of presumably 'traditional' roles, relationships and behaviour either. Instead, the serial, like many of the serials in the VNCN series, challenges the order of things in a way that has not been seen since the mobilisation drives to join the national liberation struggle; in a small way, Ha and Hang's rejection of their parents' structuring of their lives is dimly reminiscent of the rejection of the dutiful daughter role played by young women who went off and joined the Communist Party in the 1930s and 1940s. The serial also manages to celebrate modern society's opportunities to create new identities – Long has his renewal, and so does Hang; Ha is able to forge her unsuitable alliance in the face of opposition from her family.

This urban society reflected in locally made TV shows is a society characterised by fragmentation and conflict over social roles and behaviours. The forms of social relationship are in dispute or under negotiation to suit the new circumstances; for example, young people clearly no longer feel it is appropriate to subject themselves unthinkingly to the guidance of their elders (although to what extent has that ever 'really' been the case? Whether the ideal 'Confucian' traditions were in fact more ideals than reality is another study entirely). Modern urban life is affluent, or so it would appear from the serial, but nonetheless is money-centric and therefore tarnished. It is spiritually bereft and constructed in relation to its Other, the spiritually and morally rich rural. Modern urban society is also characterised by choice, though not necessarily by quality, particularly in terms of constructing an identity: as a high school student, does one choose to belong to the Four Seasons gang, delinquents who cut class and drink beer, or to the Four H group, well-behaved and studious goody-two-shoes, whose lives are shown to be built on very shallow moral ground? In the end, young people are able to construct new forms of identity for themselves, negotiating a new path between the stereotypes and obsolete models no longer held to be relevant in the contemporary process of transformation.

Notes

1 *12A and 4H* was also remarkable in that the director and co-screenwriter was himself quite young (aged twenty-five at the time of filming) and had never written or directed a television serial before. Among the enormous publicity this serial generated (discussed below), the youth of the director was often noted.

2 Known both as 'Kim-Van-Kieu' and 'Truyen Kieu', it is the most famous Vietnamese poem, composed in the early nineteenth century by Nguyen Du. It is also an epic of doomed romance, filial piety, self-sacrifice and everlasting love on a scale which puts *Wuthering Heights* to shame (Huard and Durand 1954: 272–4). Tragic romance is not a uniquely Vietnamese preference, see also Phillips (n.d.) for a discussion of trendy Japanese soap operas and their lack of happy endings.

3 I was told that*The Rich Also Cry* ended suddenly with a one-episode wrap-up which abruptly terminated every suspenseful story-line – unknown parentages, lost siblings, etc. – much to the amusement and satisfaction of many friends and acquaintances who, along with what seemed to be the rest of their compatriots with access to a television, had followed the serial avidly.

4 One small example of this is evident in a viewer letter given to me by Nguyen Khai Hung (editor of the VNCN series). It was written by an older woman to comment on another serial – *The People Who Live around Us* (*Nguoi Song Quanh Ta*). In the letter, the writer/viewer thanks the producers of the serial profusely for making the serial, and notes similarities between the lives of characters in the serial and the life of her brother and sister-in-law. She says that she cried so much while watching it that she had to watch TV with a small towel (hankie) in her hand; she writes to thank the producers for making a serial which brings her such strong feelings of love with which nothing can compare.

5 Elsewhere I discuss how these serials, *12A and 4H* included, produce and reinforce notions of certain types of femininities (Drummond forthcoming).

6 This supports the state's one- or two-child policy.

7 These apologies may also be interpreted as metaphors for a larger culpability on the part of the parents, of all Vietnamese parents, for the difficulties of socialism which they chose for the best of reasons but which has had significant negative effects for their children (lack of quality education, lack of access to higher education on basis of merit, lack of choice in employment, and more general difficulties in terms of food security, healthcare, and so on). I am not convinced, however, that this was the intention.

8 This is a stereotype which is belied by responses to a 1996 survey of local authorities in three communes of Thu Duc District, which reported that 'lack of parental concern' was the main reason behind school-age dropouts (see discussion in Drummond 1999, Chapter Five).

9 Nguyen Khai Hung, interviewed February 1998. The station had, unfortunately, disposed of all these letters from viewers by the time of my research.

10 See, for example, the discussion of nature as an actor in *The Modern American Novel* (Goldsmith 1991). See also Schmitt (1969), Fuller (1988) and Pringle (1988).

11 For example, *Doi Nha Len Pho*, a VNCN series which deals with the experiences of a flower-growing household on the outskirts of Hanoi. The family decides to sell their land and use the money to buy an apartment in the city. The serial chronicles their difficulties in adjusting to the pace of city life (this contrast is effectively if predictably underlined with peaceful shots of rural life quickly giving way to the

chaotic and noisy urban traffic). They are taken advantage of by unscrupulous, urban characters, they miss the close neighbourly ties they had in the village, and their family is almost devastated when their son becomes a heroin addict. In another very popular serial, *Ngot Ngao va Man Tra*, a rich and scheming urban family cons a sweet, studious and dutiful rural student into thinking that their mentally ill son is actually his twin brother with whom the student had fallen in love when he came on holidays to the countryside where she lived. That young man had in fact left Vietnam as a boat person and resettled in Germany, and the family takes advantage of the student's misplaced affection to dupe her into caring for the brother. This serial has been shown on TV a number of times and is also famous because the male lead committed suicide soon after it was completed, making it his last. See Thomas and Hiang-Khng Heng (2000) for a discussion of the actor's funeral and the national mourning his death produced.

12 This idealisation is pervasive, in my experience, among urbanites, increasing in intensity in positive relation to their education, sense of the aesthetic and claims to a modern, urban lifestyle, and in inverse proportion to the likelihood of their having spent any significant time residing in a rural area (with the possible exception of those urbanites who as children in the 1960s were evacuated from Hanoi to the countryside during the American war in Vietnam).

13 I am grateful to Melinda Kerkvliet for pointing out this possible reading of the character of Long. A 1997 news story about *cyclo* drivers also mentions the 'guardian angel' *cyclo* stories of stopping thieves and robberies, of even getting injured in the process (Nguyen Ba Hoang 1997).

14 Eisenstadt (1995: 200) notes, regarding the Japanese conceptualisation of nature and the role of nature in daily life and daily rituals, that: 'The basic [Japanese] attitude to nature gave rise, in daily discourse, in daily artistic activities as well as in aesthetic discourse, in the construction of gardens or homes, to a very strong emphasis on proximity to nature, on being at one with nature. … [emphasising] the quest for unity with nature.'

15 Sun (2001: 82) notes how 1990s' Chinese television dramas also display a 'Chinese ambivalence towards modernity'.

16 The hybrid nature of many features of Vietnamese culture and its iconography (e.g. the *ao dai*) is frequently remarked upon (Marr 1981; Lockhart 1996; Nguyen Van Ky 1995; Woodside 1976, particularly for his discussion of the adoption of the novel in the 1930s; Woodside 1988).

Bibliography

Abercrombie, N. (1996) *Television and Society*, Cambridge: Polity Press.

Abu-Lughod, L. (1995) 'The Objects of Soap Opera: Egyptian Television and the Cultural Politics of Modernity', in D. Miller (ed.), *Worlds Apart: Modernity through the Prism of the Local*, London and New York: Routledge.

Allen, R.C. (1995) 'Introduction', in R.C. Allen (ed.), *To Be Continued…. Soap Operas around the World*, London: Routledge.

Ang, I. (1991) *Watching Dallas: Soap Opera and the Melodramatic Imagination*, London and New York: Routledge

—— (1996) *Living Room Wars: Rethinking Media Audiences for a Postmodern World*, London and New York: Routledge.

Biltereyst, D. and Meers, P. (2000) 'The International Telenovela Debate and the Contra-Flow Argument: A Reappraisal', *Media, Culture & Society*, 22: 393–413.

Brunsdon, C. (1997) *Screen Tastes: Soap Opera to Satellite Dishes*, London: Routledge.

Bruun, O. and Kalland, A. (eds) (1985) 'Images of Nature: An Introduction to the Stud of Man–Environment Relations in Asia', in O. Bruun and A. Kalland (eds), *Asia Perceptions of Nature: A Critical Approach*, Richmond: Curzon Press, 1–24.

Chu, G.C., Schramm, A. and Schramm, W. (1991) *Social Impact of Satellite Television in Rura Indonesia*, Singapore: Asian Mass Communication Research and Information Centre.

Dao Mai Trang (1995) 'Trang Van Nghe Chu Nhat Truyen Hinh', *Thanh Nien Tap Chi*: 19.

Das, V. (1995) 'On Soap Opera: What Kind of Anthropological Object Is It?', in D. Miller (ed.), *Worlds Apart: Modernity through the Prism of the Local*, London and New York: Routledge.

Drummond, L.B.W. (1999) *Mapping Modernity: Perspectives on Everyday Life in Vietnam's Urbanising Society*, unpublished PhD thesis, Australian National University.

—— (forthcoming) 'Producing Modern Femininities: Portrayals of Vietnamese Womanhood in Local Television Dramas', in K. Iwabuchi and L. T. Reyes (ed.), *Feeling Asian Modernities*, Manila: Anivil Publishing.

Drummond, P. and Paterson, R. (eds) (1988) *Television and its Audience: International Research Perspectives*, London: BFI Publishing.

Eisenstadt, S.N. (1995) 'The Japanese Attitude to Nature: A Framework of Basic Ontological Conceptions', in O. Bruun and A. Kalland (eds), *Asian Perceptions of Nature: A Critical Approach*, Richmond: Curzon Press.

Flores-Gutierrez, M. (2000) 'Film vs. Television Versions of the Mexican Revolution: A Comparative Analysis of Political Ideology', in *Convergencia,* 7(23): 177–95.

Fuller, P. (1988) 'The Geography of Mother Mature', in D. Cosgrove and S. Daniels (eds), *The Iconography of Landscape: Essays on the Symbolic Representation, Design, and Use of Past Environments*, Cambridge: Cambridge University Press.

Goldsmith, A.L. (1991) *The Modern American Urban Novel: Nature as 'Interior Structure'*, Detroit: Wayne State University Press.

Hoang Huy (1995) '"12A va 4H": Mot Bo Phim Phan Giao Duc' ('"12A and 4H": A Film which Betrays Education'), *Giao Duc va Thoi Dai*, Hanoi: 6.

Huard, P. and Durand, M. (1954) *Connaisance du Viet-Nam*, Paris and Hanoi: Imprimerie Nationale and Ecole Française d'Extreme-Orient.

Keane, M. (1998) 'Television and Moral Development in China', *Asian Studies Review*, 22(4): 475–503.

Livingstone, S. (1998) *Making Sense of Television: The Psychology of Audience Interpretation*, Chapter Three, 'The Case of Soap Opera', London and New York: Routledge.

Lockhart, G. (1996) 'Introduction', in G. Lockhart and M. Lockhart (eds), *The Light of the Capital: Three Modern Vietnamese Classics*, Kuala Lumpur: Oxford University Press.

Lopez, A.M. (1995) 'Our Welcomed Guests: *Telenovelas* in Latin America', in R.C. Allen (ed.), *To Be Continued.... Soap Operas around the World*, London: Routledge.

Marr, D.G. (1981) *Vietnamese Tradition on Trial: 1920–1945*, Berkeley: University of California Press.

Martin-Barbero, J. (1995) 'Memory and Form in the Latin American Soap Opera', in R.C. Allen (ed.), *To Be Continued.... Soap Operas around the World*, London: Routledge.

Nguyen Ba Hoang (1997) 'Pedalling for a Living in HCM City', *Vietnam News*, HCMC: 7.

Nguyen Van Ky (1995) *La Société Vietnamienne Face à la Modernité: Le Tonkin de la fin du XIXe Siècle à la Seconde Guerre Mondiale*, Paris: L'Harmattan.

Phillips, G. (n.d.) *Trendy or Timeless? The Classical Heritage of Japanese Television Love Stories*, unpublished paper.

Pringle, T.R. (1988) 'The Privation of History: Landseer, Victoria, and the Highland Myth', in D. Cosgrove and S. Daniels (eds), *The Iconography of Landscape: Essays on the Symbolic Representation, Design, and Use of Past Environments*, Cambridge: Cambridge University Press.

Rofel, L. (1994a) 'Liberation Nostalgia and a Yearning for Modernity', in C.K. Gilmartin, G. Hershatter, L. Rofel and T. White (eds), *Engendering China: Women, Culture, and the State*, Cambridge, MA: Harvard University Press.

—— (1994b) '*Yearnings*: Televisual Love and Melodramatic Politics in Contemporary China', *American Ethnologist*, 21(4): 700–22.

—— (1995) 'The Melodrama of National Identity in Post-Tiananmen China', in R.C. Allen (ed.), *To Be Continued.... Soap Operas around the World*, London: Routledge.

Schmitt, P.J. (1969) *Back to Nature: The Arcadian Myth in Urban America*, New York: Oxford University Press.

Sun, Wanning (2001) 'A Chinese in the New World: Television Dramas, Global Cities, and Travels to Modernity', *Inter-Asia Cultural Studies*, 2(1): 81–94.

Tellenback, H. and Kimura, B. (1989) 'The Japanese Concept of "nature"', in J.B. Callicott and R.T. Ames (eds), *Nature in Asian Traditions of Thought: Essays in Environmental Philosophy*, Albany: State University of New York Press.

Thomas, M. and Hiang-Khng Heng, R. (2000) 'Stars in the Shadows: Celebrities, Media and the State in Contemporary Vietnam', in Yao Souchou (ed.), *House of Glass: Culture, Modernity and the State in South East Asia*, Singapore: Institute for South East Asian Studies.

Tu Wei-Ming (1989) 'The Continuity of Being: Chinese Visions of Nature', in J.B. Callicott and R.T. Ames (eds), *Nature in Asian Traditions of Thought: Essays in Environmental Philosophy*, Albany: State University of New York Press.

Williams, C.T. (1992a) 'It's Time for My Story': Oral Culture in the Technological Era – Towards a Methodology for Soap Opera Audience Study', in S. Frentz (ed.), *Staying Tuned: Contemporary Soap Opera Criticism*, Bowling Green: Bowling Green State University Popular Press.

—— (1992b) *'It's Time for My Story': Soap Opera Sources, Structure, and Response*, Westport: Praeger.

Woodside, A.B. (1976) *Community and Revolution in Modern Vietnam*, Boston: Houghton Mifflin Company.

—— (1988) *Vietnam and the Chinese Model: A Comparative Study of Vietnamese and Chinese Government in the First Half of the Nineteenth Century*, Cambridge, MA and London: Harvard University Press.

Zha, J. (1995) *China Pop: How Soap Operas, Tabloids, and Bestsellers Are Transforming a Culture*, New York: The New Press.

Chapter 11

Spatiality and political change in urban Vietnam

Mandy Thomas

Introduction

In June 2001, West Lake in Hanoi became a landscape over which a struggle took place between local people and foreign developers, planners, historians and environmentalists. In a dramatic move by the government, a US$32 million Austrian-funded project to clean up the waters of the capital's landmark lake was rejected following a barrage of criticism in the official media (Agence France-Presse, 30 June 2001; hereafter AFP). The largest of around twenty lakes which dot the capital and are the pride of Hanoians, the 526 hectare (1,300 acre) West Lake shelters some of the capital's plushest residential neighbourhoods on its shores. Home to more than 450 species of animals and 59 species of birds, it is seen as a major environmental and leisure amenity. Throughout Hanoi, people are joining forces with professional associations to protest against the planning and destruction of their city. These interventions are a clear departure from the previous timidity with which the populace watched the transformations take place about them.

At the same time as different groups contest Hanoi's changing architecture and street landscapes, the urban population is participating in a large-scale popular movement to reclaim the pavements and streets for their own activities and pleasures. From the roadside celebrations after football matches to pavement commercial ventures and the funerals of popular local heroes, the people are occupying the public spaces of the city for 'unofficial' activities. At the same time, the increasing rural unrest in the country has moved into the city streets. In July 2001, farmers held a protest in Hanoi over long-standing official corruption and illegal land confiscation (Reuters, 9 July 2001). Hanoians witnessing the protest suggested that this was just the beginning of complaints being taken to the streets. Hanoi here is not just a backdrop for political statement but is itself being reconstructed both architecturally and socially to define new political frameworks. In this chapter, I argue that the contestation over development in the city along with the changing role of public space can together be viewed as a powerful indicator that the public sphere and civil society have entered the Vietnamese cultural landscape. Community involvement in high-level government planning for the city, street protests against corruption and the flagrant dismissal of police attempts to order unruly activities in public spaces must be seen, together with the abandonment of interest in state-organised rituals in the monumental spaces of the city, as evidence of an emerging community politics which is grounded in the local and everyday experiences of the streets.

I begin by outlining the history of spatial meanings and landscapes in Hanoi and the recent changes that have taken place. I then document the ways in which popular culture has become enmeshed with people's activities in public spaces. The modalities through which Hanoians have critiqued development of the city in recent years are then analysed in order to draw links between the rise of public debate over housing, commercial developments and architecture in the city, with the activities of ordinary people in public spaces. I conclude by suggesting that the ideas of Habermas and Arendt are applicable to these spatial phenomena in their attention to the connection between public space and the rise of a participatory public sphere.

The changing fabric of Hanoi's cityscape

In December 2001, while walking along Dien Bien Phu Street in Hanoi, I saw a skateboarder, the first I had ever seen in Hanoi. On Dien Bien Phu, across from the Museum of Revolutionary History, is a statue of Lenin on a raised, stone platform within a larger area of paved concrete. The teenage boy was skating on the base of Lenin's statue, grinding the board along one side of it, and leaping up with the board over the entire base (Figure 11.1). When I saw him, I was on my way to visit Ba Dinh Square, the large, formal space of the state in the vicinity of many other national monuments, a space which is to a large degree defined by the huge, dark mausoleum of Ho Chi Minh at the far end. When I arrived in Ba Dinh Square, a man was jogging along the expanse of concrete in front of the mausoleum (Figure 11.2). These two activities, skateboarding and jogging, were taking place around national monuments for a very good reason. These sites were two of the rare places in Hanoi where there is flat, clear ground and few people, making them highly suitable for skating or running. The vitality of the city is made apparent through the human use of the built environment. In Hanoi, the stark monuments of the state are now being used by citizens as backdrops for activities that are apolitical. Statues and state buildings no longer hold a sacred aura for much of the populace.

In a city such as Hanoi, in the grip of a major social and economic transition, struggles over geography are over the contours of meaning in the layout of the city, buildings and public spaces. Throughout its history, different regimes have imposed different buildings, public spaces and monuments upon the landscape. And each new layer is superimposed upon remnants of earlier regimes: the earliest Vietnamese-Chinese pagodas and temples, the French colonial buildings and streetscapes, the Soviet period and the recent period of mixed architectural 'modern' forms. Through each regime, as Ainley suggests, 'architecture and design have been used as a means to exert control, across lines of class, race, gender and nation, in a myriad of ways: the imposition of physical barriers; limiting access to public, shared spaces and facilities; restrictive and inappropriate models of housing organisation; even down to the right to change colour

Figure 11.1 Skateboarder, Lenin's Statue

Figure 11.2 Jogger in Ba Dinh Square

Note: The penguin at the lower right is a dustbin, an unusual recent addition to the Square which also lessens the formality of the space.

schemes' (Ainley 1998: 63). By spatially analysing these fluctuations, it is possible to visualise the material and social form of political change and explore the multiple scales of space, 'the space of the nation, the space of the city, the space of the sect or group, as well as the space of the object, building, square or even human being' (Low 2001: 161). The links between these different spaces, from the nation to the everyday movement of people on pavements, are apparent throughout Hanoi's major public spaces and streetscapes.

Since the process of reform has been undertaken, urban space in Vietnam has been transformed not so much by architectural reconfigurations, but rather by the use of available space brought about primarily by economic transformation. Throughout most of the 1980s, many report that, even if there had been money to buy goods, there was nothing to buy. As Gabriel Thien Than, an overseas Vietnamese described it, Hanoi was an 'ascetic' capital in the 1980s (cited in Logan 2000: 217). Logan reports that, during this period,

> The once fashionable Rue Paul Bert was now an extremely depressed Trang Tien Street; the private shops and cafes had gone, replaced by the State Department Store – a 'palais de la desolation' according to Galude Palazzoli. Population densities in the Ancient Quarter had become extreme … and people were feeling that life was scarcely better now than during the war when at least they had their revolutionary ardour to cheer them.
>
> (Logan 2000: 217)

There was no street trading, only large, state-managed outlets for the distribution of goods from state-controlled cooperative farms and industries. As a result, the streets did not bustle, and, as reported to me by Hanoi residents, people were under the close scrutiny of neighbours and employers. People moved about to and from their places of study or work, but there were no hives of activity on the streets except during Tet. During this period, individuals only experienced very limited freedom of movement and were almost continuously under surveillance from neighbours and colleagues. The economic transformations that then took place led to a rapid evolution of consumption patterns, to a highly diverse, street-trading, cultural life and also to the possibility of people congregating in groups, at noodle soup shops, in parks, and with tea and cigarette sellers on the pavements. The transformations in the use of space and the corresponding dynamic city life that developed out of these spatial and economic changes have become too complex and uncontrollable to be disciplined by the police or the party despite ever-present directives and sanctions on street activities.

Embellished public space: leisure, pop culture, celebrity and protest

While cities are deeply implicated in shaping the everyday experiences of the populaces who inhabit them (Boys 1998: 217), the diversification of what people do in public space itself can constitute new public and built environments. The resurgence of an active and lively street life in Vietnam has occurred 'as users become increasingly emboldened in their occupation of this space – as an extension of domestic space, an annexation of commercial space and a space for personal expression' (Drummond 2000: 2389). Logan's description of Hanoi's recent changes reveal the disordered but decidedly spatial ways in which the city has been experiencing economic and social change:

> The economic restructuring unleashed in 1986 found its geographical focus in Vietnam's cities, but now urban development began to take place in the context of a private market in real estate and construction. This profound ideological change has led, according to one's political stance, to a new set of triumphs or a new set of disasters – or, indeed, to some of each. The changing pace and the widening scope of change soon became obvious to both citizenry and to external commentators: work practices and leisure possibilities, the composition of education curricula, the choice of available consumer goods, aesthetic tastes – all were being dramatically affected. The propaganda hoardings and advertising billboards around the city were early visual signs of change. The socialist wall posters featuring Ho Chi Minh and idealised figures of the worker, peasant and soldier disappeared. New boards went up above temples, pagodas and shop-houses for Pepsi, Fujcolour, Kenwood and Konica.
>
> (Logan 2000: 253)

In Vietnam the recent changes in the human activities in public spaces have been instrumental in signalling wider societal change and in transforming architectural spaces. These transformations are apparent in the forms of commerce undertaken in public spaces, the new forms of leisure and increasing number of people on the street, not seen during the 1980s. Where crowds were always a component of state- (stage-)managed events, now public spaces are attracting large numbers of people for supposedly non-political activities that may become transgressive acts condemned by the regime. These events include religious festivals, street celebrations after football matches, public gatherings outside law courts, and the massing of the public at the funeral of a popular young actor (see Thomas 2001). Popular culture has provided the public with the means to transcend the constraints of official, authorised and legitimate codes of behaviour in public space.

Changes in the use of public space can map the sets of relations between the public and the state, making these transforming relationships visible, although fraught with contradictions and anomalies. The shifts in the emotional valence and political meaning of the crowd in Vietnam over the last decade have allowed public space to become a site through which transgressive ideologies and desires may have an outlet. The crowd in Hanoi has undergone a huge semantic shift since the 1940s. Clearly, for the party crowds, previously the most splendid instantiation of state power, now signify the worrying possibility of subversion. Memories of the crowds that tore down the Berlin Wall, the crowds in Tiananmen Square and in 1998 at Parliament House in Jakarta would add to the concern that officials have for the power of the crowd to overturn and threaten.[1] The party has seen the impact of the potent mix of a public desire for reform and media interest in crowd formation in Eastern Europe as well as in China and elsewhere in Asia. The evidence for this is manifold. Recent rural uprisings, particularly in the northern coastal province of Thai Binh, have clearly been of continuing concern for the regime.[2] The party has had to devote considerable effort to arrest declining membership and has not been successful in promoting attendance at state-organised public events. Yet religious festivals are attracting larger gatherings of people every year and undergoing a resurgence in popularity with a rather dramatic flourishing of popular festivals and pilgrimages. Crowd behaviour at funerals and weddings as well as the phenomenon of groups of young motorbike riders racing through city streets have been increasing in frequency throughout Vietnam in recent years, and the party is increasingly attempting to curb these activities. Football crowds are also of concern to the party as they signify disrespect for authority and a loosening of party control. When Vietnam's soccer team beat Indonesia in the South East Asian Games in 1997 there was a spontaneous mass outpouring onto the streets of Hanoi and Saigon. The disruption of public order was stressed in newspapers reporting the event, as a number of people died in traffic accidents that night as a combined result of alcohol and youths racing their motorcycles. Likewise, at the Tiger Games in Hanoi in 1998, after a semi-final win by Vietnam, there were numerous arrests relating to public disorder and the setting off of firecrackers, which are now banned in Vietnam. There have even been reports of a massing of military personnel in city army barracks in preparation for possible outbreaks of civil disorder during the final of the World Cup soccer match in both 1998 and 2002 (Carl Thayer, personal communication). In June 2002, the World Cup created a sensation in Vietnam (Xinhuanet, 12 June 2002). Reuters reported that 'a few hours before the start of the 2002 World Cup Ha Noi football fans packed into cafes in their thousands around the city to watch the opening match between France and Senegal' (Reuters, 1 June 2002). Immense crowds of young people, finding all the seats taken inside the cafes all over the inner city, simply sat outside on the pavements, drinking and talking about the World Cup (VNS, 6 June 2002). While the government was keeping a watchful eye over the spectators of the World Cup, in a contradictory gesture, the state approved giant public screens around Hanoi for people to watch the matches. These new cultural spaces of post-socialism are sites where the regime recognises the loss of emotive popular appeal in the revolutionary nationalist project and, as a result, paradoxically endorses new forms of iconic consumption.

In this contemporary period, Vietnam is undergoing economic liberalisation without political democratisation. There is widespread poverty, mismanagement of the economy, systemic corruption and little change in the overall political culture. There is still no permitted dissent as the party continues to monopolise power. Elsewhere I have written about the new representational object in the media culture of Vietnam: pop celebrity (Thomas and Hiang-Khng Heng 2000: 287–312). The eager reception of the media icon constitutes not so much a challenge to state power as a shift in the ideological landscape – one over which the state can no longer maintain its dominance.[3]. Cities in Vietnam over the last decade have come to provide the physical and social space of streetscapes and public areas where previously suppressed economic, political and cultural activities are being engaged in and are openly viewed and enjoyed. Public spaces such as Ba Dinh Square, although for the most part empty, have the potential to be occupied by citizens wishing to subvert their planned meaning (McDonogh 1993: 15). Where the permissible and state-legitimated groups and organisations of the past are now crumbling (groups such as workers, military, women and youth mass organisations), new spatial configurations of people have arisen to replace them and often to undermine them. Neighbourhoods and networks of individuals may develop around the sharing of domestic or commercial space, or as interest groups with common goals and activities. In April 2001, when the renowned Vietnamese singer Trinh Cong Son (known as Vietnam's Bob Dylan) died, his funeral provided the means for the amassing of people in mourning throughout Vietnam. Like the death of Le Cong several years before (see Thomas 2001), the event marked the appeal of a local celebrity over high-ranking cadres whose funerals lack an audience. The funeral processions of these popular icons cause traffic jams, a media frenzy and a spontaneous outpouring of emotional connection that is the envy of any state mobilisation of grassroots participation. When a crowd such as that at the singer Trinh Cong Son's funeral begins to form, it is the networks of people in the spaces of neighbourhoods that are able to collect together in new allegiances and solidarities.

The formation of transgressive crowds is related to the revivifying of a public space that until recently encoded state control, not only through the restrictions on people's movement but also through an economic system that emphasised production and workspace rather than consumption and leisure space. The use of public space for everyday activities has been a catalyst for crowd formation. Trading, religious festivals, performances, music and gambling have taken place historically on the streets of Vietnam. That many of these are outlawed today has not prevented people from continuing to perform them. However, although ignoring the state's laws on street trading and performing is inevitably a form of protest, it usually never moves beyond the individual or the family. Communities of individuals for the most part have not gathered to protest together. The state has come to tolerate to some degree a more diverse range of activities on pavements, parks and streets and a more spontaneous use of public spaces for religious or other activities. In doing so, they have unwittingly allowed a spatiality that encourages new collectivities that may congeal at any moment into a crowd. The 'illegal' use of public space by individuals wishing to earn an income forms the necessary kernel for the use of public space by crowds for non-state reasons. The latter use of public space offers a fundamental challenge to the established norms of the state.

The emerging focus in contemporary Vietnam on bodily pleasure rather than bodily discipline is mapping out social and political change and providing a cartography of a nation passing through a phase of critical re-evaluation. The senses and everyday practices are presently offering up a set of tropes through which transgressive ideologies and desires may have an outlet. An efflorescence of new religious movements that explode in textures, sounds and tastes are enticing the populace away from the solemn state- (stage-)managed spectacles in which bodies of high-ranking cadres are offered up as senseless signifiers of 'nothing but' the people, the nation and the party. As Lisa Drummond has elegantly demonstrated, the contrast between 'public space' and 'private space' is becoming increasingly complicated:

> ...the distinction between public space and private space in Vietnamese cities is increasingly blurred both from the 'inside out' and the 'outside in'. By these terms I mean that, from the inside-out, families and individuals make use of so-called public space for private activities to an extent and in ways that render that public space notionally private. And from the outside-in, the state's interventions in so-called 'private' space, particularly in the organisation of domestic life, are so invasive and wide-ranging as to negate or seriously compromise a conceptualisation of 'private' space'.
>
> (Drummond 2000: 2378)

The increasing transpositions of the state's power to control the activities of both 'private' and 'public' spaces is indicative of the desire 'to force a mutual substitution of the dominant and the dominated in the power structure which leaves nothing to doubt about its own identity as a project of power' (Guha 1983: 9). In sum, there is considerable room for the exploration of unintended meanings of all forms of space in Vietnam, and for different positions to be held simultaneously in this period of increasing civil unrest in which there are numerous inversions of meaning of public monuments as well as both private and public spaces (Wainwright *et al.* 2000). At such moments, the populace 'attempt to destroy or appropriate for themselves the signs of authority of those who dominate them' (Wainwright *et al.* 2000: 28).

Conflicting spaces

The contrast between the ascetic, carceral Hanoi of the 1980s and the sensuous, lively Hanoi of the present is exemplified in the following exploration of the two key national spaces of Hanoi, Ba Dinh Square (see Figure 11.2) and Hoan Kiem Lake (see Figures 11.3 and 11.4). Ba Dinh Square is a formal, unpeopled monumental space of the state and Hoan Kiem Lake is a space of human activity, nostalgia and commerce. In 1945, Ho Chi Minh declared independence for Vietnam in Ba Dinh Square in Hanoi. Being a spectator of this formative national moment assured many individuals of a lifelong commitment to the social revolution. Ba Dinh Square today is a very different space and has been reshaped, remodelled and rebuilt under different colonial regimes. Since Ho Chi Minh occupied that site to jubilantly claim independence, the immense formal public space has been restructured to reflect 'socialist architecture', in which the

Figure 11.3 Hoan Kiem Lake, morning

Figure 11.4 Hoan Kiem Lake, afternoon

urban landscape marks an iconography of the relations between the Soviet Bloc and Hanoi (Logan 1994: 59–60). The site of Ho Chi Minh's inauguration of independent north Vietnam in 1954 is now surrounded by numerous buildings, including Ho Chi Minh's Mausoleum, a massive, isolated, solemn shrine on a barren expanse of concrete.[4] There is an overwhelming sense of remoteness and formality in the structures of Ba Dinh Square and this is reinforced by the security forces monitoring it and the wide roads surrounding it. The cement and grass expanse of the Square is flanked by several historically important buildings, including the One Pillar Pagoda built in 1049, the former colonial residence of the French Governor-General of Indochina, as well as the buildings of the National Assembly and Ho Chi Minh's Mausoleum (Tai 1995: 280).

The Square may be the politically symbolic centre of the city but, a few kilometres away, Hoan Kiem Lake with its picturesque bridge and Tortoise Pagoda is the symbolic heart of Hanoi, with its bustling street life, cafés, ice-cream stores and endless traffic. It is the popular site of morning exercises, festival activities and picnics. In January 2002, the largest commercial centre in Hanoi was opened on Hoan Kiem Lake, the US$10 million Trang Tien Plaza on the site of the former Hanoi State Department Store. The centre contains supermarkets, cafés, retail outlets and car parking (Vietnam News Service, 13 January 2002). 'The historic core [of Hanoi] is where people continue to flock from the suburbs to stroll around Hoan Kiem Lake, take part in Tet and other festivities, and enjoy the superior entertainment and recreation facilities, shops and services that exist there' (Logan 2000: 261). The two opposing public spaces, Ba Dinh Square and Hoan Kiem Lake, represent two differing sites of the struggle for control over symbolic space, the former a socially empty space of political capital and the latter a culturally and socially significant space of the people.

The changing meanings of such nationally important spaces are historically contingent and, like all spatial meaning, can only be understood through the lens of the past (Rotenberg and McDonogh 1993: xiv). Throughout the city, the ideological changes that have taken place since independence are reflected in streetscapes and government architecture, but also in the configurations of the people in public space. Sites such as Ba Dinh Square have become sites of potential political unrest, because the space itself and the political events that take place there represent a regime out of touch with the populace. By exploring how power is not only represented in buildings and urban design in Hanoi, but how that power may be subverted by the public's use of the urban landscape, it is possible to reveal the profound intertwining of urban processes with political and social change in transitional societies such as Vietnam (Low 1996; Ding 1994; DiGrigorio1995). The following international press report indicates the conscious attempt by Vietnamese demonstrators to use the city's landscape as the most meaningful and powerful stage for protests:

> Carrying signs reading 'Down with corrupt gangs,' the demonstrators said local officials had taken their land, sold it for large amounts of money, and then pushed them off the land without any compensation. 'It's corrupt all

> the way from the top down,' said one protester. 'They steal our land and they leave us nothing.' Another demonstrator, who also asked not to be identified because of fears of government retribution, said residents had tried repeatedly over the past six years to get the central government to address their complaints. 'We've come many times before but they always say next time, next time. We've even protested in front of Nong Duc Manh's house, but he doesn't listen to us,' he said, referring to the new chief of Vietnam's ruling Communist Party. The group, which included elderly people and children, walked on Sunday from Thanh Chi district, about seven kilometers from the city, hoping to convince the People's Committee to resolve their complaints. Instead, police refused to allow them to meet with a government official. Officers erected metal barriers at both ends of Le Lai street, just off central Hoan Kiem Lake, and pushed away curious bystanders. Protesters weren't arrested but an Associated Press photographer and reporter were escorted away by security officials. Groups of peasants from around the country occasionally protest at Ba Dinh Square, the seat of central government offices, when the National Assembly is in session.
>
> (Associated Press, 9 June 2001)

The contrast drawn by protestors between Hoan Kiem Lake and Ba Dinh Square is a clear form of 'tactical appropriation' of the two spaces (De Certeau 1984). Ba Dinh Square has become the site of authorised, formal, state-managed events, May Day celebrations, state funerals and state anniversaries. The state funerals for important cadres previously attracted thousands of people who lined the streets to see the funeral party pass by. Recently, only people living along the route bother to attend. Ho Chi Minh's 110th birthday celebration in May 2000 was intended to employ Ho's popular image to drum up support for the Communist Party which is struggling with its corruption-tainted and economically disaster-ridden image. Instead, the audience of the high-profile events consisted mostly of the party faithful who gathered in Ba Dinh Hall in Vietnam's National Assembly building (AAP Worldstream, 19 May 2000). Public apathy also marked the 130th anniversary of Lenin's birthday celebrations in April 2000 and the funeral of Pham Van Dong in May 2000. In Hanoi in January 1999, the public completely ignored the funeral of General Doan Khue, a Political Bureau member of the Communist Party and former Defence Minister. In April 1998, when a former Vietnamese Communist Party leader, Nguyen Van Linh, died, foreign reporters were barred from his funeral in Ho Chi Minh City (AFP, 29 April 1998). Rather than crowds of mourners lining the street, groups of security police were stationed along the roads and on corners surrounding the Reunification Hall where the body was lying in state. Likewise, the 25th anniversary celebrations of the end of the war and the reunification of north and south Vietnam, held in Saigon in April 2000, were marked by tight security and public distance (AFP August 10, 2000). In Hanoi, during the anniversary celebrations, a pro-democracy protest by thirty farmers from a southern province was held in Ba Dinh Square as police hurried to prevent the public from viewing this sign of rural unrest (Reuters, 30 April 2000).

It is thus clear that the formal ceremonies that celebrate and dramatise the rule of the party have no audience on the street. Even though these celebrations are broadcast on television, the viewing audience is unengaged. Instead, audiences, crowds and spectators are being brought together throughout the country for potentially threatening activities. For example, a major Catholic church event, the 200th anniversary of a holy sanctuary, was held in August 1998 in Hue. Seven million Catholics in the country consider La Vang to be their holiest site and over 150,000 descended on the shrine for the anniversary event. However, in May 1998, the party was already attempting to limit the number who attended, stating that there were logistical and financial reasons why it was unfeasible to encourage crowds at the site (AFP, 5 May 1998). Tourist visas to Vietnam during this period were severely restricted and even the Pope was discouraged from coming to the event. As it transpired, there was no civil unrest at the occasion itself but the state had effectively managed to persuade the organisers to reduce the numbers in attendance. Hue is the major site of religious protest in the country and, while Vietnam has embraced reform, religious groups still face restrictions. Thus, as audiences on a grand scale have abandoned attendance at party events, the party is limiting participation and therefore crowd formation at unofficial events.

In contrast to the contests over formal sites of state rule, struggles over the surrounds of Hoan Kiem Lake are focused more upon the public's notion of landscape aesthetics and history. Logan (2000: 238) reports that one of the most publicly fraught building projects to arise in Hanoi has been that of the Golden Hanoi Hotel, on the banks of Hoan Kiem Lake, 'where it was set to impinge upon key vistas of the lake, its two islands and the 1843 Ngoc Son Temple'. The building remains incomplete as public outcry over its height of eleven storeys (well over the five-storey limit for the area) forced the foreign developers into a stalemate with the People's Committee. It was claimed one of the ten most controversial and newsworthy stories of the year in 1996 (in Logan, 2000) and one which demonstrated the active involvement of civil society, where civil society designates 'those social organisations, associations and institutions that exist beyond the sphere and control of the state' (Friedmann 1998: 21). As Logan argues, this was the first time that many official protests had been made by professional associations, in particular the Vietnamese Architects' Association and the Vietnamese Association of Historical Science. These representations accurately reflected the anger of the public 'and challenged the legitimacy of actions by both Hanoi planning authorities and the foreign developers' (Logan 2000: 238). The involvement of such associations marks the active social and political presence of the people's views of the changes occurring in their city:

> Although falling short of an organised popular protest movement, the representations made by the professional associations appear to have achieved a major victory, showing that informed public opinion, even in a

> communist state such as Vietnam, could successfully force top-level intervention to protect the local heritage. This was a foretaste of what could be expected in Hanoi as *doi moi* encouraged development of an affluent middle class that was no longer prepared to remain quiet when it disapproved of official planning blunders or the destruction of key elements of the city's historical environment by private companies. Almost concurrently, in May 1996, in the village of Kim No on the outskirts of Hanoi another general outcry about planning decisions erupted into a series of angry demonstrations. In this case, the issue was the approval given to the South Korean Daewoo conglomerate to turn paddy fields into a 128 hectare luxury golf course for foreigners. These events marked an important political change – the start of serious community involvement in setting the direction of change in the city and another step towards the emergence of civil society in Vietnam.
>
> (Logan 2000: 239)

While these events on Hoan Kiem Lake signal the reconfiguring of political power and the marshalling of the people's will, the public is turning away from sites of state control and power. Today, at public political moments such as the 1998 30th anniversary celebrations in Vietnam of the Tet Offensives, the turning point in the Vietnam War, there were few spectators and no crowds. On this occasion, as James Scott (1990: 58–69) has argued, the party-state had organised a ritual that displayed its leadership and celebrated its dominance, but only to itself. Here the imposed everyday vacancy and high security of the formal space of Ba Dinh Square marks the tension between a regime threatened by a socially responsive citizenry, but needing to harness public support in elaborate parades and rituals.[5] Yet the building of a hotel on Hoan Kiem Lake could so incense the public that the regime was forced to recognise the newly emergent public sphere that was being demonstrated.

In the last few years there have been increasing reports of popular protest in Vietnam in which the local rural populace has dispensed a kind of 'natural justice' to the local police and party officials whom they accused of being corrupt. George Rude, the eminent historian of crowds and popular protest, argues that cities and not rural areas or market towns are the 'spawning ground of popular protest' (Rude 1988: 221). But rather than suggest, as many historians have, that popular protest arises from the breakdown of social ties due to migration and rapid urbanisation, he proposes that it is the continuity and stability of ties, 'the camaraderie of rebellion', that provide the grounds for popular protest and rebellion (Rude 1988: 238; see also Canetti 1984). That is, protest takes time to develop and only among a group that feels they share something in common. People may mobilise to protest against injustices but they may also engage in collective action in order to gain better conditions (Abers 1998: 56). As suggested by both Scott (1990) and Douglass (1998: 108), these forms of social unrest may not result in large-scale political protest 'but nevertheless serve as both forms of resistance to disempowerment and mechanisms to manage communities and their habitats'. And following Douglass and Friedmann, these localised protests 'will continue to be the wellsprings of political life in the coming age' (1998: 2).

Rural political protest, although increasing, is still managed by the party, who appear to have sided with the peasants and made efforts to change local governance practices. For example, in August 2001 it was announced that Vietnam's largest infrastructure project, the massive Son La hydro-electric dam would soon be under construction. The dam is expected to flood much of Muong La and several other districts in Son La and neighbouring Lai Chau in northern Vietnam. Amid concerns over safety, hand-wringing over money, and fierce debate as to whether the dam is necessary, as many as 100,000 people, mainly ethnic minorities, are likely to be displaced over the next few years as their land is flooded. But rather than resulting in overt protest, representatives of local people were accepting the dam. 'We're pleased to accommodate', said Lo Ngoc On, the Black Thai ethnic minority chairman of Muong La, spouting a well-worn party line (*South China Morning Post*, 20 August 2001). This suggests that protest is still a new and uncomfortable phenomenon in Vietnam and that accommodation to the party's wishes remains the norm. It also reveals that the incorporation of local people's thoughts into environmental planning is rare and that state-selected representatives continue to push the party line. It is only when local people can join with professional organisations such as architects, engineers and environmental groups that protest can be more readily formulated and criticisms acted upon, as in the case of the Golden Hanoi Hotel. It is in these instances that public spaces are so critical for the development of the public sphere, 'for encounters between individuals and groups who might not otherwise meet' (Ruddick 1996: 133) for the purpose of providing a forum for the interests of the public at large.

Conclusion

> Open public space is a place where people can actively engage the suffering of this world together, and, as they do it, transform themselves into a public.
>
> (Berman 1986: 485)

Berman's vision for public space as the space of encounters and social engagement is one that sees public space as instrumental in the creation and contestation of new identities. The contest in Hanoi over public places and urban redesign is that of a state unwilling to relinquish spatial power over a populace who have already voted with their feet in their abandonment of public state events over popular, unruly expressions of a public desire for entertainment and leisure. I have argued that these changing spatial practices are evidence of a significant political consciousness. Following Guha (1983: 4), I reject the idea that such activity is purely spontaneous or that political change requires the intervention of charismatic leaders or advanced political organisations. The recent socio-political turbulence in Vietnam may not be governed by organised plans on the part of those involved, but has focused upon inverting the existing power nexus in spatial terms.

The contested landscapes of public spaces and architectural monuments are cultural documents in which different power relations are being played out. The power of the state to create, define and transform the landscape of Hanoi is presently being challenged by local people. Although many of the social changes are ephemeral, such as the free-flowing movements and collections of people at certain sites, there are now opportunities for these changes to be more permanent as local people and organisations are impacting upon the city's planning bodies and development projects. Presently, citizens are amorphously grouped as 'the people', having been defined by the state through unions and organisations such as 'The Women's Union' and 'The Youth Union'. Now it seems likely that different groups in society at different stages in the life cycle, of different ethnicities, or with specific disadvantages such as the disabled – groups not determined by the state – will come forward to publicly express their particular needs and wants. In December 2001, the deputy Prime Minister himself commented on the change in the constitution of 'groups'.

> At a televised assembly session … Deputy Prime Minister Nguyen Cong Tan expressed concern about a growing number of provincial complaints being brought to the central leadership, which was impatient at the failure of local authorities to resolve them. … 'People have started forming groups,' he said. 'In the past they were formed by accident, now there are groups formed by many delegations, many provinces, which are organised, with clear goals.'
>
> (Reuters, 7 December 2001)

The social context created out of the increased number of people on the streets partaking in recreation, work and religious activities allows for the development of public opinion and debate so that 'the public organises itself as the bearer of public opinion' (Eley 1992: 290). The public are sharing views and gathering together to exchange information and ideas, allowing a 'public sphere' to develop in much the same way it did in Europe in the eighteenth century (Habermas 1974; see also Storper 1998; Abu-Lughod 1998; Holston 1998).

While Habermas argued that the growth of urban culture – eating, leisure and meeting places (see Figure 11.5) – fuelled the development of this public sphere, Arendt suggests that it is public space which allows a public sphere to flourish (Howell 1993). In Arendt's vision, public spaces have the potential to be the site for the articulation of public concerns through popular mobilisation around local issues, precisely as is occurring in Hanoi today. If landscapes are, as Duncan and Duncan (1988: 125) observe, 'the transformations of social and political ideologies into physical form', then we are set to see the erosion of the hegemonic authoring of Hanoi's public spaces by the state, and the growth of a city which more closely incorporates its citizens' yearnings for participation. In a public protest in late 2001 in Hanoi, when a group of elderly women gathered

Figure 11.5 Young people at an outside café

near Ba Dinh Square to complain that they had been robbed of land, the police and government officials watched 'but made no attempt to move the women on' (Reuters, 7 December 2001). This reveals that, as the spaces of the city change through the claims of the populace, the state may not be standing in the way.

Notes

1 Vietnamese newspaper reporting of the recent political changes in Indonesia has been kept short and never allotted space on the front page. Importantly, no photos of the mass demonstrations were permitted (Watanabe 1998).

2 In late 1997, local residents in Thai Binh province demonstrated in large numbers against corrupt local party officials. The Thai Binh disturbances had been preceded by 'unprecendented violent clashes in May and December 1996 and February 1997 between peasants living near the Hanoi airport and local authorities who attempted to resume farmland in order to build a luxury golfcourse' (Thayer 1998a: 2). At times, the demonstrations near Hanoi involved many hundreds of protesters and on one occasion there were 600 riot police present (from Reuters and Radio Australia, 31 December 1996, cited in Thayer 1998a). As Thayer argues, the Thai Binh clashes could not be ignored by the party as they could not be attributed to hostile external forces and involved thousands of people including war veterans. Further, throughout 1997, seventy-five incidents of rural unrest were reported throughout the country (*Nhan Dan*, 30 March 1998), signalling widespread local political instability and threats to public order stemming primarily from 'land rights issues, excessive taxation and corruption by local officials' (Thayer 1998a: 2–35). In response, signalling support for the majority of peasants involved in the protests, the Communist Party tried and jailed corrupt local officials and has made attempts to improve the system of local governance (Thayer 1998b).

3 The relationship between the media and new social movements in Vietnam is similar to the situation in China (see Barmé 1999; Calhourn 1989) and Korea (see Yung-Ho Im 1998).
4 Although Tiananmen Square in Beijing differs in structure from Ba Dinh Square it functions in some ways similarly in being the site of state-organised events as well as housing Mao's mausoleum (Calhourn 1989).
5 See McDonogh (1993) on the meanings of vacant spaces.

References

Abers, R. (1998) 'Learning Democratic Practice: Distributing Government Resources through Popular Participation in Porto Alegre, Brazil', in C.M. Douglass and J. Friedmann (eds), *Cities for Citizens: Planning and Rise of Civil Society in a Global Age*, Chichester: John Wiley, 39–65.

Abu-Lughod, J. (1998) 'Civil/Uncivil Society: Confusing Form with Content', in C.M. Douglass and J. Friedmann (eds), *Cities for Citizens: Planning and Rise of Civil Society in a Global Age*, Chichester: John Wiley, 227–38.

Ainley, R. (1998) 'Taking Another Look: Spaces', in R. Ainley (ed.), *New Frontiers of Space, Bodies, Gender*, London and New York: Routledge, 88–100.

Arendt, H. (1959) *The Human Condition*, New York: Doubleday.

Barmé, G.R. (1999) *In the Red: On Contemporary Chinese Culture*, New York: Columbia University Press.

Berman, M. (1986) 'Take It to the Streets: Conflict and Community in Public Space', *Dissent*, Fall: 476–85.

Boys, J. (1998) 'Beyond Maps and Metaphors? Rethinking the Relationships between Architecture and Gender', in R. Ainley (ed.), *New Frontiers of Space, Bodies, Gender*, London and New York: Routledge, 203–17.

Calhourn, C. (1989) 'Tiananmen, Television and the Public Sphere: The Internationalisation of Culture and the Beijing Spring of 1989', *Public Culture*, 2(1): 54–71.

Canetti, E. (1984) *Crowds and Power*, London: Penguin Books.

De Certeau, M. (1984) *The Practice of Everyday Life*, Berkeley: University of California Press.

DiGrigorio, M. (1995) 'Peasants, Labour Systems and Management of the Urban Environment: An Analysis of Waste Recovery in Hanoi, Vietnam', unpublished Masters thesis, University of Hawaii.

Ding, Zue Lang (1994) *The Decline of Communism in China*, Cambridge, MA: Cambridge University Press.

Douglass, C.M. and Friedmann, J. (eds) (1998) 'Editor's Introduction', in C.M. Douglass and J. Friedmann (eds), *Cities for Citizens: Planning and Rise of Civil Society in a Global Age*, Chichester: John Wiley, 1–6.

Douglass, M. (1998) 'World City Formation on the Asia Pacific Rim: Poverty, "Everyday" Forms of Civil Society and Environmental Management', in C.M. Douglass and J. Friedmann (eds), *Cities for Citizens: Planning and Rise of Civil Society in a Global Age*, Chichester: John Wiley, 101–37.

Drummond, L.B.W. (2000) 'Street Scenes: Practices of Public and Private Space in Urban Vietnam', *Urban Studies*, 37(12): 2377–91.

Duncan, J. and Duncan, N. (1988) '(Re)reading the landscape', *Environment and Planning D: Society and Space*, 6(2): 117–26.

Eley, G. (1992) 'Nations, Public and Political Cultures: Placing Habermas in the Nineteenth Century', in C. Calhoun (ed.), *Habermas and the Public Sphere*, Cambridge, MA: MIT Press, 289–339.

Friedmann, J. (1998) 'The New Political Economy of Planning: The Rise of Civil Society', in C.M. Douglass and J. Friedmann (eds), *Cities for Citizens: Planning and Rise of Civil Society in a Global Age*, Chichester: John Wiley, 19–38.

Guha, R. (1983) *Elementary Aspects of Peasant Insurgency on Colonial India*, Oxford: Oxford University Press.

Gulick, J. (1998) 'The "Disappearance of Public Space": An Ecological Marxist and Lefebvrian Approach', in A. Light and J.M. Smith (eds), *Philosophy and Geography II: The Production of Public Space*, Lanham, MD: Rowman & Littlefield, 135–55.

Habermas, J. (1974) 'The Public Sphere: An Encyclopaedia Article', *New German Critique*, 1(3): 45–8.

Holston, J. (1998) 'Spaces of Insurgent Citizenship', in Leonie Sandercock (ed.), *Making the Invisible Visible*, Berkeley: University of California Press, 37–56.

Howell, P. (1993) 'Public Space and the Public Sphere: Political Theory and the Historical Geography of Modernity', *Environment and Planning D: Society and Space*, 11: 303–22.

Lefebvre, H. (1991) *The Production of Space*, Oxford: Blackwell.

Logan, W. (1994) 'Hanoi Townscape: Symbolic Imagery in Vietnam's Capital', in M. Askew and W.S. Logan (eds), *Cultural Identity and Urban Change in Southeast Asia: Interpretive Essays*, Melbourne: Deakin University Press, 43–69.

—— (2000) *Hanoi: Biography of a City*, Sydney: UNSW Press.

Low, S.M. (1996) 'The Anthropology of Cities: Imagining and Theorising the City', *Annual Review of Anthropology*, Palo Alto: Annual Reviews, 383–409.

—— (2001) 'The Secret, the Unspeakable, the Unsaid: Spatial Discourse and Political Economic Analysis', *City and Society*, XIII(1): 161–5.

McDonogh, G. (1993) 'The Geography of Emptiness', in R. Rotenberg and G.W. McDonogh (eds), *The Cultural Meaning of Urban Space*, Westport: Bergin & Garvey, 3–15.

Rotenberg, R. and McDonogh, G.W. (eds) (1993) *The Cultural Meaning of Urban Space*, Westport: Bergin & Garvey.

Ruddick, S. (1996) 'Constructing Difference in Public Spaces: Race, Class, and Gender as Interlocking Systems', *Urban Geography*, 17: 132–51.

Rude, G. (1988) *The Face of the Crowd: Studies of Revolution, Ideology and Popular Protest*, selected essays of George Rude, edited and introduced by Harvey J. Kaye, New York: Harvester.

Sandercock, L. (1998) 'The Death of Modernist Planning: Radical Praxis for a Postmodern Age', in C.M. Douglass and J. Friedmann (eds), *Cities for Citizens: Planning and Rise of Civil Society in a Global Age*, Chichester: John Wiley, 163–84.

Scott, J.C. (1990) *Domination and the Arts of Resistance: Hidden Transcripts*, New Haven and London: Yale University Press.

Storper, M. (1998) 'Civil Society: Three Ways into a Problem', in C.M. Douglass and J. Friedmann (eds), *Cities for Citizens: Planning and Rise of Civil Society in a Global Age*, Chichester: John Wiley, 239–46.

Tai, Hue Tam Ho (1995) 'Monumental Ambiguity: The State Commemoration of Ho Chi Minh', in K.W. Taylor and J. Whitmore (eds), *Essays into Vietnamese Pasts*, Cornell: SEAP, 272–88.

Thayer, C. (1998a) 'The "Four Typhoons": Political Developments in 1998', unpublished paper presented at *Vietnam Update*, Australian National University.

—— (1998b) *Asiaweek*, 7 August.

Thomas, M. (2001) 'Public Spaces/Public Disgraces: Crowds and the State in Contemporary Vietnam', *Sojourn: Journal of Social Issues in Southeast Asia*, 16(2): 306–30.

Thomas, M. and Hiang-Khng Heng, R. (2000) 'Stars in the Shadows: Celebrity, Media and the State in Vietnam', in Y. Souchou (ed.), *House of Glass: Culture, Modernity and the State in Southeast Asia*, Singapore: ISEAS, 287–312.

Wainwright, J., Prudham, S. and Glassman, J. (2000) 'The Battles in Seattle: Microgeographies of Resistance and the Challenge of Building Alternative Futures', *Environment and Planning D: Society and Space*, 18: 5–13.

Watanabe, K. (1998) *The Yomiuri Shimbun*, 17 June.

Yung-Ho Im (1998) 'The Media, Civil Society and New Social Movements in Korea, 1985–93', in Kuan-Hsing Chen (ed.), *Trajectories: Inter-Asia Cultural Studies*, New York and London: Routledge, 330–45.

Part IV

The view from within

The changing world of Vietnamese cultural practitioners

Chapter 12

Representations of *doi moi* society in contemporary Vietnamese cinema

Dang Nhat Minh and Pham Thu Thuy

Introduction

Ever since the Vietnamese government launched a programme of economic reforms in the mid-1980s, which included the dissolution of agricultural collectives in the countryside and the opening up of the country to foreign investors, rapid social change and its consequences for the country's traditional culture and identity have occupied a central position in the official discourse on industrialisation and modernisation. Among party leaders and the country's theorists, it is generally agreed that, in order to catch up with the rest of the region, Vietnam has no other option but to modernise. However, although economic development remains the overriding goal, what really concerns the country's leaders is how to achieve material prosperity while at the same time retaining Vietnam's traditional culture and national identity. At a press conference held in Hanoi in 1998, Huu Tho, the Director of the Vietnam Communist Party Central Committee's Ideology and Culture Commission, told foreign reporters that 'Vietnam wants to develop an advanced culture with the population having a high standard of education and culture and a better community life while ensuring that the national traditional culture can absorb the essence of others' (*Vietnam News* 1998). Hence, the purpose of the resolution issued at the end of the Central Committee's fifth plenum was to devise ways of preserving Vietnam's traditional culture while gradually integrating into the regional and world communities.

Since the introduction of *doi moi* policy, the positive and negative impacts of economic changes on Vietnam's people and society at large have also been a recurring theme in Vietnamese cinema. The aim of this chapter is twofold. First, it will attempt to provide an overview of the film industry in Vietnam in the years following market reforms, and second, through a detailed analysis of the film *Returning*, it will also examine how the issues of economic reforms and cultural identity are depicted on film.

Vietnamese film industry at a crossroads

In the period 1998–2000, audiences around the world have had the opportunity to view an impressive number of award-winning films made in Vietnam, including films such as *Wharf of Widows* (*Ben Khong Chong*) by director Luu Trong Ninh, *Sand Life* (*Doi Cat*) by Nguyen Thanh Van and *Down South, Up North* (*Vao Nam Ra Bac*) by Phi Tien Son. With the outstanding success of *Sand Life* at the 2000 Asia-Pacific Film Festival held in Hanoi, one would have thought that Vietnam's film industry was entering a golden age of growth and development. The critical acclaim and the string of awards won at international film festivals in recent years have certainly done much to raise the country's cinematic profile, and to bring fame – not to mention material rewards – to a number of Vietnamese actors and filmmakers. Despite these international successes, Vietnam's film industry is fast losing the support of local audiences, at least according to prominent filmmakers such as the award-winning director Le Manh Thich. The view that the industry is in crisis was aired during the 1999 nation-wide cinematic conference marking the 40th anniversary of the release of *On the Same River* (*Chung Mot Giong Song*), the first feature film produced by the Democratic Republic of Vietnam. While celebrating the industry's numerous achievements since the 1950s, film directors and producers attending the conference could not resist making a comparison between the years prior to the introduction of open-door policy when the popularity of Vietnamese films seemed absolute and unchallenged, and the period following economic renewal, a time of steady decline, according to these directors and producers, during which local audiences increasingly gravitated toward Hollywood blockbusters, Hong Kong's martial epics and South Korea's soap operas.

For many people in the industry, this so-called decline can be traced back to the late 1980s and early 1990s when state funding for the production and distribution of feature films was drastically reduced, forcing major film studios and companies to look to private individuals and entrepreneurs for their financing and revenue.[1] In 2000, for example, the annual budget allocation was less than $500,000 for an entire film studio, barely enough for the production of two or three feature films a year. However, despite admittedly severe financial constraints, Vietnam's film industry might have regained much of its popularity with local audiences, according to some industry insiders, had it managed to overcome the most damaging of all criticisms, namely that it produced unexciting films. For large numbers of audiences inside the country, Vietnamese films have become too formulaic, relying on well-worn story-lines and familiar themes such as rural life, the country's struggles against foreign invaders and post-war socialist reconstruction. Once, Vietnamese moviegoers waited eagerly in long lines outside cinemas to see the latest productions their film industry had to offer. These days, however, a much more popular source of entertainment would be watching a rented video of a big-budget Hollywood movie full of heart-pumping action and mind-boggling special effects.

On the whole, it can be said that the system of central state subsidy has brought many benefits as well as inflicting seemingly irreversible damage on film production in Vietnam. During the period of state subsidies, the sole aim of artistic and cultural production was to serve society. Profit-making was considered a manifestation of the corrupt influences of capitalism, and was thus looked upon with disdain. For many filmmakers and producers, state subsidies freed them from mundane concerns of funding and profitability, and allowed them to focus instead on the artistic quality of their film productions. It was no coincidence that the period of subsidies saw the release of numerous art films of exceptionally high quality. However, the system of central subsidies also created inertia in cultural fields, including the film industry. One of the undesirable aspects of this system was the political pressure that the state could bring to bear on filmmakers' creative endeavours and artistic expressions, the result of which was often formulaic and predictable story-lines (Trai 1994).

It is natural that the shift to the market economy has created many problems for movie production and distribution in Vietnam. Prior to 1989, all those who worked in the film industry often felt satisfied with their jobs, even though life was hard. Nowadays, film production and distribution requires a vast amount of resources and capital which the state simply cannot provide. Since the abolition of state subsidies, the problem of shortages in production capital has been compounded by turbulent changes and uncertainty. Film companies must find ways to survive and adapt to new conditions. The easiest way to do so is to attract investment capital from private entrepreneurs, many of whom have since replaced the state as the main source of funding for film production and distribution in Vietnam. However, private investors usually become involved only for profit and, to be profitable, films have to be inexpensive to produce as well as able to appeal to the popular taste. According to some critics and observers of the industry, local Vietnamese audiences today enjoy films in a different manner compared to audiences of two decades ago: increasingly, films have become commercial products made for popular entertainment rather than education or aesthetic appreciation (Dung 1999; Hoa 1999; Kim 2000; Lan 1998).

Meanwhile, a new breed of film directors are taking advantage of a government policy introduced in the early 1990s which allowed private individuals and entrepreneurs to invest in film production, in an attempt to reverse declining profitability. One example that comes to mind is director Ly Huynh, who has been compared to Hong Kong action director John Woo. A well-known actor for nearly twenty years before taking up directing and producing films in 1989, Ly Huynh is among the few filmmakers in Vietnam today who can claim to have made a profit – though moderate compared to more lavish foreign productions – from his feature films. Talking with a newspaper reporter in 2000, the Saigon-based director dismissed the widely held view among some circles of filmmakers that high-quality art films must necessarily be commercial failures, while those movies which are box-office hits must be totally devoid of artistic merits. For Ly Huynh, critical acclaim and commercial success are not mutually exclusive. There is nothing to prevent filmmakers and/or producers aiming for both. Although the situation may look bleak now, as younger and more affluent audiences continue to seek alternative entertainment venues, director Ly Huynh refuses to believe that Vietnam's film industry is on the brink of collapse. According to him, local audiences still love to watch movies on the big screen. All it takes to fill cinemas around the country is simply to show films of high artistic quality that also have the potential to excite and educate audiences. To be able to produce such films is therefore the most difficult challenge facing Vietnam's film industry as it enters the twenty-first century.

Doi moi cinema

Many filmmakers and observers of the industry today would agree that, during the last decade of the twentieth century, Vietnamese cinema has unequivocally outgrown socialist realism in terms of content as well as stylistic conventions. However, it remains a widespread and sincere conviction among certain circles in the film industry that the most important task of filmmaking is to express in filmic language the concerns and aspirations of ordinary people, to explore the effects and consequences of rapid economic change on personal as well as social relationships. Despite enormous financial constraints on film production and distribution since the late 1980s as a result of market reforms and the abolition of the state subsidy system, Vietnamese cinema has managed to make a favourable impression on international audiences with an impressive number of critically acclaimed and award-winning feature films, such as *Returning*, which won the Special Jury Prize at the Pacific and Asian Film Festival held in Sydney (Australia) in 1995; *A Thousand Mile Journey* by Saigon-based director Le Hoang winning third prize at the Bergamo International Film Festival in Italy in 1998; and more recently, *Sand Life* by director Nguyen Thanh Van, which was voted best feature film at the 45th Asia-Pacific Film Festival held in Hanoi in 2000.

One of the latest art films from Vietnam to be screened in cinemas around the world in 2002 is the controversial *Season of Guavas* by Dang Nhat Minh. A moving story of a middle-class family evicted from their Hanoi home during the campaign of urban land reform in north Vietnam in the late 1950s, the film delves into a period in Vietnamese history that remains politically sensitive, perhaps one reason why it took two years for the government to approve the script. With the empathy and candour which have almost become the director's trademark, *Season of Guavas* 'shows life as it is', with scenes depicting members of the Hanoi traffic police chasing away street vendors and peddlers as part of a recent campaign to beautify the capital city.

At present, cultural production including filmmaking is no longer completely subsidised by the state. Consequently, the products of these cultural activities have become subject to the laws of market competition. If film-making was ever considered in Vietnam a non-profitable branch of cultural production, attitudes are fast changing, as the critical and commercial success of some Vietnamese films have shown that culture and arts can be highly profitable if such products meet the expectation of audiences. When arts participate in the market, there are bound to be adverse effects, but opportunities also exist for innovation, development and expansion. This seems to be precisely the case of Vietnamese cinema in the period following *doi moi* or economic renewal.

Returning: themes and issues

Winner of the Special Jury Prize at the 39th Asia-Pacific Film Festival held in Sydney (Australia) in 1995, *Returning* is essentially the story of a young Vietnamese woman searching for love and personal fulfilment in an increasingly materialistic society. While assigned to a teaching post in a southern coastal town in the 1980s, Loan – the main character – has a brief love affair with Hung, a deeply troubled and discontented young man who is being pressured by his domineering father into leaving the country illegally. After the affair ends, with Hung's reluctant departure as one of the boat people, Loan returns to her family in Hanoi where she meets Tuan, a former classmate and childhood friend who has just come back from his studies in the Soviet Union. Before long they are married, and the couple move to Saigon. In this land of opportunity, Tuan immerses himself in the frenetic race to move up the corporate ladder, while Loan becomes increasingly dissatisfied with her role as a simple housewife. The marriage inevitably breaks down as Loan once again returns alone to Hanoi, where she at last finds happiness and fulfilment in the love of her family and the innocent smiles of her young students.

If the definition of an art film (*phim nghe thuat*) in Vietnam is one which endeavours to portray the lives of ordinary people, their joys and heartaches, and to bring into sharp focus the contradictions and problems of a rapidly changing society, then *Returning* is an excellent example of the new wave of art cinema which has emerged since the introduction of market reforms in the 1980s. Although at first glance it might appear a simple love story, *Returning* is in fact a sensitive and thoughtful portrayal of the impact of rapid economic change on traditional moral values and social attitudes.

Each of the three main characters in the film represents a different set of ideals regarding personal aspirations and behaviour in a new era of economic development. For instance, Tuan is depicted as an intensely ambitious person who works hard to accumulate wealth and to achieve upward social mobility in terms of lifestyle. At his best, Tuan can be said to be the epitome of Vietnamese urban youth today, for he possesses the intelligence, the dynamism and the resourcefulness that are the basic ingredients for success in a fiercely competitive environment. The character Loan, on the other hand, represents an entirely different set of values. In stark contrast to her husband's pragmatic and materialistic thinking, which is conveniently summed up by his assertion that 'society is made up of nothing other than goods and services', Loan is a romantic at heart who values love and family attachment above the acquisition of wealth and power. This perhaps explains why she feels such a strong attraction toward Hung, and *vice versa*, when they first met during her sojourn in the south. Having lived among affluence all his life, Hung looks upon money with a mixture of indifference and disdain. Indeed, he realises very early on that wealth and material success do not automatically lead to happiness and personal fulfilment. The feeling that somehow he has wasted his life remains strangely palpable, even when he returns from Australia as the representative of a foreign corporation to sign a major business deal with Tuan's company.

From our discussion of the plot-line above, it becomes clear that *Returning* is an attempt to explore in cinematic language the moral problems facing the individual living in a country which is undergoing rapid economic and social change. The pervasive message seems to be that, while a commodity-based economy undoubtedly creates wealth for the people and renders the nation powerful, it would, however, result in the break-down of family and social relationships if accompanied by an excessively utilitarian way of life, in which profit and other practical considerations hold sway over human feelings and moral norms. In other words, affluence, without compassion and concern for one's fellow human beings, runs the risk of impoverishing the spiritual life, and destroying traditional ethical values.

Hanoi: a timeless city

From the point of view of many Vietnamese people, Hanoi is not only the country's capital, but also the seat of culture and learning, the spiritual heart of the whole nation. It is perhaps for this reason that the city, which was founded in 1001, has often been portrayed in literature as well as on film as a place of cultural refinement unsullied by rampant consumerism and a materialistic way of life. In the film *Returning*, for instance, the city appears timeless, with its tree-lined streets dotted with people dressed in conservative, dark colours, quietly moving along on their bicycles. In this eternal city, the cradle of Vietnamese national spirit, even the *cyclo* drivers are soft-spoken and gentle in manner. Wearing a green pith helmet and old army clothes, the *cyclo* driver who takes Loan to her parents' house on both occasions when she returns to Hanoi, calmly speaks of his poverty without shame or self-pity. Already forming in his mind, however, is the perception that Ho Chi Minh City – or Saigon, as its inhabitants would call it – is an entirely different place. In the more tranquil and slower-paced environment of Hanoi, he might find it not too difficult to maintain a modicum of dignity in the face of abject poverty, but in Saigon one needs to have money – and plenty of it – otherwise 'why should anyone want to go there?'.

The quiet dignity of Hanoi and its people also finds expression in Loan's elderly parents. A long-retired cadre, her father refuses to sit at home and while away the hours watching television or feeling sorry for himself. Instead, he becomes actively involved in social work, participating in local community projects and helping less fortunate families. Similarly, Loan's mother runs a tiny stall selling sweets and stationery to children in the neighbourhood, not for profit but simply to keep herself busy and useful. Though far from being well-off, Loan's parents lead an extremely happy and contented life, growing old together in the house that saw the birth of their children. Significantly, in the film Loan always appears to be most cheerful when she comes home to her parents in Hanoi. The first thing she does upon arriving is to perform a personal cleansing ritual beside the well in the garden at the back of the house – a ritual marking her actual as well as symbolic *returning*.

Saigon: a land of contrasts

If Hanoi is depicted in the film *Returning* as a place where love and the ethics of personal dedication take precedence over the acquisition of wealth, Saigon is seen as the centre of frenetic commercial activity. Not only is it the land of opportunity, as those who are eager to take advantage of market-oriented liberalisations would like to believe, but it is also a land of contrasts – contrasts between rich and poor, between country and city, and between past and present.

In stark contrast to the almost rural appearance and atmosphere of Hanoi, the streets of Saigon, as seen in the film, are a constant hubbub of honking motorcycles, flashing neon lights and blaring pop music. The policy of *doi moi* has transformed the city, reviving its long forgotten image as the 'pearl of the Orient'. However, market reforms have also contributed to a growing polarisation between rich and poor, resulting in the degradation of moral values and the deterioration of personal as well as social relationships. Consider, for example, the sharp contrast between the scene in which a balding middle-aged businessman gets drunk in a high-class bar amid a bevy of attractive young girls, all dressed provocatively, and the scene where a crippled former soldier earns his living by singing old songs and selling lottery tickets to people who are hardly any better off than himself. For all its newly refurbished hotels and restaurants, its flashy discotheques and nightclubs, in the film *Returning*, Saigon is portrayed as a place of social inequity and injustice.

Saigon seems to have a negative impact on the main characters in the film. As a result of living in the city where 'every human activity is governed by the laws of supply and demand' and where 'the strong survives and the weak perishes', ambitious individuals such as Tuan now have only one value: getting rich by any means. Corrupted by his own unquenchable desire for money and power, Tuan becomes a cold-hearted and calculating person whose only concern is to further his own career. Loan, on the other hand, becomes a lonely prisoner in her own luxurious home. Having resigned from her teaching job at the request of her husband, she now leads an extremely isolated and empty life amid Vietnam's largest and most crowded city; her little dog and the maid are her only contacts. All around her, people seem to be sucked into a whirlpool of money, consumer goods and pleasure-seeking, giving in to their greed and losing their sense of responsibility toward fellow human beings, many of whom still live in densely packed slums in the shadow of modern buildings and office towers.

Past and present

Under the difficult conditions brought about by the war with the United States in the 1960s and early 1970s, one might have thought that people caught up in the common struggle would share the genuine and positive commitment to revolutionary ethics that calls for self-sacrifice and personal abnegation in the interests of national salvation and liberation. However, as tentative market reforms heralded a new era of economic transformation, the solidarity and revolutionary fervour that characterised the war years were increasingly superseded by new standards of personal and collective aspirations and behaviour. If in the past the ideals for personal action and behaviour which demanded selfless sacrifice and abnegation had helped the Vietnamese revolution triumph against incredible odds, in the context of market-oriented reforms, individual initiative and interest now constituted the main driving force behind Vietnam's modernising efforts. In other words, individual efforts to achieve material success have become no less important than selfless acts of patriotism were in the past for, by improving one's own living conditions, one is contributing to the prosperity and enrichment of the whole nation. Among many of the younger generation in Vietnam today, not only is it desirable to work for a strong and prosperous country, but also to look directly to one's own interests, material comfort and well-being in the process.

In *Returning*, the character Tuan, who abandons his studies in physics to pursue a more profitable career in economics, represents the thousands of dynamic entrepreneurs eager to take advantage of the government's market-oriented reforms. For him, Saigon, or Ho Chi Minh City, is the place to be as it is the engine behind Vietnam's new economic growth, the gateway through which foreign capital, technology and ideas make their way into the country. While the nostalgic types sit at home reminiscing about long-gone times of heroic endurance and selfless virtues, Tuan and others like him work hard to accumulate wealth, which in turn allows them to enjoy a sensuous and luxurious urban lifestyle.

Under the new economic conditions, the ideals of personal sacrifice and dedication to an unselfish cause – ideals which flourished in times of scarcity and hardships – are no longer pursued. The new way of life brought about by economic development is also fraught with danger, however. This is clearly demonstrated in the film's portrayal of Tuan and his moral downfall as he conspires with Hung, recently returned to the country as the representative of a foreign company, to defraud the state-owned enterprise of which he is one of the senior executives. It seems that Tuan is but one more example of the numerous individuals in *doi moi* society who have let themselves be corrupted by their newly acquired wealth and power.

One of the most salient features of Vietnamese traditional culture is arguably its emphasis on gratitude and compassion. A person is expected to show respect and gratitude not only toward his ancestors and parents, but also toward those who have sacrificed their lives to protect the country against foreign aggression. The ideal of compassion, on the other hand, results from a long process of integration of indigenous values with imported religious teachings such as Buddhism. In *Returning*, these traditional moral norms are pitted against an aggressively utilitarian and materialistic world-view in which economic efficiency and practical considerations take precedence over human compassion and dignity. Take, for instance, Tuan's callous indifference toward his wife's long-dead brother, a revolutionary soldier who was killed during the war and now lies buried in the province of Long An, southwest of Ho Chi Minh City. Despite having lived in Saigon for three long years, Tuan never once visits his brother-in-law's grave to pay his respects. Not only that, he often dismisses such gestures as overly sentimental and a complete waste of time. Like many of the younger generation, Tuan prefers to spend his time and energy on more profitable activities than pondering the meaning of war and the sacrifices of revolutionary generations in the past. The lack of respect and compassion for the dead is not restricted to successful individuals like Tuan alone, however. Due to a superstitious belief among taxi drivers, according to which terrible misfortune will befall the person who carries people's ashes or remains in their car, the driver hastily departs the military cemetery after he discovers that Loan and her father intend to take the dead soldier's remains back with them to Ho Chi Minh City, leaving father and daughter stranded in Long An as the night approaches.

It seems that not all those who live in the new era of economic reforms are selfish and heartless, however. A section of the population still look with favour and nostalgia upon the more simple days when people were united by hardships and a common sense of purpose. The elderly man who kindly offers to accommodate Loan and her father for the night is a case in point. Asking for neither thanks nor payment, his main reason for helping them is because he also lost one of his own sons in the war.

While compassion unites people suffering the same loss and anguish, it also does much to obscure the line of ideological demarcation. In one of the most moving scenes of the film, a former Saigon soldier, maimed by the injuries he received in the war, sings of war and suffering to a bleary-eyed audience, exhausted by their daily toil and struggle, as Loan sits hugging the canvas bag containing the remains of her dead brother, a soldier fighting on the opposite side.

> With mud on the soldier's uniform and boots,
> Amid gunsmoke and bleary eyes,
> After a night of combat, all I need is a kind word.
> Why do you not sing for those who are still busy fighting?
> All we see are trees, not the carefree bars and cafes,
> Sing for the mothers who pine for their sons,
> Sing for those who fell last night.
> A path snakes through the dense jungle,
> A soldier's life is a hard one.
> I've heard the sounds of war since the day I was born,
> So now I'm fighting to bring peace to my country.
> Your words move me deeply,
> Do not sing like the birds high up in the trees,
> Show that you're sincere about what you are singing,
> Show the same feelings a soldier has for the jungle. [2]

Conclusion

For all the artificial devices employed in filmmaking, cinema does not exist simply as pure fantasy. It forms part of society's reality; it gives voice to the concerns, the joys and the sorrows of ordinary people during their day-to-day existence. Neither is cinema speaking to its audience in purely escapist terms. More often than not, cinema – especially what some circles among filmmakers and producers in Vietnam call art cinema – communicates with audiences using images and concepts embedded in contemporary lore regarding *doi moi* and its impact on urban lifestyles. As part of the new art cinema which has emerged since the introduction of reforms and liberalisations in the late 1980s, the film *Returning* seeks to illustrate the growing popular perception that economic renewal, or *doi moi*, might not turn out to be the panacea to the country's numerous problems as it moves toward modernisation and industrialisation. Although people's living conditions have greatly improved in recent years thanks to market reforms, the resulting utilitarian and materialistic way of life in urban centres has also taken its toll on traditional values such as compassion, generosity and a sense of responsibility toward one's fellow human beings. As indicated by the discontent and disillusionment experienced by the film's main character, material wealth itself cannot solve all human problems. Though economic growth has brought about in Vietnam some degree of social progress and higher standards of living among certain sections of the population, it has also engendered rampant consumerism, the rise of money worship and a lifestyle driven solely by self-interest and practical considerations. As the country enters the twenty-first century, it seems genuine progress and modernisation can come about only if they include social justice, ethical behaviour, compassion and a moral lifestyle.

Notes

1 For a more detailed discussion of changes in the financial structure of film production in Vietnam, see 'Dien Mao Dien Anh Viet Nam Nhung Nam Doi Moi' (Aspects of Vietnamese Cinema during the *Doi Moi* Years) by the film critic Ngo Phuong Lan.

2 Entitled 'Jungle of Low-Hanging Leaves' ('Rung La Thap'), this was a popular song in Saigon in the early 1970s.

Bibliography

Le Nhu Hoa (1999) 'The Relationship between Vietnamese Feature Films and Audiences from the Perspective of Consumer Culture', *Culture and the Arts*, 181: 62–3.

Ngo Phuong Lan (1998) 'The Changing Face of Vietnamese Cinema during Ten Years of Renovation 1986–1996', in D.G. Marr (ed.), *The Mass Media in Vietnam*, trans. Pham Thu Thuy, Canberra, Department of Political and Social Change, Research School of Pacific and Asian Studies, Australian National University.

—— (1999) 'Dien Mao Dien Anh Viet Nam Nhung Nam Doi Moi' (Aspects of Vietnamese Cinema during the *Doi Moi* Years), *Que Huong*, 2&3: 62–5.

Ngoc Trai (1994) 'Culture and Market', *Vietnam Social Sciences*, 4(42): 76–83.

Pham Vu Dung (1999) 'The Movie Industry in 1998 – Observations Based on a Few Figures' in *Dien Anh Viet Nam–An Tuong va Suy Ngam* (Vietnamese Cinema – Impressions and Reflections) (editor unknown), Hanoi: Van Hoa Dan Toc Publishing House.

Tran Luan Kim (2000) 'Elements in the Revival of the National Film Art', *Van Hoa*, 19 June: 5–6.

Tuong Lai (1993) 'The Role of Individuality in Vietnam's Emerging Dynamism amidst Recent Renovation,' *Vietnam Social Sciences*, 36(2): 10–16.

Vietnam News (1998) 'Party Ideologist Talks with Foreign Press', 25 August 2000.

Chapter 13

Let's talk about love

Depictions of love and marriage in contemporary Vietnamese short fiction

Phan Thi Vang Anh and Pham Thu Thuy[1]

> They'll lose their way within dark sorrowland,
> Those passionate fools who go in search of love.
> And life will be a desert reft of joy,
> And love will tie the knot that binds to grief.
> To love is to die a little in the heart.[2]

Introduction

After years of languishing on the fringe of mainstream literary production, the topic of love has once again emerged as a pervasive and indispensable feature of Vietnamese fiction. The change came in the mid-1980s when the Vietnamese government began introducing various reform measures, including allowing writers more freedom in terms of artistic expression and the choice of subject matter. Since then the Vietnamese literary scene has been flooded with novels and short stories dealing with the subjects of romantic love and marriage in contemporary settings. Although writers' preoccupation with these topics may not in itself warrant detailed discussion, the persistence of certain themes and images regarding romance and marriage in Vietnam nowadays, as well as the literary techniques used for conveying them, deserve a systematic examination.

The present chapter will deal exclusively with short fiction, partly because this literary genre has in recent years surpassed the novel in terms of popularity and stylistic development. Perhaps the growing popularity of short fiction in Vietnam has much to do with the fragmentation and increasing speed of life in this country following economic reforms. More and more people living in urban areas now want information and entertainment delivered fast, and in a format that can be quickly absorbed. New developments in the Vietnamese literary scene during the past decade have also seen an increasing number of writers turning their talents to short fiction. One of the most important reasons for many writers to lean toward short fiction is that, unlike the novel, short stories require minimal investment in terms of time and effort, leaving writers time to pursue careers in other areas such as publishing and journalism.

In this chapter, we will examine works by some of the most well-known and popular writers of short fiction in Vietnam today, including women writers such as Le Minh Khue,[3] Nguyen Thi Thu Hue, Vo Thi Xuan Ha, Vo Thi Hao and Y Ban. Although short stories written and published in the 1990s will form the bulk of the analysis, a few stories from the 1980s have been included for the purpose of comparison and contrast. For clarification, it should be noted that terms such as 'love story' and 'romantic fiction' are used interchangeably in this chapter to denote literary works dealing with the topics of love, romance and marriage. Before looking more closely at the short stories selected for analysis, however, it may be useful to examine briefly how depictions of love and marriage in Vietnamese literature have changed since the early twentieth century.

Love and marriage in early novels

Depictions of love and marriage in Vietnamese literature have undergone a remarkable transformation since the early decades of the twentieth century. The most significant changes took place in the 1920s with the appearance of the first romantic novels written in the romanised national script (*quoc ngu*). One of the most well-known romantic novels produced during this period was *To Tam* (Pure Heart) written by Hoang Ngoc Phach (1896–1973).[4]

By the 1930s, the notion of romantic love had become closely linked with intellectuals' demand for social reforms. Motivated by a sense of cultural crisis, writers and intellectuals of this period – most of whom had grown up in the French or Franco-Vietnamese educational system – used the novel to attack those aspects of traditional society which they perceived as obstructive to Vietnam's progress and development. Not surprisingly, the extended family and the traditional marriage institution became the foremost targets of the intellectual offensive, as these represented the essence of traditional society. Although love and romantic relationships continued to be an essential feature of many fictional works of this period, as evident in the novels of the Self-Reliance Literary Group, the focus shifted to socially relevant issues such as the plight of women in the traditional marital order. One of the most emotive works on this subject was *Doan Tuyet* (Breaking Off) written by Nhat Linh (1906–63), a leading figure of the Self-Reliance Literary Group.

It was not until the emergence during the 1960s and early 1970s of numerous women writers from the southern cities – some of whom were extremely talented and not afraid to break into more taboo areas – that romantic love became fully developed as a literary theme. Amid all the violence and destruction of the war, love seemed to provide an escape from the general feelings of despair, frustration and disillusionment. In his survey of southern literature prior to reunification, the writer Vo Phien describes how love and romance became almost an obsession for many southern novelists during these years (Vo Phien 1992: 139). Compared to the literature on love in previous decades, the most significant change was the increasingly explicit depiction of the physical aspects of love in southern romantic fiction. Women writers such as Nguyen Thi Hoang, Tuy Hong and Le Hang were among the first to explore unorthodox notions of love and previously ignored aspects of female sexuality. One of the most controversial novels of this period was *Vong Tay Hoc Tro* (The Student's Embrace) by Nguyen Thi Hoang. Other best-selling writers of romantic fiction in southern Vietnam prior to 1975 include Chu Tu, whose novel *Yeu* (Love) was replete with unconventional love relationships, and Le Hang, a young female author who shot to fame with romance novels depicting passionate affairs in affluent, urban settings. Thus, in the decade before reunification, the topic of romantic love seemed to enjoy tremendous growth and development in the literature of south Vietnam.[5] According to Vo Phien:

> it was the strange combination of political and social disorders, disasters and tragedies of war, new thoughts and trends from the West, that turned this confused time, amazingly enough, into a time when both amorousness and unruliness were of paramount importance.
>
> (Vo Phien 1992: 140)

A socialist definition of love

In contrast to the explosion of romantic literature in southern cities during the war, official literary production in north Vietnam maintained a deafening silence on the topic of love. For many northern writers, this was an extremely difficult period, as their artistic freedom was being subsumed by the greater needs of the socialist revolution and the war against the United States. This does not mean, however, that they had completely lost all enthusiasm for love and romance as a literary theme. Admittedly, the vast majority of fictional works produced in north Vietnam during the 1960s and 1970s revolved around the struggle for national liberation, the socialist transformation and the collectivisation of the countryside – topics which conformed to the dictates of socialist-realist literature. Nevertheless, at the heart of many of these fictions was always a love story, although love was represented in a highly didactic and formulaic manner. More often than not, it was closely bound up with the socialist 'one for all and all for one' ideology. Love was not considered true and lasting if it encouraged people to place their own happiness above that of the community or the nation at large.

Although love was never entirely banished from the official publications of post-war Vietnam, as was the case in China during the Cultural Revolution (Louie 1989: 51), it was so narrowly defined that complex human emotions and desires played almost no part in romantic relationships. This situation was about to change in the latter half of the 1980s, however, with the appearance of love stories that focused on the inner world of lovers – their passions, joys and sorrows.

In love and war

By the late 1980s, with the liberalisation of many aspects of Vietnamese society including literature and the arts, the country's literary scene had witnessed the appearance of numerous short fictions that adopted a less didactic and prescriptive approach in their depiction of romantic love. More often than not, these stories unfold against urban settings, and are filled with characters for whom the war is only a memory or an image in a distant dream. Nevertheless, war continues to be an important feature of many romantic short stories written during the 1980s, especially when it is the cause of the lovers' separation and sufferings. Unlike the war fiction of the previous two decades, however, these stories seek to describe not heroic battle scenes, but the impact of war on the emotional life of its victims, portraying the anguish of those who have had their dreams of love and happiness destroyed in the ashes of war. 'Du Phai Song It Hon' (Even if We Must Live a Little Less), written by Da Ngan in 1985, is a case in point.

Niem, the central female character, was engaged[6] to Thinh shortly before he left to regroup to north Vietnam in 1954. As war erupted, Niem and Thinh lost touch with one other. A few years later, Thinh fell in love with and married another woman, thinking that Niem had been killed in the war. Following the reunification of the country, however, Thinh discovers Niem is still alive and has been faithfully waiting for his return all these years. He is now confronted with the agonising choice between the woman who is the love of his life and the family that means everything to him. Niem too finds herself torn between her love for Thinh and a gnawing sense of guilt, knowing that her own happiness is built on the sacrifice and suffering of three innocent people, Thinh's second wife and his two children in Hanoi.

In numerous short fictions produced in the 1980s, authors seek to bring to the fore the moral and political circumstances which impact heavily on romantic relationships. During the American war, and even well into the post-war era, love was routinely equated with patriotic ideals, altruism and self-sacrifice. Increasingly, however, the message that comes across from romantic short fiction is that the pursuit of love is emotionally and morally worthwhile. Everyone has the right to seek out love and happiness even if by doing so they are defying the political and ideological norms of the times.

Love and marriage

Moving into the 1990s, love is no longer an abstract idea but has become concrete, a problem confronted by real people in everyday life. A growing number of short stories have begun to discuss the social and cultural expectations placed on women in terms of marriage, as well as the potential conflict between different sets of social attitudes towards love and marriage. Traditionally, love was often thought to develop naturally between husband and wife following marriage. From the standpoint of modern society, however, it is romantic love and sexual attraction that may eventually lead to matrimony, and not vice versa. Nevertheless, these two seemingly opposing sets of views also have one thing in common, which is the underlying belief that a person can only find fulfilment and true happiness through marriage. For many people in contemporary Vietnam, being unmarried still carries a social stigma. Family and friends usually regard unwed individuals as unfulfilled, and they often become the targets of solicitous match-making efforts.

Written in 1991, 'Cho Duyen' (Waiting for a Match) by Nguyen Thi Minh Ngoc is a rather cynical examination of the notions of love and marriage in contemporary Vietnam. It is the story of four unmarried sisters in an old-fashioned, southern family, told from the viewpoint of one of the women. Although good-looking and well educated, none of the sisters has managed to find a suitable marriage partner. Nevertheless the women are quite content with their lives, and have made it clear that they have no wish to get married just for the sake of it. In the end, however, the reason that prompts them to reluctantly co-operate with their condescending and meddling relatives is the strong belief that it would make their parents happy.

> As for us, like those people who stay up later than twelve o'clock at night and no longer feel sleepy, we don't consider getting married as important any more. We are only aware of one thing and that is my mother feels sad, although she keeps it inside and hidden from everyone else … My mother lives simply, having no need for money or material things. The best way to make her happy, and thus fulfil our filial duty, is perhaps for at least one of us to be married to a good man.
>
> (Nguyen Thi Minh Ngoc 1996)

In a slightly satirical tone, the author of 'Waiting for a Match' turns on its head the traditional concept of *duyen* or predestined relationship. Here *duyen* no longer stands for predestined love. Instead, it denotes one of the most pragmatic principles governing the marriage market: take whatever you can before it is too late. When a woman reaches a certain age, love becomes as irrelevant to marriage as a piece of pretty garnish to a starving person. Thus the need to find a suitable husband before time runs out must take precedence over any emotional considerations. It is not love or romance but a stable marital relationship that women of a certain age should aim for. Not surprisingly, when the narrator expresses her doubt and concern over getting married to a man she does not love, the advice from relatives is unanimous: 'get yourself a husband first, love will come later'.

The view that marriage is the main source of a woman's happiness is also the theme of 'Giai Nhan' (Belle), written in 1993 by Nguyen Thi Thu Hue. The short story revolves around Sao, a beautiful single woman in her late thirties who one day wakes up to herself and the emptiness in her life.

> There was a thump on the door. Sao was stunned. She spinned around to make sure that there was really someone knocking on her door. There it was again. Louder this time. Who could it be? It was an unfamiliar knock. 'Oh God', Sao moaned, her whole body shaking. Please, please let it be the man of my dreams. I swear, I swear I will love him with all my heart. And I

> will marry him, one way or another. I can't stand this loneliness any more. I don't need anything now except a family. Sao felt her heart beating wildly as if it were going to burst out of her chest. I will embrace that man and never let him go. I will always keep him for myself, whoever he may be.
>
> (Nguyen Thi Thu Hue 1994: 150)

Apart from the vivid depiction of the woman's emotional crisis and loneliness, a striking feature of 'Belle' is the temporary removal of the inherent connection between romantic love, sex and marriage. Having a sexual relationship with and falling pregnant to her former boyfriend do not make Sao feel compelled to marry him as she probably would if the story were set in an earlier time. The author is not trying to promote women's personal freedom through sexual liberation, however. While focusing on the issues of women's autonomy and sexuality, Nguyen Thi Thu Hue nevertheless expresses a deep scepticism of the belief that sexual freedom can lead to happiness and personal fulfilment. Like many other women writers in contemporary Vietnam, the author seeks to illustrate the risks women take in challenging the social norms of female sexuality. On the surface, Sao appears to be leading a life of complete and perfect freedom, initiating and ending relationships whenever it suits her. In reality, however, she is no more than a sexual object for the enjoyment of men who quickly abandon her for younger and more beautiful women. For all her freedom, Sao cannot escape the superficiality and frivolity that seem to characterise the majority of her relationships, just as she is now unable to escape the loneliness that has engulfed her life. In short, the story's message seems to be that the source of a woman's contentment is not to be found in sexual liberation, which sometimes serves only to increase her vulnerability, but in true love, which ultimately leads to marriage and a serene family life. For those women who challenge this perception, loneliness and despair await, as Sao belatedly finds out.

Love in a material world

Ever since the government introduced a policy of reforms in the mid-1980s, the issue of economic forces corrupting people's moral outlook and behaviour has been brought to the fore in literary and artistic production in Vietnam. Apart from drawing attention to the problems of social stratification and the widening gap between rich and poor, literary works also focus on the increasingly materialistic attitude among some young men and women in urban areas, especially where marriage decisions are concerned. Although marriage for love remains the dominant romantic ideology, a growing number of young urbanites are giving consideration to the strain that material deprivation could exert on a union between two poor individuals. These concerns are reflected in numerous short fictions dealing with the subjects of love and marriage.

Written in 1990, 'Chon Vo' (Choosing a Wife) by Cao Linh Quan tells the story of a penniless young man, Son, who is faced with the agonising choice of marrying for love or for money. While deeply in love with Hanh, a pretty girl with all the qualities that would make her an ideal wife and mother, Son nevertheless finds himself reluctant to propose to her mainly because she comes from a poor family. Although she is studying to be a nurse, there is no guarantee of a job after graduation. Despite the fact that they truly love each other, if they married it would be the case of 'two small hardships making one big poverty', according to Son. Another girl, Thuy, has also fallen in love with him. Four years older than Son, Thuy is the youngest daughter of an affluent family, but unfortunately, she is a hunchback. As Son continues to weigh the pros and cons, arguing with himself about which is worse, following his heart and living in poverty or marrying a hunchbacked woman and never again worrying about his financial situation, it becomes clear that this is not so much a love story as a thinly disguised attempt to satirise the younger generation and their attitude towards love and marriage. Most glaring is the notion that love alone is quite enough to ensure personal happiness and fulfilment. In a world fraught with uncertainties, money not only offers security but can also take the place of real human emotions in a relationship. For those who lived in Vietnam during the war – as represented by uncle Duong in the short story – such a view is symptomatic of the moral decay that has become a problem among Vietnamese youth in recent years. According to uncle Duong,

> The girl's hump is a congenital disability; it is perhaps harmless. But the hump in your soul is much more dangerous, a malignant tumour. If it became cancerous, no doctor or healer in the world could help you then!
>
> (Cao Linh Quan 1992: 89)

Extramarital love

Romantic short fictions produced in the 1990s are also conspicuous in their preoccupation with extramarital love affairs. Marriage and family life are generally depicted as fraught with disappointment and bitterness. Perhaps this is an attempt on the part of writers to reflect a sad reality in Vietnamese urban life in recent years: a rapidly climbing divorce rate. In 1999, every counsellor at the Centre for Marriage and Family Counselling in Ho Chi Minh City received about 200 calls per month from men and women seeking advice on marital problems. Newspapers and popular magazines regularly receive letters from readers, both male and female, who are desperately unhappy in their relationships. In response to this growing social trend, more short-story writers are turning their attention to the clash between romantic expectations and the mundane realities of everyday life, as well as its impact on conjugal relationships.

Written in 1998, 'Sau chop la giong bao' (After Lightning Comes the Storm) by Y Ban revolves around a married woman who yearns for love and passion. During a business trip away from home, the central female character, a worldly career woman who is married with a small daughter, felt a strong attraction for her co-worker, a man whom she described as having a 'kind face'. Amid all the emotional turmoil, the woman begins to re-examine the true state of her marriage. To her dismay, she finds that the marriage has been dead for some time as far as romance and passion are concerned.

> In their married life, she and her husband had had many conflicts and disagreements, but they had always been able to resolve their differences peacefully. Still, years of peaceful compromise had taken all the passion out of their relationship. Her husband had become like a close relative, her own flesh and blood; someone who is not much different from her father, her brothers and sisters, or her daughter. She cared for him and looked after him, but she could no longer feel the fire coursing through her veins when he touched her. At about the same time as she began to notice a definite 'ossification' of her feelings toward her husband, she started to have very unusual dreams at night. In these dreams, it only took a glance or a slight touch from a man, a complete stranger, to send her into a state of supreme ecstasy. Every time she had such a dream, she always woke up the next morning feeling utterly refreshed and revitalised. But it was never her intention to search for the lover in her dreams among the men whom she encountered every day in real life. She looked at all men with indifference and disdain.
>
> (Y Ban 1998)

For the woman in this story, married life has resulted in the slow death of her carefree innocence and passion for life. She has a pleasant voice and loves to sing, but her singing always draws sarcastic remarks from her husband and mother-in-law. The oppressive monotony of everyday life has also reduced the intimacy and passion between her husband and herself.

> She took off her clothes and stared at her own body. Before she could form an opinion about it, her husband had entered the bathroom. She was completely taken by surprise because they had not bathed together for quite a while, at least not since she had the baby. With his clothes still on, the husband took her in his arms. He was about to say something but changed his mind. He bent down and kissed her. Like a reflex action, she turned her head to avoid his kiss, for it had also been a long time since they kissed each other. The husband held her face firmly in his hands and kissed her. He whispered in her ear:
>
> – Do you still love me?
>
> She froze as she searched for an answer to her husband's question. Do I still love you? She did not even know if she still loved him. She only knew that she needed him but right now her heart was aching for someone else. She still cared for her husband very much – of that she could be certain. And

> she was afraid of hurting him. Tears streamed down her face. The husband hugged her tightly against his chest, and then left her without saying a word.
> (Y Ban 1998)

The possibility of love, however, has transformed the central character from an experienced and indifferent woman to 'an innocent and carefree girl who has never known disappointment or misery'. And all because the man with the 'kind face' has encouraged her to sing and to express herself. He has made appreciative comments on her looks, and has 'really seen' her when to everyone else she has become nothing but a shadow. Coming back to work at her office after the trip, the woman spends her day anxiously waiting for the man to ring, daydreaming and reminiscing about the nice things he has said to her in that honeyed voice. When the man finally rings, however, she starts to have doubt about the whole adventure, wondering where it would lead her.

In 'Con Mua Cuoi Mua' (The Last Rain of the Monsoon), a short story written by Le Minh Khue in 1991, love becomes a metaphor for the utopian search amid the moral and spiritual wasteland of contemporary society. The idealism and romanticism of the lovers involved in an adulterous relationship contrasts starkly with the apathy and sordidness that have come to characterise the world in which they live. It is the story of Mi, a successful engineer who is widely known among her friends and colleagues as a loving, devoted wife and mother. During one of her work assignments at a construction project, however, Mi meets and falls instantly in love with Binh, also an engineer and married with a family of his own. The story is narrated by Duc, a mutual friend of the lovers, in a detached and unemotional voice that contrasts sharply with his friends' torrid affair. As the construction project begins to wind up, both Mi and Binh are faced with the agonising choice of terminating their extramarital relationship or leaving their families.

Here love is once again invested with the power of rebirth and renewal. It is portrayed as having the almost magical ability to transform dowdy married women into vivacious young girls. Through Duc's eyes, we witness the rapid changes that come over Mi soon after her first encounter with Binh. Although an extremely attractive woman, Mi has long lost the incentive to make herself beautiful to members of the opposite sex. According to Duc, she is 'always busy, always a mess'. Love, however, has transformed Mi into a different person, so much so that even a close friend like Duc can scarcely recognise her. Suddenly radiant and lovely as a young girl, her face 'fresh from the cool breeze, the mist, and the moonlight', Mi walks, talks and breathes with a new vitality that only love can bring. Even her voice has changed; it is now 'full of new sounds'.

Throughout Le Minh Khue's story, the contrast between romanticism and mundane reality is achieved using various methods. The love affair between the two engineers, for example, unfolds against the dreary and heavily polluted background of the construction site. The contrast is also made apparent through the opposing personalities of Mi and her confidant Duc. Transformed by love, Mi begins to dream of a life less ordinary, an existence far removed from the sordidness that she encounters on a daily basis in the housing project in Hanoi where she lives with her family. On the other hand, Duc, who believes that 'real life is such a powerful shock it could even break stones', seeks to protect his friend by constantly deflating her romantic aspirations. This is illustrated in one of their late-night conversations, when Mi has just come back from her amorous rendezvous with Binh:

> She looked at the pile of magazines and newspapers on the table. There was a picture of a new president who was not yet forty. He looked strikingly handsome, and people said he was very talented too. You would know just by looking at his picture that he was an extraordinary person, the shining star of a large country on the other side of the hemisphere.
>
> Mi gazed at the picture for a long time.
>
> – I can't understand these people! How are they different from us? They are so far away, unreachable. How would it feel to be the wife or lover of such an important man? It must be very special and extraordinary. Surely it has to be like that!
>
> – It would probably be the same as with anyone else.
>
> – How could that be? It must be happiness. True happiness. Such a man would know how to love a woman. Love from the bottom of his heart. True love.
>
> – He wouldn't have the time, believe me. He has to carry out his presidential duties.[7]
>
> (Le Minh Khue 1996: 343)

When Mi expresses her desire to run away with Binh, unsurprisingly Duc advises against it. In his view, having an extramarital affair is normal, sometimes even necessary, but love should not be allowed to enter the equation. Duc believes that Mi is going through a crisis that will soon work itself out when she returns to her ordinary daily life. If Binh and Mi run away together now, he warns, they will eventually find their lives beset with the same monotony, frustration and disillusionment. According to Duc,

> ...even if you go to the moon or to the planet Mars, you could never escape. That's how we are. After a while, you would return to your present state of mind.
>
> (Le Minh Khue 1996: 349)

However, Mi desperately wants to believe in the possibility that love can somehow deliver her from the 'tyranny of the ordinary', the overwhelming power of everyday trivialities to sap one's life of all meaning and purpose. At first, she cannot accept that life could ever be the same again:

> But I will die. If things go on like this forever, there will be nothing left for me. I can feel myself eroding a little each day. I will become stupid, lethargic and housebound. I will become ugly and mean, shouting at my son, fighting with neighbours, counting every cent like a penny-pincher. In only another ten years I will turn into a forty-year-old hag and no one will recognise me any more.
>
> (Le Minh Khue 1996: 350)

Eventually both Mi and Binh realise that they must end the relationship. Significantly, it is not the fact that they are already committed to different people that ultimately separates the lovers. Rather, both seem to have resigned themselves to the belief – Duc's belief – that unhappiness and disappointment are part of the human condition and that any attempt to resist is futile. In a calm and down-to-earth tone, the narrator advises Mi to be content with the fact that she is alive, healthy and whole, shielded from poverty, hunger and the worries of everyday life. Mi seems to accept her friend's argument as she settles back into her normal daily routine as a wife, a mother and a working woman.

Since the early 1990s, many short-fiction writers have begun to focus their attention on the failings of marriage in real life, particularly the breakdown of communication and the loss of intimacy between spouses, as we have seen in 'After Lightning Comes the Storm'. The issues of marital unhappiness and infidelity also become a vehicle for expressing authors' dissatisfaction with the state of their society, as illustrated by Le Minh Khue's 'The Last Rain of the Monsoon'. Despite differences in narrative styles and methods of characterisation, the short stories discussed above share a number of notable thematic similarities. For example, the central female character is always portrayed in the beginning of the story as feeling utterly unhappy due to the absence of romance and passion in her marriage. Furthermore, marriage is often depicted as a constant battle to resolve the conflict between the female protagonist's desire to reassert her self-identity and the need to fulfil the roles society has imposed on her.

As many short-fiction writers in Vietnam nowadays are women, the stories are often told from the point of view of the female character. Many emphasise the instability and impermanence of romantic relationships in the face of mundane reality, and adopt a cynical attitude toward marriage that is often depicted as an emotional deadlock rather than a happy ending. Such pessimism and cynicism are pervasive not only in the works of Le Minh Khue, who has become well known in recent years for her preoccupation with the theme of lost idealism, but also in the fiction of Vo Thi Xuan Ha, who tends to depict relationships between the genders as fraught with tension and disappointment, as we shall see below.

Significantly, the stories above seem to convey a similar 'message': that the promise of happiness and emotional fulfilment in an extramarital affair proves illusory in the end. Romance outside the bounds of marriage represents a mere diversion from and not a solution to the marital and emotional problems of the central characters. Sooner or later, people who cheat on their partners, or contemplate doing so, will have to return to reality and resume their roles as dutiful wife or loving husband.

Love, sex and gender relations

In recent years, many women writers of short fiction have turned their attention to the unfathomable gulf between males and females regarding love and sex. For writers such as Vo Thi Hao, a woman's search for love and romance always ends in disillusionment. Although men talk about love, their love only extends as far as the bedroom. Written in 1993, Vo Thi Hao's story 'Vuon Yeu' (The Garden of Love) depicts the problems many young women have distinguishing between love and sex, particularly when there are some men who would unscrupulously manipulate their need for love and take advantage of them. The female protagonist in this story is an innocent young girl who dreams of a perfect love. However, her romantic visions are quickly shattered by crude sexual encounters in the public park, which she has thought to be the 'Garden of Love'.

> We walked and walked in the Garden of Love until we could find a spot under a tree. And he said: 'Sit down, baby!' I sat down, but not too close to him. I started to tremble with excitement and anticipation. As I was trying awkwardly to smooth the creases on my clothes, he suddenly pulled me closer, sat me in his lap, and then it began. I shook like a leaf and was almost suffocated by that first kiss. I kept my eyes shut for a long time before opening them to look over his shoulder. Up there the moon was smiling. Faint stars dotted the lilac-coloured sky. A white cloud with a reddish fringe was rolling up and then suddenly unfurled into the shape of a torn sail gliding across the sky. 'Why a torn sail? Can a boat reach its shore with a torn sail?'
>
> Still dreaming about the white cloud, I suddenly looked down and was shocked to see his experienced hands already on my breasts. Breasts which I have tried to hide by stooping my shoulders and wearing bras so thick I could hardly breathe. And now … Such images of love-making had not even begun to enter my imagination!
>
> I sat right up and angrily pushed him away: 'You don't respect me at all! Mother!' He looked at me in surprise: 'Why are you acting in this way? Don't you understand anything about love?' 'Yes, I do. But not like you. You have humiliated me … ' I wept bitterly. He said: 'Such is love, baby. Look around you. People are silent because they are all busy!'
>
> Through a veil of tears, I looked around. The faint shapes of couples standing and sitting in unusual positions were now becoming more visible. Sadly I realised that he was right.
>
> Was this supposed to be the Garden of Love? I could not pluck up the courage to leave the garden and go home, so I huddled up like a porcupine with its quills ready to bristle at a touch. Where were the souls of those who

> had died for love? I could no longer hear their tender whispers nor feel their poignant longing for rebirth. They were here just ten minutes ago. Or have they flown away with the torn sail?
>
> Our conversation suddenly became as exciting as cold fish soup. 'This is the third time I fell in love. Believe you me, love is like this. I don't want to be jilted again. My intentions are honourable: I want to marry you.'
>
> I had never been in love before, so I did not have enough knowledge in this area to argue with him. Still I felt like something precious had been stolen from me. I felt utterly empty.
>
> (Vo Thi Hao 1995: 55–6)

In a short story entitled 'Nha Co Bas Chi Em' (Three Sisters), writer Vo Thi Xuan Ha explores the notions of love and marriage from the perspective of three very different women. Phuong, the eldest sister, is a thirty-nine year old teacher who dresses conservatively and leads a quiet lifestyle dominated by a strict routine of work and regular visits to her mother. Despite her good looks, Phuong has never been involved in a romantic relationship before. Now as she approaches middle age, Phuong has resigned herself to life as an old spinster. Nghi, the second sister, works as a newspaper reporter but also likes to dabble in poetry in her spare time. Married to a medical doctor with two children, Nghi appears to have a perfect family life. In reality, her husband is a cold man more interested in his work than his pretty wife. After having a few of her poems published, Nghi suddenly becomes known as a young and upcoming poetic talent. The passionate love poems have also awakened a mysterious longing in her heart. Before long, she meets and falls in love with a much younger man, plunging headlong into an extramarital affair in the hope of satisfying her romantic fantasies. Hong, the youngest sister, has been married twice. For the past three years, she has been made a virtual prisoner in her husband's house in Saigon, waiting hand and foot on her in-laws. With the help of her friends, Hong finally broke free from that oppressive household and is now working at a nightclub. Her objective is not simply to earn a lot of money but also to find herself a nice Westerner who is willing to marry her and take her out of the country. In her most recent visit home, Hong informs her mother and sisters that she has found someone, a Belgian businessman thirteen years her senior, who has agreed to tie the knot with her. Completely disenchanted with love and romance, Hong criticises her sister Nghi for entangling herself in an affair that she suspects will lead nowhere except to more heartache. Hong advises her sister:

> Let me find you a Western husband. You'll never have to worry about anything any more. Love is a waste of time. Forget about him. What's more, the men in our country are all bastards. It's all right to be lovers but as soon as the word marriage is mentioned, they'll begin weighing and measuring as if they're buying breeding stock.
>
> (Vo Thi Xuan Ha 1995: 4)

With sinking heart, Nghi realises that Hong's view about men in their society, though harsh and judgmental, may not be completely groundless. Take Giang, her young paramour, for example. Lately, she has detected a subtle change in his attitude toward her. Gone are the ardent looks and the passionate kisses. In their place is an outright refusal to make any kind of permanent commitment.

The author seems to be suggesting that, for some men, love is like an adventure that must be enjoyed while it lasts. This attitude contrasts starkly with the romantic ideals regarding love which have been imparted to many women since their youth. For all her education and success in the material world, the character Nghi remains subservient to Giang merely because she wants him to return the love and respect she feels for him. Her very propensity for love makes her vulnerable to emotional and sexual exploitation.

As her idealised image of love and romance is shattered, Nghi cannot return to her former existence as a devoted wife and mother. In her deepest despair, Nghi sees death as the only way she could ever be united with Him, the personification of her romantic ideals. As she writes in a suicide note to her mother:

> He is my arrogant and ambitious youth. He and I have found each other across the great expanse of space, and will belong to each other for all eternity. For I have fallen out of step with this world. There is not even a tiny place for me on this planet. I have fallen into the abyss. There is nothing there. Who knows, perhaps I will be resurrected and will catch up with him in another world full of light and hope.
>
> (Vo Thi Xuan Ha 1995: 7)

Underlying Vo Thi Xuan Ha's story is a very pessimistic outlook which explodes the myth of a perfect, all-fulfilling romantic love. In many ways, 'Three Sisters' represents another attempt to explore the theme of women's desire and the consequent frustration in their search for 'true love'. Once again, the main female character is shown wandering aimlessly through an emotionally unsatisfying marriage, all the while suffering from some inescapable and unrealised desire.

Conclusion

Compared to the didacticism of socialist-realist fiction of the late 1970s and early 1980s, short stories dealing with the topic of love in the last decade of the twentieth century have exhibited a much more profound understanding of the complexities of love and the human condition in general. Love has undergone a dramatic transformation from a narrowly defined abstract idea to concrete emotional and moral dilemmas confronting men and women in a rapidly changing society. Interestingly, the majority of romantic short fiction produced in Vietnam today seems to focus on urban women and their experiences in love and marriage, at the expense of their rural counterparts. This could be explained partly by the fact that some of the most well-known and popular writers of short fiction nowadays are also women living and writing in an urban environment. While there is little evidence to suggest that Vietnamese women writers like to project their own image onto the central characters, it is hard to ignore the emergence of a recurrent pattern of characterisation in contemporary, romantic short fiction. In many love stories, the female protagonist falls into one of the following different categories of urban women. The first type is the educated and independent career woman, who leads a stable, if not affluent, married life but nevertheless yearns for love and romance, sometimes committing adultery in the hope of fulfilling her romantic fantasies. More often than not, this type of female character is also highly sensitive and passionate, making her vulnerable to unscrupulous men. Even when she is condemned to wander the emotional wasteland of a burnt-out marriage, she still retains a fierce belief in the transforming and redeeming power of true love. The second type of protagonist is the disillusioned woman whose painful past experiences with love have made her sceptical about any permanent commitment from men. Often portrayed as exceptionally beautiful and intelligent, she uses sex to manipulate men for her own purposes. At first glance, the two types of female characters appear to be located at opposite poles: one seems to devote her life to the quest for 'true love' while the other seeks to establish her autonomy and freedom through sexual relations with wealthy and powerful men. Despite surface appearances, both types of women often find themselves trapped in an unfulfilling pattern of gender relations that continually puts them in the weaker position – a predicament from which they seem unable to escape despite their beauty, intelligence and education.

Unlike fictional works dealing with love and marriage written in the early decades of the twentieth century, contemporary short stories have given much more prominence to the conflict and friction inherent in a romantic relationship, particularly the gulf between the sexes in their perceptions of love and romance. Typically, women are portrayed as sensitive and emotional individuals who are prepared to sacrifice much in the name of love. From their perspective, love is the most wondrous gift, and as such it must be cherished and treated with respect. However, these stories suggest that men are interested in only one thing: sexual gratification. In their eyes, love is just a euphemism for lust, part of the language of seduction. Short fictions by Vo Thi Hao in particular often depict the vulnerability of young women in negotiating between traditional concepts of love and marriage and modern standards of sexual behaviour.

Perhaps reflecting the increasing social problem in contemporary Vietnam of marriage breakdown due to infidelity, extramarital love affairs constitute a major theme in romantic fiction. Significantly, infidelity is no longer depicted predominantly as a transgression against the sanctity of marriage by the male sex. In contrast to the old story-line of married men engaging in adulterous relations with single women, extramarital affairs in contemporary short fiction usually involve two married persons. The traditional stereotype of the wronged wife is also fast becoming outmoded. As evinced in the short stories above, married women are depicted as flesh-and-blood individuals with real emotional and sexual needs. Susceptible to the same desires as men, they are driven to commit adultery by the lack of passion and intimacy in their marriages. For these women, it is not sexual gratification but the need to regain their self-identity, which has been buried underneath layers of marital and social roles, that prompts them to look for love and romance outside marriage.

Since a large section of Vietnamese society nowadays continues to hold to the view that for women the greatest source of happiness lies in the domestic rather than the public sphere, romantic love becomes the key for women to reach the eternal paradise of marriage. A growing number of short-fiction writers, especially women, are beginning to question whether modern notions of love and marriage truly bring happiness and fulfilment. Many address the devastating effect of romantic illusions and their consequences for the emotional life of women, married or otherwise. Contemporary short fiction dealing with love and romance in general, and the stories analysed in this chapter in particular, vary widely in their approaches, overtones, thematic development and other stylistic qualities. However, they all seem to share one essential feature – women's desire to be appreciated, cherished and respected by the men they love, by their family and by society at large.

Notes

1 All translations in this chapter are by Pham Thu Thuy, unless otherwise noted.
2 'To love is to die a little in the heart' (Yeu la chet o trong long mot it) by Xuan Dieu, translated by Huynh Sanh Thong (1996).
3 Some of Le Minh Khue's best short stories have been translated into English by Dana Sachs and Bac Hoai Tran. For a more detailed discussion of Le Minh Khue and her works, see Dana Sachs (1999).
4 The novel *Tinh Mong* (Dream Love) by Ho Bieu Chanh (1885–1958) appeared even earlier than *To Tam*. Published in 1923, it deals with an incestuous love affair resulting in an unwanted pregnancy. Arguably the first modern romantic novel in Vietnam, *Tinh Mong* did not achieve the kind of popularity nor generate such controversy as *To Tam*.
5 The growth of romantic literature in south Vietnam prior to 1975 was supported by a rapidly expanding market for love stories and romance novels. So great was the appetite for romantic fiction among southern urbanites during this period that local literary production had to be heavily supplemented with translations of love stories by foreign authors such as Françoise Sagan of France and Ch'iung Yao of Taiwan.
6 Among Vietnamese of the older generation, an engagement is considered as binding as matrimony.
7 This translation is by Pham Thu Thuy. For a different translation, see Karlin (1997: 97–116).

Bibiography

Cao Linh Quan (1992) 'Chon Vo' (Choosing a Wife), in *Ngay Thuong* (Ordinary Days), Hanoi: Thanh Nien Publishing House, 84–100.

Da Ngan (1996) 'Du Phai Song It Hon' (Even if We Must Live a Little Less), in Nguyen Tat Hoa (ed.), *Nhung Cau Chuyen Tinh* (Love Stories), vol. 2, Hanoi: Culture Publishing House, 657–69.

Ho Anh Thai (1998) 'Creative Writers and the Press in Vietnam since Renovation, in David G. Marr (ed.), *The Mass Media in Vietnam*, Canberra, Department of Political and Social Change, Research School of Pacific and Asian Studies, Australian National University, 58–63.

Hoang Ngoc Thanh (1991) *Vietnam's Social and Political Development as Seen through the Modern Novel*, New York: Peter Lang Publishing.

Huynh Sanh Thong (trans.) (1996) *An Anthology of Vietnamese Poems*, New Haven, CT: Yale University Press.

Karlin, Wayne (ed.) (1997) *The Stars, the Earth, the River – Short Fiction by Le Minh Khue*, Willimantic, CT: Curbstone Press.

Le Minh Khue (1996) 'Con Mua Cuoi Mua' (The Last Rain of the Monsoon), in Nguyen Tat Hoa (ed.), *Nhung Cau Chuyen Tinh* (Love Stories), vol. 2, Hanoi: Culture Publishing House, 335–56.

Louie Kam (1989) 'Love Stories: The Meaning of Love and Marriage in China 1978–81', in Louie Kam (ed.), *Between Fact and Fiction*, Broadway, NSW: Wild Peony.

Mong Binh Son and Dao Duc Chuong (1991) *Nha Van Phe Binh – Khao Cuu Van Hoc Viet Nam Thoi Ky 1932–1945* (Literary Criticism by Writers – A Study on Vietnamese Literature in the Period 1932–45), Hanoi: Literature Publishing House.

Nguyen Dinh Hoa (1994) *Vietnamese Literature: A Brief Survey*, San Diego, CA: San Diego State University.

Nguyen Thi Minh Ngoc (1996) 'Cho Duyen' (Waiting for a Match), *Nhan Dan*, online. Available: *http://www.nhandan.org.vn/* [accessed 14 August 2000].

Nguyen Thi Thu Hue (1994) 'Giai Nhan' (Belle), in *Truyen Ngan Hay 1993* (Outstanding Short Stories of 1993), Hanoi: Literature Publishing House, 140–54.

Sachs, Dana (1999) 'Small Tragedies and Distant Stars: Le Minh Khue's Language of Lost Ideals', *Crossroads*, 13(1): 1–10.

Vo Phien (1992) *Literature in South Vietnam 1954–1975*, trans. Vo Dinh Mai, Melbourne: Vietnamese Language & Culture Publications.

Vo Thi Hao (1995) 'Vuon Yeu' (The Garden of Love), in *Nam nguoi dan ba va bon nguoi dan ong* (Five Women and Four Men), Hanoi: Youth Publishing House, 51–61.

Vo Thi Xuan Ha (1995) 'Nha Co Ba Chi Em' (Three Sisters), *Nhan Dan*, online. Available: *http://www.nhandan.org.vn/* [accessed 14 August 2000].

Y Ban (1998) 'Sau chop la giong bao' (After Lightning Comes the Storm), *Nhan Dan*, online. Available: *http://www.nhandan.org.vn/* [accessed 14 August 2000].

Chapter 14

Doi moi and the crisis in Vietnamese dance

Cheryl Stock

> I think it is the right time because it is *our* time, [we are] ready. And for the next future.
>
> (Pham Anh Phuong, Vice-Director, Vietnam Opera Ballet Theatre)

This statement was made in 1996 when there was a mood of optimism in some dance circles about the potential for positive change through *doi moi*. Whilst primarily an economic policy to encourage free-market reform, it was believed that *doi moi* would also have a beneficial effect on the arts.[1] However, in an article about theatre development in Vietnam, Catherine Diamond quoted the director of a *Cai luong* company as saying that *doi moi* meant the opening of one door and the closing of another (Diamond 1997: 372).[2] The evidence since then might

Figure 14.1 Nguyen Minh Thong in *Through the Eyes of the Phoenix*

well suggest a revolving rather than an open door, a door which returns to its original position whilst appearing to move on.

This view of *doi moi* was formed during my work as a director and choreographer on eleven intercultural projects in Hanoi from 1988 to 2000. Dancers from the national dance company, Nha Hat Nhac Vu Kich Viet Nam (Vietnam Opera Ballet Theatre), with whom I regularly work, have complained that, whilst their material conditions are improving because of their 'left-hand job' – mostly tourist shows of 'traditional dance' in hotels – they feel 'jobless' in their 'right-hand job', or their principal work as dance artists.[3] This tension is a symptom of the arts becoming increasingly driven by economics, but the underlying problems of the arts under *doi moi* are more complex. How does Vietnam reconcile the conflicting elements of global capitalism, consumerism, nationalism, communism and traditional values both in practical and philosophical terms? Kolko (1997: 43) claims that under *doi moi*, 'Vietnam is drifting aimlessly in many crucial social and institutional areas' and that, 'not withstanding impressive economic growth statistics, there is a profound crisis in motivation and morale'. Templer puts it more succinctly in referring ironically to *doi moi* as 'market Leninism' (1999: 2). How these opposing doctrines are affecting dance artists in Vietnam is a key to gaining some insight into the upsurge of dance activity on the one hand and artistic stagnation on the other.

Economic effects of *doi moi* in professional dance

The current crisis in the dance profession is in many ways a microcosm of the larger schisms facing Vietnam. As Andree Grau comments, the making of dances is not simply 'an exercise in the organisation of movements, but … a symbolic expression of cultural organisation which reflects, in part, the values and the ways of life of the human beings who create them' (1993: 24).

One of the policies of *doi moi* which directly affects dance is *xa hoi hoa* (literally 'socialisation') or, in Western terminology, privatisation. Former Director of the Performing Arts Department of the Ministry of Culture and Information, Bui Gia Tuong defines socialisation in the arts context as meaning 'that the society has the responsibility to financially support the organisation and not the government'. He adds the crucial rider that 'the government guides [some companies] in terms of their artistic content but does not assist them financially' (Bui Gia Tuong 1998). The rationalisation through 'socialisation' includes plans to reduce the enormous number of song and dance companies in the hope of encouraging greater quality, but without any incentives or the freedom to engender any increase in quality.[4] The lack of strategies to effect a transition from total subsidy of major companies to greater self-sufficiency is a partial reason for the crisis in dance. Plans to upgrade and update skills, approaches and training through overseas study are thwarted by the exclusion of the arts from almost all aid programmes, whilst at the same time continuing state control and censorship of professional arts discourages innovation and new ideas within the country. Government initiatives to improve the previously deplorable material conditions of artists are beginning to have a positive impact, but these improvements are restricted to buildings and equipment, with the already pitiful wages reduced in real terms because of higher living costs brought about by the market economy.

Political control of culture

Political control of culture is enshrined in party and therefore government legislation (Communist Party of Vietnam 1996: 70). The cultural plenum in July 1998 was quite explicit in writing that this meant 'the monitoring of cultural activities in terms of timely intervention of wrong-doing and application of effective corrective measures' (*Vietnam News* 1998: 8). Deputy Director of the Vietnam Cultural Institute, Pham Hung Thoan (1998), explained the nature of political control in dance:

> Firstly the value of dance is measured by the reactions of the leaders of the country because they provide the budget for dancers' salaries, for the theatres, for rehearsals, for productions. The dance must therefore fulfil the needs and expectations of the Ministry…

Staff and indeed artists talk about companies 'belonging' to the Ministry of Culture and Information under which company members are permanent government employees (Pham Thi Thanh 1997). Bui Gia Tuong (1998) gave the following indication of the encompassing nature of this control:

> We decide which artists and organisations will be able to enter the country and which Vietnamese ones will tour inside and outside the country. We also document and report on all the performing arts and make decisions about approving, or not approving the content of programs.

Although controlling information on the Internet and via satellite dishes or preventing free association with the millions of visitors now entering the country is a battle which the government is losing, the cumulative effects of such a controlling environment upon artists continue to have detrimental results on creativity (Bui Gia Tuong 1998). All performing arts festivals and awards continue to be run directly by the state, and the increasing number of competitions organised by the Vietnamese Dance Association, which attract cash prizes and afford future opportunities, adhere strictly to government policy in their entry guidelines. Such guidelines make reference to acceptable content and style, as well as nominating set repertoire works. A more subjective but nonetheless effective means of control is the kind of self-censorship, often unconscious and ingrained, that artists themselves apply in order to be able to keep making, performing and touring works in their own country. Working outside the societal and political structures is extremely difficult, especially for dance artists whose art form depends largely on its ensemble nature and a visible infrastructure.

Working within these structures and strictures often means working around them, which dissipates creative energy (Ngoc Cuong 1997).[5]

Artistic challenges under *doi moi*

Whilst it may be true that a stable and growing economy provides a more conducive climate for artistic development, the philosophical shifts in thinking required to engender creativity are not simply a result of economic policies, nor can a lack of artistic development be blamed entirely on government control of the arts. Dancers, choreographers, scholars and bureaucrats have been concerned for a decade about the growing crisis in Vietnamese dance. Dance critic Thai Phien (1997) acknowledges that audiences for dance have decreased dramatically, and that globalised mass entertainment now available in many urban homes is only partly to blame. He believes that those working in dance should take some responsibility for lack of audiences because of the boring and repetitive choreography they produce.

In December 1997, the Vietnamese Dance Association held a conference in Hanoi to discuss how to improve the quality of dance. In terms of the art form, its greatest concern was low choreographic standards and a proliferation of works devoid of ideas in form and content. Many older choreographers and directors who received intensive training in the 1970s and 1980s cited inadequate technical knowledge of dance as well as a lack of specific knowledge of the traditions on which choreographers drew for their work, resulting in superficiality, monotony and homogenisation (Thieu Hanh Nguyen 1997: 47). Vu Hoai, a choreographer with a deep knowledge of ethnic minorities in the Son La area where he lived for thirty-four years, also identified as one of the serious problems a lack of understanding of the essence of the ethnic dances on which much choreography is based (Vu Hoai 1997).

Trung Kien, Vice-Minister of Culture and Information, reiterated similar concerns in a 1998 interview, when he said of Vietnamese choreographers, that 'their understanding of traditional dance is very limited, very poor. If they don't explore in more depth, we will continue to see superficial works. I love dance so much but I cannot bear to see those works performed' (Trung Kien 1998). Cong Nhac, Artistic Director of Vietnam Opera Ballet Theatre, cited not only poor conditions and lack of infrastructure but also the 'restrictions placed on the nature of the work by the government [which] prevents development' (Nguyen Cong Nhac 1997).

The lack of challenging choreography and unadventurous content is naturally having a detrimental effect on the technical standard of dancers. Vice-Minister of Culture and Information, Trung Kien, is well aware of the problem, remarking in frustration: 'in some artistic groups under the Ministry, they do not practice at all. They just go onto the stage and perform because the choreographers give them such simple movements to perform'. Up to seven years full-time training at the Vietnam Dance School produces technically accomplished dancers but students lack incentive to attain the high technical standards required for graduation when they perceive it is neither needed nor valued in the profession. Experienced, highly skilled dancers such as Thu Lan complain, 'Vietnamese dancers are not lazy; it is just that we have nothing to do' (Luu Thi Thu Lan 1997).

Whilst professional dance in many ways appears to be stagnating, fundamental changes in people's lives and attitudes have occurred as a result of *doi moi*. The power that new-found consumerism exercises over artists who grew up in a closed world of poverty should not be underestimated. The ability to earn a decent living on the open market in clubs or tourist hotels for little effort is attractive to artists, reducing the drive to maintain high standards in either performance or choreography. These 'left-hand' jobs also reduce the time available for more serious artistic pursuits.

Hong Phong, a young dancer who has worked in major companies as well as in commercial venues in Saigon and Hanoi, feels strongly about the devaluation of the dance profession in Vietnam:

> I will never do cheap dancing because I believe dance should be about beauty. I will only do the work I want to, and … because you have to work really hard, it must be paid well. I feel very offended when professionals like us who have studied for seven years have to dance with people who have only trained for three or four months. The Vietnamese situation is not like the Western one where you need qualifications to get work. If your father is in a high level position he can help you, and these people can earn more money than we can.
>
> (Nguyen Hong Phong 1998)

The extent to which these issues are affecting professional dance begs the question: is it possible for Vietnamese dance to emerge as a revitalised artistic force in a consumer-obsessed Vietnam, which still tightly controls its cultural products by re-enforcing outdated formulas overlaid with a superficial gloss of mass-media commercialism?

Questions of history: dance and revolution

To attempt to answer this question, it is necessary to understand the historical context in which dance was professionalised and what conditions have led to its present state. Prior to the war of independence against the French in the 1950s, there was no professional infrastructure for dance. Despite a rich folk dance tradition among the fifty-four ethnic groups including the majority *viet* or *kinh*, the only professional dance was the court dance practised in the former Imperial capital of Hue and the dance component of traditional theatre forms such as *Tuong* (classical court opera), *Cheo* (folk opera) and from the 1920s, *Cai luong*. The first dance training institution *Truong Mua Vietnam* (Vietnam Dance School) was set up in Hanoi in 1959 by the government, with a group of artists, some of whom had trained in China in the early 1950s and who were assisted by Russian-trained visiting Chinese and Korean experts. Together with a basis of ballet training, a 'traditional' syllabus was devised by codifying forms of ethnic dances collected during visits to ethnic villages over two decades. This syllabus was documented in written form, and is still simply referred to as 'the book'. Classical ballet and 'traditional' dance thus became the basis for Vietnamese professional dance training and remain so today.

However, the driving force for professionalising dance was a revolutionary one. War provided the conditions for the first widespread professional practice where large numbers of artists were deployed in Army Ensembles performing as part of military strategy. From the late 1950s to the mid-1970s, 'Vietnamese culture concentrated on the heroism of the arts' (Trung Kien 1998). Nguyen Cong Nhac (1997) provides the following blunt description of artistic propaganda:

> The arts were used to serve the war. Whatever we did, we had to encourage the soldiers, to make them strong, to impart appropriate opinions and ideas through our work, and to make them hate the enemy. We had to help them win the war with our art … our first priority was to have a common purpose, and all convey the same message in our work. We had to forget about having individual opinions and ideas.

Yet many of the artists who danced during the war spoke of the love and knowledge of ethnic dance which they discovered at the time and how the experience of learning dance from villagers in remote areas helped inform their choreographic work and style. Of the thirty-four dance artists aged over forty-five whom I interviewed in Hanoi and Saigon, twenty-eight mentioned their dance experiences as members of Army Ensembles, but only when asked directly. Vietnamese artists tend not to dwell on the past, preferring to deal with the present and look to the future.

Apart from the beginnings of what is now a widespread, nationalised, traditionally based dance form, the late 1950s and early 1960s saw the first, full-length Vietnamese 'ballets' in the form of revolutionary dance dramas using classical ballet vocabulary. *Tam Cam* (the name of two women from a Vietnamese legend) and *Ngon Lua Nghe Tinh* (a story of the revolution in Nghe Tinh) were both directed by a Korean teacher and director, Kim Te Hoang, with choreography devised by the performers, several of whom are now or have been directors of dance companies. At that time, the only national song and dance company was Doan Ca mua Quan doi Nhan dan trung uong (People's Army Song and Dance Company) which annually travelled abroad, mainly but not exclusively to socialist countries. The Vietnam Opera Ballet Theatre was established in 1959 along with the Vietnam Dance School but was still in its formative stages. Wartime stories abound of dancers working as part of the performing arts 'cells' in the jungles and tunnels. Vu Minh Nguyet (1998), Director of the Dance School in Saigon, vividly recalls her experiences in the Vietnam/American War, revealing how valued artists felt, in contrast to the present situation:

> It was a very hard time but we were happy we could still dance. War raged throughout the country and it was our destiny to do this. We even opened a dance school in the jungle in Tay Ninh! When we moved to Cuu Chi we

> had to live in the tunnels and we also performed in the tunnels. We danced Vietnamese stories with ballet technique; imagine standing in arabesque in an *ao ba ba* (peasant dress of loose black pants and brown shirt)! The government took special care of artists during the war. There was a saying at the time, 'It is sad if one soldier dies, but there is triple sadness if an artist dies.' Government officials were really respectful of artists because they could not imagine anyone studying that hard for eight years.

Training for students also continued throughout the war and, when the bombing of Hanoi intensified, making it too dangerous to study in the capital, the School shifted to a northern village. According to the Director of the Vietnam Dance School, from 1966 to 1971 the students lived with village families and trained in a converted animal barn (Nguyen Thanh Thuy 1997). This legacy of war as the formative professional experience of the current dance directors and leaders is not to be underestimated in terms of the ensuing malaise, in which a theatre of resistance and propaganda has given way to an artistic lethargy in an institutionalised, post-war authoritarian state.

Post-war Soviet influences

Closure to the West followed the end of the war and a historical distrust of China, which flared up again in the 1979 border war between the two countries, saw Vietnam turn to the Soviet Union for assistance. This played out what Henry Kamm (1996: 131) refers to as the 'eternal natural law that makes a weak country forced to choose between two mighty friends elect the one with whom it shares no common history or border'. The Soviet Union was extraordinarily generous in its financial assistance for dance, not only footing expenses for training inside and outside the country, but providing shoes, costumes and production costs for over a decade. As a result of such encompassing cultural aid, there occurred what Vietnamese/Australian composer Le Tuan Hung (1994: 242) refers to as the 'Cultural and Ideological Revolution' whose aim was to build a new culture 'by blending indigenous and Soviet sociocultural concepts and practices' into a form known as *dan toc hien dai* (modern national). In dance this meant choreographing works which were a blend of ballet steps and Western classical compositional techniques with decontextualised Vietnamese folk and court dance forms. Thus, developing dance in Vietnam meant 'Sovietising' training, choreographic and philosophical approaches, aesthetics and even content.

Independence and peace brought a new cultural imperialism, resulting in sweeping changes in the arts. Of the fifty-four dance professionals I interviewed in Hanoi, Saigon and Hue in 1997 and 1998, thirty-nine had received intensive training in the Soviet Union, from periods of two to eleven years, with qualifications at diploma, degree, masters and doctoral levels. Courses were rigid with no deviation from the set syllabus. Many interviewees had trained at GITIS, the prestigious National Theatre School in Moscow where, in addition to Russian classical ballet techniques and allied practical and theoretical areas, it was compulsory to study such political subjects as Russian Communist Party history, military theory, Marxist philosophy and the 'science of Communism' (Vu Duong Dung 1998). This kind of inflexible and absolute education, perpetuated in Vietnamese government cultural training institutions, has ill-equipped artists for exploring alternative choreographic and teaching approaches in the rapidly changing environment of today's Vietnam.

The past and current professional dance training of four to seven years' full-time study of daily, Soviet-style, ballet classes has a powerful acculturating effect upon young students' bodies and minds. This is compounded by the fact that the concurrent training in twenty of the fifty-four Vietnamese ethnic and court styles has less time allocated to it than the ballet training, even though the vast majority of graduates work in traditionally based companies. The over-riding conventions of a highly codified technique inevitably alter the kinetics, aesthetics and stylistic norms of the cultural dance styles, despite concerted attempts by teachers to differentiate between ballet and 'traditional' dance.

Institutionalisation and stagnation

The national experiment of blending the new, Soviet-based, Western knowledge with old cultural forms began to stagnate as the arts quickly became institution-

Figure 14.2 Minh Phuong with students of the Vietnam Dance School

alised. As Soviet aid decreased then ceased altogether with the collapse of communism from 1990, an artistic malaise set in which paralleled the political and ideological paralysis. Dissident voices in literature and the visual arts had no counterpart in the dance world.[6] As a communal art form reliant on years of unquestioning, repetitive training and government support, dance bred few radical ideas or new visions, a trait compounded by very little access to alternative ideas. The choreographer and Director of the October Ballet Company in Saigon, Tran Van Lai (1998), sums up the situation with these words:

> Our country had a closed policy for a long time … That is why Vietnamese choreography is so strongly influenced by Russian and Chinese styles; not only in the choreographic know-how and skills, and staging, but even the way the mind works. I wish we could have had an open policy a long time ago so we could have access to the dance and culture of many countries and then we would have time to select it and make our own style.

Lack of money and incentive also meant that, during this later period of closure, full-length or substantial works were rarely produced, and even now much choreography consists of short works ranging from three to ten minutes, suitable to include in a variety-show format or at party conferences.

Dilemmas in dance training

The *doi moi* arts policy has induced a dichotomy between improved material conditions, at least for the urban elite, but without a sustained investment in the art form of dance, leading one to ask if dance in Vietnam can survive other than as a commercial form. Dance requires years of intensive training, and one of the problems in Vietnam at present is the lack of teachers. Duong Dung, in his early forties, told me he was the youngest teacher at the national Vietnam Dance School and that most adequately trained teachers were about to retire. It was difficult to recruit teachers 'because the teaching salary is so tiny, nobody wants to work here' (Vu Duong Dung 1998). In addition, many dance artists interviewed mentioned that the country's only tertiary teacher training course at the Theatre and Film Institute in Hanoi was of such poor quality that it fulfilled its quota of students by accepting provincial students who had very little dance training. The four-year degree is offered only every four years, with student intake averaging around ten. Deputy Director Hoang Su (1997) admitted that sometimes the course has not been offered at all due to lack of enrolments. Others commented that the course was inflexible, boring and irrelevant to changing professional needs. Bui Thuc Anh studied at a tertiary institution in Australia and therefore has a source of comparison. She is particularly scathing, but others who have not had access to training outside Vietnam feel similarly.

At the pre-tertiary training level there is now a greater drop-out rate and more absenteeism, a situation that was rare before *doi moi*. Director of the Saigon Dance School, Minh Nguyet, cites 'health reasons' caused by an inability to cope with the pressures of intensive vocational training in addition to increased academic school work (Vu Minh Nguyet 1998). In Hanoi, prior to *doi moi*, the majority of dance students lived at the School with housing, food and clothing provided by the government, and recreational programmes organised by the School. Nowadays, according to a teacher at the Vietnam Dance School, students miss many classes because they are too tired to attend after earning money in clubs and restaurants at nights. Disturbed by the lack of concentration amongst students and deprived themselves of artistic stimulation and professional development, teachers report that they feel physically exhausted and professionally burnt out.

The centralism of dance training is a major problem as it tends to breed uniformity and mediocrity. Since its inception in 1959, all vocational dance training in Vietnam has depended on the system set up at the Vietnam Dance School in Hanoi. Its 'branch' in Saigon is expected to follow an identical syllabus, with an abridged form of this national training occurring in provincial centres. Very few private schools exist, and those that do are recreational, money-making ventures. The only other source of training is after-school classes at government youth and recreation clubs, now teaching mainly hip-hop and other social dance styles.

Encouraging diversity of practice and training is therefore an urgent priority to promote a dynamic dance scene. Regional differences in *mua dan gian* (ethnic folk dance) have invariably been cited to boast of the richness of Vietnamese traditional culture, and yet regional diversity in contemporary professional settings of other dance genres has been actively discouraged. Commenting on the Saigon Dance School's plans, the Director Vu Minh Nguyet (1998) confided:

> I hope we can develop our course independently of Hanoi because we have identified different needs and skills here. Basically we have to teach the same syllabus as in Hanoi, and they often visit from Hanoi to 'control' us!

Changing the 'system'

It is therefore not surprising that one of the most striking impressions of the dance profession in Vietnam is the low morale and lack of energy. This is partially a result of disempowerment by a system that provides no incentives for the hard work or talent of its best artists. Chu Thuy Quynh (1998), Director of the Vietnamese Dance Association, admitted that 'the salary is always the same whether you are talented or not, and because you are a government employee you get the same as every other employee'. Breaking the nexus of a sinecure which has bred laziness and indifference is not limited to the arts and is one of Vietnam's endemic problems, as well as a source of the much publicised corruption in the country. In relation to dance, as Trung Kien has pointed out, increasing salaries 'for talented dancers who want to work' does not solve the problem of 'the working methods of the management' (Trung Kien 1998). Just as demoralising as unfair wage structures are artists' reliance on an unwieldy administrative bureaucracy staffed by former artists or cadres with no training in financial, marketing or administrative procedures. Management training still appears mainly relevant to propping up government policy and dominant ideologies. Planning tends to be ad hoc to accommodate 'directives' from the Ministry of Culture and Information, which can lead to sudden and frequent interruptions to normal company business. This has bred a mentality of reacting rather than initiating and planning. A common experience which directly affects programming is the demand for a small number of dancers from a company to go to a neighbouring country to provide a Vietnamese dance programme for up to three months at only a few days' notice. Dancers Pham Anh Phuong, Bui Thuc Anh, Bich Huong and others from a number of arts companies have described such experiences.

Many artists and directors identify the urgent need for training in contemporary administrative skills, and a complete overhaul of management practices, but this is accompanied by a sense of despair about the 'system' ever changing to accommodate such reform. Young artists in particular feel powerless to effect change as well as feeling unsupported by the existing structure. Dancers Quoc Tuan, Minh Thong and Thu Lan in particular voiced these frustrations on returning home from overseas study. Individual initiative is also regarded with suspicion, especially by those who have already risen to prominence through seniority and the existing system.

Minimal programming and the drop in morale and energy to keep up technical standards makes it difficult when working with visiting artists, 'because in Vietnam no one is ever asked to work at that high level', according to senior dancer Phung Quang Minh (1998). Choreographer and dancer, Tran Quoc Tuan (1997) similarly speaks of an internal complacency that changes as soon as there are opportunities to tackle creative and technical challenges introduced into the country from outside. However, these energising challenges tend to evaporate when foreign guests leave, with little encouragement to develop any new ideas introduced.

Dance as commodity: new ideas or just new economic potential?

Nevertheless, the opening of Vietnam's doors to a range of previously inaccessible influences has been responsible for renewed energy amongst some artists and teachers. There is excitement at the increasing potential to engage in a greater diversity of artistic ideas through exchanges into and out of the country. Whilst providing short-term stimulus, these visits do not yet address the long-term needs of professional development, and restructuring of training.

Some independence of practice has occurred under *doi moi*, but in dance this is limited to commercial and tourist shows which are primarily economic in motivation. Under *doi moi* nationalisation of tradition has been largely replaced by commercialisation of tradition. In Saigon, highly trained dancers and choreographers literally run from one commercial venue, throwing a coat over a costume and climbing on their motorbikes, to arrive in time for their slot as 'Vietnamese traditional dancers' at the next venue. Their ten-minute appearance may include a hip-hop number followed by the 'golden tray dance', a theatricalised and acrobatic version of a shamanistic ritual (*len dong*) of the Mekong delta region. Early next morning, these same dancers rehearse for their 'right-hand job', which will result in perhaps one or two performances in a major theatre. It is difficult for dancers in Vietnam to separate these two worlds, and it has become a way of life in all the major centres. Of course, this situation is not unique to Vietnam, and the effects of tourism and globalisation, together with decreasing arts subsidies in many countries, make this the scenario for artists from all over the world. The difference in Vietnam is the lack of any audience for concert dance, and the current political and socio-cultural difficulties in making non-commercial work independently.

Commercialisation of dance is causing noticeable changes in product and practice in both market and cultural tourism.[7] Culturally specific dances are shortened, simplified, often mix genres in style and costume, accelerate tempi and replace original musical accompaniment with internationally accessible alternatives. The already standardised national repertoire of these dances thus becomes even more undifferentiated. Once dance becomes no more than a commodity that the 'consumer' experiences only once or twice; there is not the same pressure to maintain clarity, difference or a level of expertise. Pham Thi Thanh, theatre director and former Deputy Director of the Performing Arts Department cites the one-off nature of tourist audiences as a negative factor in the maintenance of quality and the development of Vietnamese theatre artists: 'Because there is not a regular ongoing audience the performers do not have to improve their performance the way you must when the same audience returns again and again and can make comparisons' (Pham Thi Thanh 1997). Competition with karaoke, disco and club culture makes market tourism competitive and responsive to audience preferences for instant entertainment gratification. The drop in standards is exacerbated by the fact that most commercial traditional dance groups are privately run, where monetary considerations ensure that quantity takes priority over quality.

There is a view that traditional dance forms, no longer attended by local audiences, may find it hard to survive at all in the new Vietnam without the support of foreign audiences in tourist environments. However, some have suggested that in those villages capitalising on cultural tourism, folk forms which were in danger of disappearing have not only been revived but are resisting the kind of homogenising tendency seen in city companies.[8] Whether these still relatively isolated pockets of indigenous culture can survive the onslaught of globalised culture is, however, doubtful.

'The breath of contemporary dance'

Apart from commodified versions of 'traditional' dance and the introduction of popular dance styles via video and television as current influences on choreographers and dancers, *doi moi* has seen the introduction of contemporary dance. Describing his view on the development of dance in Vietnam, Deputy General Secretary of the Vietnamese Dance Association, Trinh Xuan Dinh (1998) stated that, after 1975, 'we had a really good Russian classical system but somehow were missing the breath of contemporary dance'.

The Australian company Dance North, of which I was Artistic Director, introduced the first Western-style contemporary concert dance to Vietnam in January 1988. Although *doi moi* had ostensibly been underway for a year, the country was still bleak for visiting foreigners. Movement was restricted, contact with ordinary Vietnamese difficult, and suspicion and poverty were everywhere. Nevertheless the huge, run-down theatres in which we played in Saigon and Hanoi were full, and contacts were made with dance and theatre artists who were keen to access anything new. For the following twelve years I returned almost every year, for periods of four to twelve weeks, to teach and choreograph in Hanoi. After several visits teaching and creating works for Nha Hat Tuoi Tre, the mime component of the Youth Theatre, the Vietnam Dance School and the Vietnam Opera Ballet Theatre, I opted to work solely with the more experienced and trained dancers of the latter.

Rather than creating the kind of contemporary works pertinent to my Australian context, I sought a dialogue with the existing Vietnamese dance context. As a result, the new works created in collaboration with Vietnamese artists in Hanoi consciously blended the dancers' classical and traditional training and aesthetics with the contemporary style I introduced via daily classes and my choreography.[9] These intercultural collaborative experiments, which

Figure 14.3 Nguyen Cong Nhac in *Through the Eyes of the Phoenix*

included exchanges to and from Australia, lasted from 1988 until 2000, culminating in the first season of new, contemporary but traditionally based works by Vietnamese choreographers, composers and designers.[10]

During the first eight years of *doi moi,* there were few opportunities for professional contemporary dance to develop or be seen.[11] Mainly due to financial constraints and restricted entry for foreign artists, it was difficult to bring in long-term resident teachers to introduce new forms of dance training inside the country, or for Vietnamese dancers to train for extended periods outside the country.

The French connection

Since the mid-1990s, overseas opportunities in contemporary dance training and performance have come predominantly from France, Vietnam's former colonial ruler. This has been possible through generous scholarships provided by the French government for Vietnamese dancers. Scholarship recipients are almost exclusively drawn from the Vietnam Dance School and the Vietnam Opera Ballet Theatre.[12]

Philippe Cohen, Director of Choreographic Studies at the Lyon Conservatoire, has been visiting Vietnam regularly since 1993 to improve the predominantly classical dance training of Vietnamese dancers. He has stated that he has no interest in pursuing any areas of traditional dance, dismissing the 'extreme Sovietisation' of national dance styles as totally irrelevant to the needs of Vietnamese dancers of the future (Cohen 1999). In his work in Vietnam, he chooses not to work with local composers, designers or musicians, preferring to bring staff from France and to use extant recorded music. The exceptions have been a programme of neo-classical works, *Danses de Moussons* (1999), for Vietnam Opera Ballet Theatre, with costumes by a young Hanoi fashion designer, Vu Thu Giang, and a version of *The Nutcracker* in 2000 which incorporated Vietnamese costume influences and some traditional Vietnamese dance steps, albeit to the music of Tchaikovsky. Although not engaging with the local culture, Philippe Cohen has nevertheless made a positive contribution to dance in Vietnam in raising the technical standard of the dancers, their morale and confidence. He has also raised the company's prestige and audience numbers.

Despite France being internationally renowned for its cutting-edge contemporary dance and the fact that scholarships offered by France to Vietnamese dancers have been mainly for contemporary dance study, the 'new' repertoire produced by Cohen for the Vietnam Opera Ballet Theatre has consisted of neo-classical and conservative modern dance works. New ideas are now beginning to circulate amongst some in the dance profession, but the money and power being invested by the former colonial power in Vietnam is for French productions with which to grace the lavishly restored Hanoi version of the Paris Opera House. Naturally, the Vietnamese government and the company itself wish to raise their profile amongst the large foreign community now living in Hanoi, who flock to see such works.

A paradox of French involvement in dance in Vietnam is seen in the work of French-Vietnamese artist Ea Sola who has produced four major works there, the most acclaimed being the first, *Drought and Rain*. Ea Sola chooses not to work with trained dancers because of what she describes as mental rigidity, a result of their Sovietised and nationalised training. Creating what she views as a national language of gestures, Ea Sola draws on the energy of the body and the subtlety of gesture she sees as quintessential to the peasant culture of Vietnam. Not surprisingly, she is appalled by the 'diplomatic' official cultural programmes in Vietnam sponsored by the French government (Ea Sola 1999). Ea Sola's unique contribution to Vietnamese music and dance derives from a deeply personal artistic journey of cultural identity. Her ideas and works are important in Vietnam in bringing a unique and innovative approach to revitalising Vietnamese traditions, which counters the re-Europeanisation of the professional dance sector through the 'official' French dance programmes.

For the Vietnamese dancers who have studied in France and Australia, lack of opportunities to engage creatively with the revitalising influences they have brought back into the country has been frustrating. Le Vu Long (1998) echoed the sentiments of many of the dancers when he observed:

> luckily in our company we have a lot of dancers and choreographers who have gone abroad to train and they have new ideas, but at the moment we do not have *real* choreographers. Well, we have some, but not many who are good. We cannot choreograph regularly because we need a group of choreographers so they can spark off each other, and then the quality of work may improve.

Positive developments: actual and potential

At the time of writing there are promising changes taking place. The Vietnam Opera Ballet Theatre, with new premises close to the city centre, has recruited many new young graduates, expanded its performance commitments, and has begun to incorporate some contemporary technique classes to complement their daily, classical ballet training regime. In 2001, Ha The Dung returned from France with Le Vu Long and Nguyen Hong Phong (Nguyen Minh Thong had returned earlier as had Tran Quoc Tuan, after also studying in France) and together they staged the first full programme of contemporary dance choreographed solely by Vietnamese artists. The success of this programme has led to plans to form a contemporary dance group directed by The Dung under the umbrella of the Vietnam Opera Ballet Theatre.[13] There are plans for new productions with international guest choreographers for this new group and possibly a tour to France. However, much depends on continued support from both the Vietnamese Ministry of Culture and outside sources such as the French government, which continues to give scholarships for dancers to study and work in France. Although contemporary dance was only added to the curriculum of the Vietnam Dance School on a trial basis in 2001, Ha The Dung and Pham Anh Phuong began teaching modern dance styles, which they had picked up from myself and in Australia, at the Army Dance School in

1991. This school feeds the Army Song and Dance Company which remains one of the three biggest companies in Vietnam, with between 100 and 150 members of which approximately one-third are dancers. There are also fourteen smaller provincial army troupes. Quite a lot of interchange occurs between dancers of the army companies and other government companies, as the Army Dance School training is a four-year version of that taught at the Vietnam Dance School, with some crossover in teaching staff. Contemporary dance is currently taught at both the Army Dance School and the Vietnam Dance School by Ha The Dung, Nguyen Minh Thong, Tran Quoc Tuan, Nguyen Hong Phong and Le Vu Long (all male) (Nguyen Cong Nhac, e-mail communication, 11 September 2001a). Thus it is the army, instrumental in the development of professional dance in the 1950s and 1960s through its wartime artistic troupes, which has in peacetime provided the first opportunities for aspiring young dancers to train in new techniques.[14]

It is too early to predict how widely the more individualistic contemporary dance forms will be absorbed into and influence the highly codified training as it now exists. Since contemporary dance consists of a series of philosophies and approaches manifest in a variety of techniques, it resists the kind of uniform syllabus that still pervades educational thinking in Vietnam. The hierarchy within Vietnamese dance and the absence of an independent dance scene make it problematic for dancers to work in the more exploratory ways experienced outside the country. Nevertheless, many choreographers now incorporate into their work elements of contemporary dance styles and vocabulary they have observed in the work of visiting companies and artists. Dancer and choreographer Nguyen Minh Thong (1997) commented that this tendency 'is really a big problem. People make modern works here now but they have no training in the style so it is like eating rice without chopsticks.'

There is another significant element to the mixture of current influences on Vietnamese dance, which began with the 1998 production of *Realising Rama*, an initiative of the ASEAN Cultural Council. This project used dancers from every ASEAN country, drawing on their contemporary and traditional backgrounds. Produced by Nestor Jardin and choreographed by Denise Reyes from the Philippines, this production featured Pham Anh Phuong and Nguyen Minh Thong, amongst its diverse cultural cast and premiered in Hanoi in December 1998 for the ASEAN Summit. During 1999 and 2000 it toured to all the ASEAN countries. A four-year intercultural dance production, *Realising Rama* may be the beginning for Vietnamese dance artists of exposure to other Asian countries more experienced at employing contemporary processes and techniques in re-inventing their artistic traditions.

Although these recent developments are positive for Vietnamese professional dance there are two sobering realities. The significant opportunities of the last five years have been reserved for a small number from the two elite, Hanoi-based, national dance institutions, with no access for struggling companies in Saigon and elsewhere. It would also seem that the French training connection has been abruptly severed by the Vietnamese government since at least four outstanding dancers have opted to stay illegally in France where they can pursue the kind of dance career unavailable in Vietnam.

In the long run, losing some of Vietnam's best dancers to a former colonial power can be no more controlled than the global flows of communication and information which have entered the country as a result of *doi moi* opening its doors to global capitalism (see Carruthers 1998: 4). Whilst the state attempts to restrict these flows through a policy of cultural control, artists still find ways to tap into them as a potent source of revitalisation.

Yet as individual dancers and choreographers begin to effect change, management remains ineffectual. Dancer/choreographer and rehearsal director of the Vietnam Opera Ballet Theatre Ha The Dung and his colleagues cannot survive as full-time members of staff. The Ministry of Culture and Information subsidises around fifty performances per year but the amount of money per performance is so little that the national company is unable to sustain that number of performances, unless it includes the private tourist and commercial appearances organised by individual company dancers.[15]

The gap between desiring change and effecting change

In the foreseeable future it would seem impossible therefore for dance artists to completely escape the schizophrenia of opposing forces which are shaping their contemporary practice. These include privatising the arts for short-term gain versus long-term investment in creative development, unchallenging superficial work versus long years of intensive training, valuing commercial considerations in arts practice versus the devaluation of the artist in society, and the prescribed nature of existing practice and training versus the desire for more independence and freedom in those areas. At a deeper level, there is the need to break away from institutionalisation yet a continuing dependency on it. Commitment to large-scale fundamental change is thwarted by the easy option of hitching a ride on the *doi moi*-induced commercialisation of upmarket 'traditional' arts entertainment. Even with access to alternative ideas from overseas, implementing them is still a problem. Vice-Director of the Vietnam Opera Ballet Theatre, Pham Anh Phuong (1998), who has had several overseas study and performance opportunities, remarks that 'we understand and see the systems of different countries, and want to change to something similar, but how to get out of the current one?'.

Thus, Vietnamese dance artists themselves identify two major issues which are impeding change. One is the inappropriateness of the current infrastructure and training, and the second is the apparent inability to turn ideas and words for change into actions. Many of the reasons for this have been examined, but it is Vietnam's outspoken literary dissident Duong Thu Huong who comments most tellingly on the gap between what is said and what is done:

> Our people are very strong in times of war. We have what it takes to support deprivation, losses, massacres. These qualities come from our traditions. But

> to live in a civil society, with a full awareness of individual value, our people is [sic] still very young and naïve. Notions like democracy, the rights of man, are seen as something distant, luxuries. Vietnam is not a normal country. Its abnormality is its own; it is not the same as China's for example. The Vietnamese are more supple than the Chinese, and behind that suppleness lies a certain pragmatism. You might say that Vietnam is always ready for compromises based on pragmatic considerations. But the Vietnamese and Chinese have much in common. The essential is the gap between action and word. What they say is one thing, the reality another.
>
> (Cited in Kamm 1996: 144)

Renewal from within

The major choreographic challenge for Vietnamese dance is to find new forms to support contemporary ideas in a rapidly changing world, and at the same time to rediscover aspects of traditional culture which can be meaningful today. This challenge is not unique to Vietnam, but the particular circumstances surrounding it are. The most effective ways to face such a challenge are likely to be internal ones, emanating from artists inside the country. Outside stimulus will undoubtedly refocus the mind, offer skills and alternatives, and provide a mirror in which similarities and contrasts can be reflected, but will not provide ultimate solutions to the dilemmas of Vietnamese dance.

On the negative side, an increasingly pragmatic government with a continuing agenda of nationalism and cultural censorship is unlikely to invest in cutting-edge artistic practice, or even conservative, contemporary dance productions that do not show immediate returns or that depart radically from the status quo. Nor in the continuing economic crisis is sponsorship for cultural activities likely, especially when nervous foreign investors are giving Vietnam a wide berth. It is also doubtful that in the short term the increasingly consumerist, urban middle class will form the critical mass necessary to provide an audience for concert dance or independent practice, from where new artistic developments in dance generally emerge.

Exposure to new ideas and thinking via information technology, visiting artists and teachers, greater opportunities to travel and a higher standard of living are positive changes in dance artists' lives. Vietnam has rapidly become one of the West's most popular destinations and there are a greater number of artists visiting from an increasing number of countries and artistic backgrounds, sometimes out of curiosity and sometimes on cultural exchanges. More diverse opportunities for collaborative exchanges will provide more models for employing contemporary processes and techniques to re-invent artistic traditions. The dynamic interaction that results from such stimulus can be an energising catalyst. That there is an identifiable albeit small number of artists initiating original creative projects and introducing new training approaches provides grounds for some optimism for the future of Vietnamese dance in the market-driven climate of *doi moi*.

interestingly when there is an international collaboration, the media is all over them

Notes

1 *Doi moi* literally means 'new way' or 'renovation' and was introduced in December 1986 by the Vietnam Communist Party in an attempt to begin to redress the devastating economic effects of closure of the country since the end of the American (Vietnam) War and reunification in 1975. It involves market-driven reform and stringent International Monetary Fund conditions in order to borrow money and receive aid. The quotation from Pham Anh Phuong (1996: 7) was recorded in a personal interview, Melbourne, 30 July. This and the following interview quotations are taken from unpublished transcripts of personal interviews recorded by the author during doctoral research from 1996 to 2000, predominantly in Vietnam, but also in Australia and France.

2 *Cai luong* refers to 'renovated theatre', a neo-traditional form which evolved in the 1920s in the south as a result of French colonial influences, combining elements of traditional theatre forms with Western staging and naturalistic techniques whilst maintaining the convention of sung text.

3 The reference to the left- and right-hand jobs refers to a well-known Vietnamese expression. It was used by dancer Tran Van Hai, from the Vietnam Opera Ballet Theatre, in a personal interview in Hanoi, 1 January 1998 (translator, Vu Mai Thu). The 'jobless' reference occurred in many conversations but is recorded in a personal interview with Tran Quoc Tuan, in Hanoi, 11 December 1997 (translator, Tran Thanh Mai), who said, 'In my job now, I feel like I am jobless, I have nothing to do.'

4 According to the Department of Performing Arts of the Ministry of Culture and Information, there are sixty-two *Doan Ca Mua Nhac* (Song and Dance Companies) of which fifty-six have dance groups. Director of the Department, Bui Gia Tuong, was quite specific about the government's restructuring of the performing arts: 'In the current situation Vietnam has too many companies. There are about 140 companies of which 110 are provincial, another twelve central (metropolitan), and there are fourteen army companies. So now the government wants the provinces to retain only the companies of good quality. It is a priority to keep the traditional companies, but they must be seen to be effective in their activities' (Bui Gia Tuong 1998).

5 The late Doan Long, choreographer and director, told me: 'We do have the right to say what we want; it is how you say it that is the problem. In order to solve this dilemma, you cannot approach it head on, you have to go in different directions and talk with different people because it involves a lot of issues and has to be tackled comprehensively' (Doan Long 1998).

6 Duong Thu Huong is one of the most well-known literary dissidents in the West. Formerly an extremely popular novelist, her campaigning for human rights and her publicly voiced disapproval of the path that communism was taking in Vietnam led to the banning of her books and film scripts and she was placed under house arrest on and off for many years. Still living in Hanoi, she is almost invisible as a public figure though her work is available on the black market and she has become something of a *cause célèbre* in the West. Her dogged courage and determination to remain in her homeland as a dissident is much admired, albeit somewhat secretly, by many in Vietnam.

7 In this context, 'market tourism' describes the delivery of a product, which appeals to tourists for whom the experience of seeing a performance is a form of holiday entertainment, often during the consumption of a meal or social drinking. This differentiates it from 'cultural tourism' where a more discerning audience deliberately seeks out an arts or cultural experience.

8 This more positive aspect of the effects of *doi moi* on folk traditions was mentioned by Vu Hoai, Pham Thi Thanh, Be Kim Nhung and Huu Ngoc in interviews, and by many others in informal conversations. With regard to the court arts or classical Vietnamese dance, Doan Nghe Thuat Cung Dình Hue, the Hue Royal Arts Company, has been set up specifically to serve the needs of cultural tourism and 'not

as a commercial enterprise' according to its director Tran Thanh Thuong (1998). In addition to performances of recreated court arts in the restored Royal Theatre of the former Imperial Palace, a priority will be to 'concentrate on upgrading the training of the performers'. For this purpose a new centre is being established where students will train in the court arts. So whilst market tourism is creating a situation of down-grading of training, cultural tourism in this instance is investing in improved training.

9 Two major works *Em, Nguoi Phu Nu Vietnam* (known in English as 'Land of Waiting Souls') (1995) and *Through the Eyes of the Phoenix* (1997) drew on the talents of Vietnamese composers, writers, designers and the Vietnam Theatre Orchestra as well as traditional music ensembles. See Stock (1999, 1998a, 1998b).

10 Pham Anh Phuong, principal dancer with the Vietnam Opera Ballet Theatre, worked for a year in Australia as a dancer with Dance North in 1990. In 1993, Dance North spent five weeks in Hanoi working on an extensive exchange involving 200 dancers, musicians and actors in a programme of new works, and in 1996 the Vietnam Opera Ballet Theatre performed at the Green Mill Dance Festival in Melbourne with a touring version of *Em, Nguoi Phu Nu Vietnam*. Since 1999, Pham Anh Phuong has been Vice-Director of the Vietnam Opera Ballet Theatre. In addition, some dancers from Vietnam have furthered their studies in Australia, and Australian teachers have made short visits to Hanoi since 1991, mainly from the Victorian College of the Arts and the Queensland University of Technology.

11 The late 1980s and early 1990s also saw the first works in Vietnam of French-Vietnamese artist Ea Sola. Her work has been controversial amongst dance artists who were angered by her much publicised statement to the Director of the Performing Arts Department that 'there was no Vietnamese dance before I came' (a 'rumour' confirmed in personal communication with Bui Gia Tuong, Hanoi, 27 January 1998). Ea Sola's first two productions using non-dancers, whilst receiving international acclaim, have had little impact on the development of the dance profession in Vietnam as dance artists have not had the opportunity to work with her or observe rehearsals (which are always closed), their only contact being as audience members and perhaps meeting her.

12 The following information was provided by the Vietnam Opera Ballet Theatre in late 1999, when there were two male dancers, Le Ngoc Van and Phuong Hoang, employed by Ballet de Marseille and L'Esquisse at the National Choreographic Centre in Angers. In addition, a further five dancers were studying in Lyon or Istres (Vu Long, Hong Phong, Hoang Thanh, Hoai Ngoc and Thu Lan) with three having returned from France (Minh Thong, Quoc Tuan and The Dung). With the exception of the mainstream Lyon Conservatoire, the other centres are known for their contemporary and postmodern approaches. In 1998 and 1999, two female dancers, Tran Ly Ly and Bui Thuc Anh, were studying in Australia, and one dancer in 2002. Of the twelve dancers studying overseas since 1996, only four have been women.

13 The four choreographers were Nguyen Minh Thong, Ha The Dung, Nguyen Hong Phong and Le Vu Long, all of whom studied contemporary dance with myself and in France. Their connections in France have been with the Coline Company and Ballet Atlantique (Nguyen Cong Nhac 2001b).

14 This analysis refers to training rather than choreographic opportunities. It is the Vietnam Opera Ballet Theatre that has led the way in terms of developing new styles of choreography and has been enormously supportive of new work, predominantly in its on-going support of foreign choreographers, in tandem with encouraging new contemporary work within the company.

15 Ha The Dung (2001) reported that groups of Vietnam Opera Ballet Theatre dancers can sign separate contracts for commercial and private performances as long as they inform the company. They are not obliged to pay any share of income earned from these contracts to the company. These commercial appearances are counted in the

Vietnam Opera Ballet Theatre's report to the Ministry as official performances in order to make up the number required by the Ministry to maintain current subsidies.

Bibliography

Bui Gia Tuong (1998) Personal interview (translator, Tran Thanh Mai), Hanoi, 21 January.

Carruthers, Ashley (1998) 'What Bugs the State about Truong Tan?', *TAASA Review*, 7(3): 4–5.

Chu Thuy Quynh (1998) Personal interview (translator, Tran Thanh Mai), Hanoi, 4 February.

Cohen, Philippe (1999) Personal interview, Lyon, 9 February.

Communist Party of Vietnam (1996) *VIIIth National Congress Documents*, Hanoi: The Gioi Publishers.

Diamond, Catherine (1997) 'The Pandora's Box of "Doi Moi": The Open-Door Policy and Contemporary Theatre in Vietnam', *New Theatre Quarterly*, XIII(52), November: 372–86.

Doan Long (1998) Personal interview (translator, Tran Thanh Mai), Hanoi, 8 January.

Ea Sola (1999) Personal interview, Paris, 31 January.

Grau, Andree (1993) 'John Blacking and the Development of Dance Anthropology in the United Kingdom', *Dance Research Journal*, 25(2): 21–8.

Ha The Dung (2001) Personal correspondence (translator, Graham Alliband), 6 September.

Hoang Su (1997) Personal interview (translator, Tran Thanh Mai), Hanoi, 20 December.

Kamm, Henry (1996) *Dragon Ascending: Vietnam and the Vietnamese*, New York: Arcade Publishing.

Kolko, Gabriel (1997) *Vietnam: Anatomy of a Peace*, London and New York: Routledge.

Le Tuan Hung (1994) 'The Dynamics of Change in *Hue* and *Tai Tu* Music between 1890 and 1990', in M. Kartomi and S. Blum (eds), *Music-Cultures in Contact: Convergences and Collisions*, Sydney: Currency Press.

Le Vu Long (1998) Personal interview (translator, Tran Thanh Mai), Hanoi, 6 February.

Luu Thi Thu Lan (1997) Personal interview (translator, Tran Thanh Mai), Hanoi, 11 December.

Ngoc Cuong (1997) 'Some Thoughts on the Quality of Dance Works', report for the Department of Performing Arts, Hanoi, 25 November.

Nguyen Cong Nhac (1997) Personal interview (translator, Tran Thanh Mai), Hanoi, 9 December.

—— (2001a) Personal correspondence, 5 September.

—— (2001b) Personal correspondence, 11 September.

Nguyen Hong Phong (1998) Personal interview (translator, Tran Thanh Mai), Hanoi, 12 January.

Nguyen Minh Thong (1997) Personal interview (translator, Tran Thanh Mai), Hanoi, 13 December.

Nguyen Thanh Thuy (1997) Personal interview (translator, Tran Thanh Mai), Hanoi, 27 December.

Pham Anh Phuong (1996) Personal interview, Melbourne, 30 July.

—— (1998) Personal interview, Hanoi, 2 January.

Pham Hung Thoan (1998) Personal interview 1998 (translator, Tran Thanh Mai), Hanoi, 5 January.

Pham Thi Thanh (1997) Personal interview (translator, Tran Thanh Mai), Hanoi, 22 December.
Phung Quang Minh (1998) Personal interview (translator, Tran Thanh Mai), Hanoi, 21 January.
Stock, Cheryl (1998a) 'Dancing the Dual Phoenix: Collaborating across Cultures', *The Korean Journal of Dance Studies*, 2(Fall): 109–27.
—— (1998b) 'Questions of Gender and Power in Professional Dance in Vietnam: A Western Choreographer's Perspective', *Brolga*, 9.
—— (1999) 'Moving Bodies across Cultures: An Analysis of a Vietnamese/Australian Dance and Theatre Project', *Australasian Drama Studies*, 34(April): 47–68.
Templer, R. (1999) *Shadows and Wind: A View of Modern Vietnam*, London: Abacus.
Thai Phien (1997) Personal interview (translator, Tran Thanh Mai), Hanoi, 23 December.
Thieu Hanh Nguyen (1997) 'Preserving the Soul of Dance', *Vietnam Economic News*, 52: 47
Tran Quoc Tuan (1997) Personal interview (translator, Tran Thanh Mai), Hanoi, 11 December.
Tran Thanh Thuong (1998) Personal interview (translator, Phan Thuan Thao), Hue, 16 February.
Tran Van Lai (1998) Personal interview (translator, Tran Thanh Mai), Hanoi, 25 January.
Tran Van Hai (1998) Personal interview (translator, Vu Mai Thu), 1 January.
Tran Xuan Dinh (1998) Personal interview (translator, Tran Thanh Mai), Hanoi, 6 January.
Trung Kien (1998) Personal interview (translator, Vu Mai Thu), Hanoi, 11 February.
Vietnam News (1998) 'Vietnamese culture; product of aeons of creativity, struggle', 16 August: 8.
Vu Duong Dung (1998) Personal interview (translator, Tran Thanh Mai), Hanoi, 7 January.
Vu Hoai (1997) Personal interview (translator, Tran Thanh Mai), Hanoi, 7 December.
Vu Minh Nguyet (1998) Personal interview (translator, Nguyen Tan Loc), Saigon, 19 February.

Index